Repair Your Home ...In No Time

Brooke C. Stoddard

que

800 East 96th Street
Indianapolis, Indiana 46290

Repair Your Home In No Time

Copyright © 2005 by Que Publishing

All rights reserved. No part of this book shall be reproduced, stored in a retrieval system, or transmitted by any means, electronic, mechanical, photocopying, recording, or otherwise, without written permission from the publisher. No patent liability is assumed with respect to the use of the information contained herein. Although every precaution has been taken in the preparation of this book, the publisher and author assume no responsibility for errors or omissions. Nor is any liability assumed for damages resulting from the use of the information contained herein.

International Standard Book Number: 0-7897-3339-0

Library of Congress Catalog Card Number: 2004117481

Printed in the United States of America

First Printing: April 2005

08 07 06 05   4 3 2 1

Trademarks

All terms mentioned in this book that are known to be trademarks or service marks have been appropriately capitalized. Que Publishing cannot attest to the accuracy of this information. Use of a term in this book should not be regarded as affecting the validity of any trademark or service mark.

Warning and Disclaimer

Every effort has been made to make this book as complete and as accurate as possible, but no warranty or fitness is implied. The information provided is on an "as is" basis. The author and the publisher shall have neither liability nor responsibility to any person or entity with respect to any loss or damages arising from the information contained in this book.

Bulk Sales

Que Publishing offers excellent discounts on this book when ordered in quantity for bulk purchases or special sales. For more information, please contact

    U.S. Corporate and Government Sales
    1-800-382-3419
    corpsales@pearsontechgroup.com

For sales outside of the United States, please contact

    International Sales
    international@pearsoned.com

Executive Editor
Candace Hall

Development Editor
Lorna Gentry

Managing Editor
Charlotte Clapp

Project Editor
George Nedeff

Production Editor
Megan Wade

Indexer
Erika Millen

Proofreader
Dan Knott

Technical Editor
Ben Helmuth

Publishing Coordinator
Cindy Teeters

Multimedia Developer
Dan Scherf

Interior Designer
Anne Jones

Cover Designer
Anne Jones

Cover Illustration
Nathan Clement, Stickman Studio

Page Layout
Michelle Mitchell

Graphics
Laura Robbins

Repair Your Home ...In No Time

Contents at a Glance

Introduction 1

Part I: Home Repair Basics
1 Getting Ready 9
2 Preparing a Maintenance Plan 19

Part II: Essential Home Repairs, Area by Area
3 Walls and Floors 29
4 Doors and Windows 61
5 Plumbing 89
6 Simple Electrical Repairs 125
7 Painting and Wallpapering 149
8 Outdoor Repairs and Maintenance 185
A References and Resources 211
  Index 213

Table of Contents

Introduction 1

Part I: Home Repair Basics

1 Getting Ready 9

Assembling a Basic Toolkit 10
    Choosing Essential Tools and Equipment 10
    Adding Work-aids and Some Special-Purpose Tools to Your Toolkit ... 12
    Adding More Tools 13

Stocking Up on Basic Supplies 14

Caring for Your Tools 15

Surviving the Home Repair Store 16

Summary 18

2 Preparing a Maintenance Plan 19

Creating a Home Maintenance Plan 20
    Listing Seasonal Maintenance Tasks 20
    Anytime List of Repairs and Maintenance Tasks 22

Maintaining an Apartment 23

Calling In the Pros 25

Summary 26

Part II: Essential Home Repairs, Area by Area

3 Walls and Floors 29

Repairing Walls 30
    Working with Wall Surfaces 30
    Choosing and Using Wall Fasteners 33
    Repairing Plaster 35
    Patching Drywall 40
    Working with Grout and Ceramic Tile 43

Repairing Floors 48
    Repairing Hardwood Floors 48
    Repairing Resilient Flooring 52

Summary 59

4 Doors and Windows 61

Making Basic Window Repairs 62
    Understanding the Anatomies of Double-Hung, Casement, and
    Sliding Windows 62
    Freeing a Stuck Window 64
    Improving Sash Movement 65
    Installing and Repairing Window Weatherstripping 66
    Removing a Broken Window Pane 69
    Installing a New Pane 69
    Making Small Wire Screen Repairs 71
    Making Small Fiberglass Screen Repairs 73
    Replacing a Screen on a Wooden Frame 73
    Replacing a Screen on a Metal Frame 74

Repairing Doors and Door Latches 76
    Installing or Repairing Weatherstripping 77
    Fixing a Loose Hinge 78
    Shimming a Hinge 79
    Repairing a Door Latch by Filing the Strike Plate 80
    Repairing a Door Latch by Repositioning a Door Stop 81
    Recognizing Types of Door Locks 82
    Installing a Cylinder Lock 82
    Installing a Deadbolt Lock 84

Summary 87

5 Plumbing 89

Understanding Plumbing in Your Home 90
    Your Water Supply and Main Shutoff Valve 90
    The Hot and Cold Water Lines 90
    Drains and Vents 90

Basic Plumbing Tools and Materials 92
    Putting Together a Basic Plumbing Toolkit 92
    Plumbing Materials to Have on Hand 93

Shopping at a Plumber's Supply Store 94

Taking Care of Simple Plumbing Chores 95
    Replacing Clothes Washer Hoses 96
    Replacing a Shower Head 96
    Cleaning a Faucet or Spray Hose Nozzle Aerator 97
    Installing a Water Filter 99
    Caulking a Tub 99

Dealing with Sinks 101
   Adjusting a Pop-Up Stopper 101
   Removing and Cleaning a Pop-Up Stopper 103

Clearing Out Clogs 104
   Removing and Cleaning a Sink Trap 104
   Using a Plunger to Unclog a Toilet 106
   Using a Plumber's Snake to Unclog a Drain 107

Stopping Drips and Repairing Faucets 108
   Repairing a Compression Valve Faucet 110
   Repairing a Stem Valve Packing Leak 111
   Repairing a Ball Faucet 112
   Repairing a Single-Handle Cartridge Faucet 113
   Repairing a Disk Faucet 115
   Replacing a Faucet 116
   Replacing Supply Tubes 118
   Replacing Shutoff Valves 120

Solving Toilet Tank Problems 121
   Changing a Toilet Tank Flapper 121
   Installing a Toilet Inlet Valve 123

Summary 124

6 Simple Electrical Repairs 125

Putting Together Your Toolkit 125

Working Safely with Electricity 127
   Understanding Basic Principles of Electrical Wiring 127
   Working Safely with Electrical Circuits 128
   Checking Circuits with a Voltage Tester 129

Minor Repairs and Improvements 132
   Making Simple Wiring Connections 132
   Replacing Cords and Rewiring Plugs 135
   Repairing and Rewiring a Lamp 137
   Installing a New Light Fixture 138
   Installing a Chandelier 140
   Installing a Single-Pole Dimmer Switch 142
   Installing a Three-way Dimmer Switch 144
   Adding a GFCI Receptacle 145

Summary 147

7 Painting and Wallpapering 149

Painting, from Setup to Cleanup 150
    Your Painting Tool Set 150
    Choosing the Right Paints 152
    Choosing Brushes and Rollers 154
    Proper Painting Preparation and Techniques 156
    Painting Walls and Ceilings 163
    Painting Windows 164
    Painting a Door 166
    Taking a Break and Cleaning Up 166
    Hiring a Professional Painter 170

Working with Wallpaper 170
    Gathering Your Wallpapering Tools and Equipment 170
    Choosing and Buying Wallpaper 171
    Getting Your Room and Walls Ready for Wallpapering 173
    Pasting the First Piece 176
    Hanging the Second and Subsequent Strips 177
    Wallpapering an Inside Corner 178
    Papering Around an Outside Corner 179
    Papering Around Windows, Doors, and Entryways 180
    Dealing with Electrical Outlets and Switchplates 182

Summary 183

8 Outdoor Repairs and Maintenance 185

Problems Underfoot 186
    Fixing Cracks and Bad Patches in a Driveway or Walk 187
    Sealing Concrete 188
    Staining a Deck 188

Working on Walls 190
    Repointing Brick 191
    Fixing Wooden Siding 193
    Repairing Vinyl Siding 195
    Repairing Aluminum Siding 196
    Power Washing a Wall 198
    Painting Exterior Siding 199

Repairs on High: Working with the Roof and Gutters 203
    Detecting Roofing Problems 203
    Repairing a Composition Shingle 204
    Replacing a Composition Shingle 205
    Cleaning Gutters 207

Summary 208

A References and Resources	**211**
Index	**213**

About the Author

Brooke C. Stoddard has worked as a carpenter and home repair contractor as well as a writer and editor. He has written for and edited many of Time-Life Books' home repair and improvement series. He is also the author of *Building* (1994), a coauthor of *A Consumer's Guide to Home Improvement, Renovation and Repair* (1990), and the editor of *Country's Best Log Homes Magazine*. He and his wife have renovated an 1860s frame townhouse and a 1910 brick colonial.

Acknowledgments

My hat doffs to the skilled editors and artists at Que Publishing: Candy Hall for charting the course, Lorna Gentry for aligning my thoughts and tuning my syntax, Laura Robbins for crafting the exacting drawings, and George Nedeff for producing. *Omnes Sine Qua Non.* Lucky for me they were there, for, as we carpenters hopping from joist to joist have often heard: Build on a Firm Foundation.

We Want to Hear from You!

As the reader of this book, *you* are our most important critic and commentator. We value your opinion and want to know what we're doing right, what we could do better, what areas you'd like to see us publish in, and any other words of wisdom you're willing to pass our way.

As an executive editor for Que Publishing, I welcome your comments. You can email or write me directly to let me know what you did or didn't like about this book—as well as what we can do to make our books better.

Please note that I cannot help you with technical problems related to the topic of this book. We do have a User Services group, however, where I will forward specific technical questions related to the book.

When you write, please be sure to include this book's title and author as well as your name, email address, and phone number. I will carefully review your comments and share them with the author and editors who worked on the book.

Email: feedback@quepublishing.com

Mail: Candace Hall
Executive Editor
Que Publishing
800 East 96th Street
Indianapolis, IN 46240 USA

For more information about this book or another Que Publishing title, visit our website at www.quepublishing.com. Type the ISBN (excluding hyphens) or the title of a book in the Search field to find the page you're looking for.

Introduction

Whenever something went wrong in Louis XIV's gigantic home Versailles, he just called on one of his minions to fix it. Of course, this was a man who didn't dress himself in the morning—he stood there with his limbs about him and had other people do it for him.

You and I are not so fortunate. We dress ourselves, and when something goes wrong in our homes, we either bend our own backs to the work or face an expensive bill from a professional.

There's not much satisfaction writing a big check to a house-calling plumber or electrician, but there can be a lot of satisfaction in looking back on a job you've done, knowing it has been done properly and thinking about the money you're not forking over to a person who charges a lot for what you have just finished yourself.

Yes, two facts are certain in this world: Things will go wrong in your home, and people will charge you money to fix them. But you can do many of the fixes yourself *if you know how to do the work properly.*

That is where *Repair Your Home in No Time* comes in. It gives you information you need to make repairs and fixes quickly and effectively, saving you hundreds—even thousands—of dollars.

Who This Book Is Written for

This book is for persons who don't have a lot of free time, who don't really want to create a home workshop in the basement, or who don't devote large chunks of a weekend to home improvements. Rather, we have written this book for busy persons, ones who want to get the job done and then get on with their lives.

This book is also written for persons who do not have a lot of experience in home repairs, who do not have chests full of expensive tools, and who do not have bodybuilder-type sons waiting around for home-style challenges.

This book is for persons who need to make fixes with a minimum of fuss, help, time, and expense.

What This Book Will Do for You

We don't pretend that home repairs are fun or easy for everyone, although some people do find at least some of them fun and some of them easy. But everyone should understand that home repairs not only save you money, aggravation, and time, but also make your home more valuable. A new chandelier, tongue-and-groove flooring, or a new faucet makes your home more convenient, enjoyable, and attractive for you, but it also makes it more attractive to others at the time when you eventually might want to sell your home.

My own experience with home repairs has taught me this: One of the highest hurdles—often *the* highest hurdle—is right at the beginning: fear of the unknown and fear of failing. After you get over these fears, you discover that much of the work is rather easy and that after you have done a repair once, you'll have the confidence to do it again.

Let me give you an example. You might have a faucet leaking at the spout. If you look at that faucet and have no idea how it works or what might be the source of the leak, you can imagine all sorts of watery and cut-finger disasters if you plunge in taking the faucet apart. But if you understand *how* the faucet works, disassembling and reassembling it is rather fun, sort of like playing with puzzles when you were a kid.

If the faucet is a stem faucet, the basic fix is merely replacing a washer that is held in by a screw. When you have done that once, you'll feel it's so easy that you'll think of going around and replacing all the washers in all your stem faucets.

And here's another thing that will motivate you. The washer you put in and that stops the drip might cost all of 20 cents, and the repair might take just 5 minutes. If you were to succumb to the rather defeatist attitude that the faucet is too bewildering or that you do not have the proper tools, your recourse is to call a plumber. He's going to charge heaven knows what just to drive to your home and walk through the door. He could be gone in minutes but still charge you $35. So, there you have it: 20 cents and 5 minutes or $35, plus the 5 minutes it takes to greet the plumber at the door, walk him to the problem faucet, and write him the check.

Avoiding the plumber and making an effective repair yourself is really a matter of understanding how the faucet goes together, what goes wrong, and how to fix the problem.

Our job is to move you from someone who does not understand a system to having the confidence to fix problems in that system.

INTRODUCTION 3

How to Use This Book

You'll get the most out of this book if you follow a couple simple suggestions. Read all of Part I, "Home Repair Basics." It contains material on what every home should have by way of tools and materials. It also discusses a maintenance plan. This part is important because, if you take some regular maintenance steps, you'll avoid the breakdowns that are more costly and complicated to put right.

You can use Part II, "Essential Home Repairs, Area by Area," more as a reference book. It is the heart of this volume and describes repairs that are commonly needed around the home. When something needs attending, merely find a reference to the problem in the index and go to the indicated page to read about the solution. It would be a good idea, however, to read the introductory material of a chapter in which the pages on the solution are found. The introductory material generally discusses how the system of the problem area works (the water supply system in Chapter 5, "Plumbing," for example, or electric circuits in Chapter 6, "Simple Electrical Repairs") and what sorts of tools and materials are needed for most fix-it work.

How the Book Is Organized

As mentioned, this book is organized into two parts. The first part reviews the basic tools and materials that everyone should have around the home, the ones that everyone is going to use eventually, which is why you should have them on hand and not have to run out to the store when their use is urgently needed. This part also reviews the kinds of stores where you can purchase tools, supplies, and materials; how to shop effectively in those stores; and how to get your questions answered.

Part I includes a section on keeping home repairs to a minimum. This, of course, means doing the small chores around the home so problems don't crop up in the first place—as they so often do at the worst possible times. Many people shy away from maintenance not because they don't like work, but because they do not have confidence that they can perform what is called for either efficiently or correctly. This section assures you that you can do much of what must be done to prevent problems in the first place.

Part II is the core of the book. It addresses repairs and maintenance by house system (plumbing, electrical, and so on) or by location (outdoors, for example). You do not have to read it straight through, and you do not have to read all of it. Rather, you can treat it as a reference. When you have a lamp to rewire, just find the section on rewiring lamps. Follow the step-by-step instructions and—voilà—a repaired lamp.

Every home needs the kind of repairs that are covered in this section. You will end up using it a lot.

We have placed information about the kind of work around the home that is less frequently needed—or not needed at all—but which can make your home less expensive to maintain (for example, by adding attic insulation), better looking (upgrading the door and window trim), and more amenable (adding a patio) on our website.

One chapter is filled with ideas about saving energy. Another provides step-by-step instructions for carrying out some home improvement projects that are not particularly difficult but which can make your home both more enjoyable and worth more in the marketplace. The two online chapters, "Saving Energy" and "Simple Home Improvements," can be accessed by going to www.quepublishing.com. Enter this book's ISBN (without the hyphens) in the Search box and click Search. When the book's title is displayed, click the title to go to a page where you can download these chapters.

Special Elements

To help you with the maintenance and repairs you will be doing around the home, we've included lots of helpful elements. For example, many sections begin with a You'll Need list of the tools and materials you will need to complete the job.

We also have sprinkled the book with different kinds of tips, notes, and cautions. These point you to ways of saving time or money, sparing yourself aggravation, estimating what your materials costs are going to be, and more. We have especially noted the precautions you should take to save yourself from injury or harm.

As you read through the book, you'll also notice some graphic icons in the page margins. We use these icons to call out specific types of information of special interest or importance. Here's what those icons mean:

Short Cuts. The Short Cut icon indicates ideas that allow you to save time or money. These might be ways to temporarily solve a problem until you have more time to go back and properly resolve it or a means of getting the job done for less money than you might have expected.

Pro's Tip. The Pro's Tip icon points to methods some professionals use to make the job easier or ensure the repair lasts longer.

Estimator's Calculator. An Estimator's Calculator icon points to ways of determining about how much your project is going to cost in materials. Information marked by this icon can also help you estimate how much time you are likely to have to spend on the project.

Call the Pro. The Call the Pro icon indicates a situation when your best option might be to stop your work and call in a professional. This option can actually save you time, aggravation, and (in the long run) money.

INTRODUCTION

Above and Beyond. The Above and Beyond icon points to ways you can go beyond the repair or task at hand. It might suggest an upgraded material or a way of creating something better—even stunning—rather than simply "fixing" the existing problem. Your friends will be amazed by some of the improvements you'll learn in these tips.

Finding Your Way

With home repairs, you really only need a few things: knowledge of how the damaged element goes together, the right tools for taking it apart, the right parts for putting it back together properly, the proper amount of time, a reasonable measure of patience, and a suitable amount of confidence.

This book tells you about how the elements of your home work, the proper tools for various jobs, and how to obtain the suitable parts. This knowledge should give you confidence. Then if you supply the time and the patience, you'll see that you can handle a good deal of jobs around the home for which professionals would charge you dearly.

Some people actually like home repair work. And it's not too difficult to understand why. For one, it often saves a good deal of money, better spent on meals out, vacations, college tuition, you name it. But many find home repair work satisfying because it gives them results they can see, feel, and enjoy—often for years to come. In an era when a lot of career work is shuffling papers, going to meetings, selling retail, or brokering financial products, much of the work around the home makes something you can step back from, look at when the day is done, and feel a good measure of satisfaction over. The splintered floorboard now looks perfect, the door has a new brass lock, the bathroom sink sports new brassy-colored faucets, the baby's room is bright with balloons-and-birds wallpaper, and the living room has new built-in bookshelves. These are all things that please the eye and give satisfaction to the soul.

You can do it. Read. Add patience and time, and you've got it.

Part 1

Home Repair Basics

1 Getting Ready 9

2 Preparing a Maintenance Plan 19

1

Getting Ready

No one is born with a talent for repairing things, and everyone starts off with no skills at all. Some people grow up in households that have tools and parents who are handy, but even youngsters in these homes learn by picking up and doing. Everyone learns that way.

So, if you are new to the field of home repairs, take heart that everyone was once in your shoes. What you need are basic tools and some experience. In this chapter, I list basic tools and supplies for your home or apartment. These are things everyone is going to need some day to perform simple maintenance and repair tasks around their home or apartment. Tools from the succeeding lists can be added as needed, and tools in the specialty chapters (on plumbing, electrical, and so on) can be added if you get into that kind of work. The basic tools will get you a long way and keep you from having to call a professional for many home repairs, saving you from paying those high hourly rates.

Tools are useless, of course, if you cannot find them, so you need to be consistent about returning them to your tool bucket or tool holder. If a friend borrows one, make a note of the tool, the friend, and the date; it's scary how quickly you can forget where a tool is. And tools are almost useless if they have been abused or allowed to become blunt, rusted, or bent. When you own a tool, keep it in good condition, or your next job with it is going to be far harder than it should be.

In this chapter:

* Learn which tools to pull together to create a basic, expanded, or deluxe home repair toolkit.
* Stock your toolkit with the right supplies.
* Practice simple methods to keep your tools clean and in good shape.
* Learn how to navigate the big box home repair center experience, so you get in and get out efficiently, with the tools and supplies you need.

You learn how to store tools safely in this chapter and how to keep your supplies in cool dry places so they do not become spoiled or mildewed.

Finally, take note of the section on shopping at stores. There are ways to be efficient and ways to be inefficient. Shopping in home improvement stores is something you should do as quickly as possible because it takes time away from getting the repair done. And that keeps you from doing the things in life you would rather be doing.

To do list

- ❏ Learn the tools and equipment you should include in a basic toolkit.
- ❏ Determine which extras you might want to include to make your basic toolkit more functional.
- ❏ Learn about some of the special tools and equipment you might need to perform special home repair tasks.
- ❏ Choose from some professional tools you might need for larger projects.

Assembling a Basic Toolkit

Everyone should have a collection of tools and supplies necessary to perform common home repair tasks. The following sections suggest some basic tools and supplies you can pull together to make your own home repair toolkit. I've also suggested some tools and supplies that you can add over time, as you begin working on more than the most basic tasks.

Your toolkit should be portable so you can take it with you to the site of the repair. No matter how carefully you plan a repair, there's usually a tool or material that you want when you're right in the middle of the task. You can store many of the tools I've suggested here right in your tool bucket (one of the tools recommended). This means they are handy right where and when you need them, so long as you've carried your toolkit to the task at hand.

Other tools you'll store in a place that is out of the way but nevertheless convenient when you need it. Hopefully, this will not be a damp place because some steels rust. Store your tools logically and where you can see them readily. My father always used to tell me, "Put the tool back where you found it." It's good advice, especially if you have a spouse or children who uses tools from time to time, too. In any event, you'll always know where your tools are; little is more aggravating than needing to use a tool but not being able to find it.

Choosing Essential Tools and Equipment

No matter what kind of home repair tasks you tackle, you can count on using certain tools over and over again. The list of tools in this section are those that I recommend *everyone* include in a basic home repair toolkit.

CHAPTER 1   Getting Ready

Here is my recommendation for putting together a basic toolkit:
- **Protective wear**—Safety is critical, so make sure your toolkit includes some basic safety gear. Have a good pair of eye protectors, which are clear plastic and can even fit over a pair of eyeglasses. Buy dust masks. These will not block harmful chemicals but can prevent large dust particles, sawdust, and insulation fibers from reaching your lungs. Also stock your toolkit with a pair of lightweight cotton gloves; these can save your fingers from small cuts and abrasions.
- **Tool bucket**—This is what you carry your tools and materials around in. Get one with a comfortable grip and plenty of pockets for tools.
- **Hammer**—For basics, buy a medium-weight hammer with a curved claw for removing nails. It should have a comfortable grip. Buy a good one; a hammer can last a lifetime.
- **Screwdrivers** —Purchase a set of both Phillips and flat-head screwdrivers (a Phillips screwdriver has a cross-shaped blade, unlike the straight blade of a flat-head screwdriver); a basic set contains three of each. Don't get the cheapest screwdrivers you can find; cheap Phillips screwdrivers wear at the tips at the first stubborn screw. Instead, buy screwdrivers at least in the middle price range.
- **Tape measure**—A 25-foot, retractable tape measure with 1" wide blade is a good choice.
- **Torpedo level**—This is a short level—about 9 inches long—for checking plumb (exactly vertical) and level (exactly horizontal). This tool is useful for checking your picture frames for level.
- **Power drill**—Cordless power drills that operate on a rechargeable battery are handy, but corded ones are fine, too (and don't need recharging). Buy a drill that is variable speed and reversible—that is, spins counterclockwise as well as clockwise. Also, be sure the drill has a 3/4" chuck (the end into which you set the drill bit). If you buy a cordless drill, get one with two batteries, so you always have a charged battery available. Your cordless drill also should be rated at 3.5 amps or higher, so it provides ample power to turn stubborn screws. Buy a set of 15-twist drill bits; these are the most common kind and drill through both wood and metal.
- **Pliers**—To start, have three types of pliers: *Regular* pliers have blunt tips and can be set in two positions to grip nuts, bolt heads, and so on. *Channel-lock* pliers adjust the width of their grip by moving one jaw down a series of channels; they are used to grip larger items such as small pipes and plumbing connectors. *Needle-nose* pliers have sharp, pointed tips; are essential for electrical work; and come in handy for snaring or gripping small objects.
- **Nippers**—Nippers resemble pliers but have a wide, slightly curved head that can grip the upper part of a nail projecting from wood. When you roll the curved head down along the wood while gripping the nail, the nail is pulled out of the wood. Nippers can also be used to cut through small metal items.

- **Utility knife**—These handy knives, also known as *box cutters*, have a pointed blade. Buy one that can retract the blade into the handle/body when the tool is not needed. The body also stores spare blades.
- **Putty knife**—Putty knives have a flat, flexible metal blade set into a flat handle, and they're used to smooth plaster and putty repairs or to scrape flaking paint or built-up gunk from flat surfaces. Make sure the blade is somewhat flexible and that the handle is comfortable.
- **Chisels**—Buy a set of four wood chisels, each with a different width, and treat them with care. You'll find many uses for these tools, and most require that the chisel blades are sharp and straight. Look for a set that comes with tip guards or plastic pouches for guarding the blades when they are not in use. Buy at least one cheap wood chisel for rough work; call this your "junk chisel."
- **General-purpose handsaw**—Some saws are called *cross-cut* saws (for cutting across the grain), and some are called *rip saws* (for cutting along the grain). Buy one that is of general purpose—that is, does both adequately well. To find a general-purpose saw, look at the label or ask a salesperson.
- **Step ladder**—Everyone needs a sturdy three-step stepladder, if for nothing else than to change light bulbs. Collapsible metal ones are sturdy and store easily. For more on ladders, see Chapter 8, "Outdoor Repairs and Maintenance."
- **Stud finder**—This handy device detects the metal or wood studs behind plaster, wallboard, or paneling. A stud finder comes in handy when hanging shelves, railings, or other heavy materials on walls.
- **Rasps and files**—Every toolkit should have a rasp for shaping wood and a file for trimming metal. Rasps and files are metal pieces about 10" inches long with rough surfaces for scraping. They come in differing sizes and styles. Begin with general-purpose ones and add others as jobs demand over the years. Buy a handle. A single handle can be used for a number of rasps and files whose ends (tangs) can fit in or be taken out.

Adding Work-aids and Some Special-Purpose Tools to Your Toolkit

When you have gathered the tools above into a basic toolkit, you might want to add the following over time and as your budget allows. They allow you to do more jobs in comfort and with greater efficiency:

- **Knee pad**—These thick foam pads come in a rectangular shape and often with a grip for easy carrying. They pad and protect your knees when you must kneel to work, and they take the knee ache out of many jobs.
- **Combination square**—A combination square has a 12" rule that slides in a body, a portion of which is at a right angle to the rule. It serves as both a ruler and an aid in drawing a line for making a right-angle cut.
- **2-foot level**—A 2-foot level is usually made of metal and has bubble indicators for showing true vertical and horizontal. It serves for projects too large for a torpedo level. Some have inches marked along one edge.

CHAPTER 1 Getting Ready

- **Block plane**—Hand planes for smoothing wood have hand grips on the top and delicate blades protruding from the bottom and come in many types. A block plane is small and is gripped by just one hand. Larger and longer planes are for smoothing the edges of doors and wood to be used in furniture.
- **Clamps**—Clamps come in many styles and sizes. Screw clamps have C-shaped bodies and a threaded portion that rises or retracts through one end. Choose screw clamps of medium size. Eventually you will use them for gluing pieces of wood together.
- **Coping saw**—A coping saw is shaped somewhat like a *D* with a grip protruding from one end. One side of the *D* is a thin wood-cutting blade meant for cutting small pieces of wood, including thin pieces of trim.
- **Hacksaw**—A hacksaw is needed for cutting metal. Sturdy ones hold the blade stretched in a frame. Others are smaller and have a blade projecting from a handle; these come in handy in tight spaces.
- **Tool apron**—These are like kitchen aprons but of tougher fabric and with a couple of pouches for nails, screws, and small tools. Not the least of their service is protecting the clothes you are wearing underneath.
- **Tool belt**—Tool belts are handy when your job requires you to leave your tool bucket behind (as when you are standing on a stepladder). Simple ones do nicely. Buy one with spaces for your utility knife, hammer, and various nails or screws. Tool belts hold more tools than a tool apron, which makes them handy, but they do not protect clothing, which is why you might want to buy both.
- **Sanding block**—A sanding block makes sanding less stressful on your fingers and helps you sand the surface more smoothly than you can do with your fingers alone.
- **Bench vice**—These attach to a bench and hold objects for cutting, planing, smoothing, and so on.

Adding More Tools

As your repairs and projects become more complex, consider buying the following for your repository of tools. They deal with angled wood cuts, larger sanding and drilling jobs, tasks that raise dust, and more:

- **Miter box and backsaw**—A miter box allows you to make 90° and 45° cuts more easily and accurately. You use a backsaw (meaning a saw with a reinforced top edge, or back) with the miter box, which has slots to guide the backsaw blade.
- **Folding rule**—Folding rules are wooden rulers hinged and folded into 8" sections. In some locations they are easier to use

> **note** *Pro's Tip* — Inexpensive miter boxes are made of hardwood or plastic, but after long use the slots become worn and wide and thus somewhat inaccurate. Metal ones are expensive but useful if you are going to be doing a lot of miter cuts. Professionals use combination power circular saws and miter gauges (these are called *power miter saws* or *chop saws*); buy one only if you are renovating a house.

than tape measures. Ones with a sliding 7" extender in the first folded section make them good for exactly measuring interior distances, such as across a door opening inside surface to inside surface.

- **Power sander**—If you are going to be doing a lot of sanding, you might as well buy one of these and save your arm and fingers. Power sanders come in various configurations.
- **6" joint compound blade**— A joint compound blade is like a putty knife but wider. These come in handy for working with drywall joint compound, grout, and the like.
- **Extra drill bits**—If you are going to drill into the mortar between bricks or concrete block, buy several sizes of masonry bits. For making holes larger than twist bits can, buy spade bits, which have a wide, flat blade with a sharp, pointed tip for centering the bit. For drilling holes into wood for screws, use a *counterbore bit*. In one motion, one of these shapes a hole for the threaded part of the screw, the smooth shank, and the slanted screw head. These come in different or adjustable sizes for different sizes of wood screws.
- **Respirator**—If you are going to be sanding a lot of drywall joints, doing demolition, or creating a lot of sawdust (which some people are allergic to), buy a respirator. These filter the air better than dust masks and have replaceable filters. Match the filter to the job (screening out sawdust, drywall compound, and so on).
- **Cedar shims**—These wide, tapering shingles of cedar are not for roofs but rather for general woodworking and repair around the home. Cedar shims are used where any wood has to be shimmed just a bit (a door trim shifted slightly, for example). They are shaped easily with the blade of a utility knife.

Stocking Up on Basic Supplies

Alongside tools, everyone needs some rags, sandpaper, oils, and other basic supplies for performing common home repair tasks. Keep some of these items in your tool bucket; store the remainder in a place where you can gather them easily. And be sure to keep your supplies orderly, so they remain clean and usable:

- **Sandpaper**—You'll use sandpaper to sand rough wood finishes or smooth plaster repairs. The amount of material the sandpaper can remove is determined by the coarseness of its grit. You can buy an assortment of grits in one pack.

> **caution** Take care not to store oils and lubricants near any appliance that produces a flame, such as a gas water heater or gas or oil furnace.

- **Single-edge razors**—These blades have one edge topped with a ridge of blunt steel so you can hold it in your hand and scrape with the other edge. You can also buy holders, also called *scrapers*, into which single-edge razors fit. They make it easier on your hand

for large jobs, and the blade can be retracted into the body for safety when the holder is not in use.
- **Nails and screws**—Buy an assortment as well as a small plastic chest of drawers in which to store them.
- **Oils and lubricants**—Buy one can of penetrating oil for loosening stubborn nuts and one can of lubricating oil, such as WD-40®, for lubricating parts.
- **Bucket and rags**—You'll need a small plastic bucket to catch water and debris during plumbing repairs and emergencies. Rags are useful on countless jobs.

Caring for Your Tools

The old adage is, "Be kind to your tools and they will be kind to you." It's true.

Some tools require special care; otherwise, they very soon will not be up to their jobs and have to be replaced. Cutting tools especially require care and attention to keep their blades sharp and intact. Chisels need to be handled carefully to preserve their sharp edges; otherwise, they are of little use. When not in use, keep chisels in their pouches or with their tip guards on. For tough or indelicate work, use a "junk chisel." Take care to protect the teeth of all handsaws. Don't saw into old nails or even set saws down carelessly. Their sharp teeth make sawing easy for you; if they lose their cutting edges, your arm is going to have to work much harder.

Pay attention to any tool with steel parts. These include combination squares, framing squares, levels, handsaws, and clamps. Keep them clean and store them in dry places. Use steel wool to scour away any rusting, and occasionally wipe the metal parts with light oil to prevent rust from forming.

> **tip** Keep your tools clean for two reasons: A clean tool is more enjoyable and safer to use, and a clean tool will have a longer useful life. Wipe tools off after using them. Putty knives especially get build-ups of gunk. Wipe both the blade and handle clean after every use.

Things You'll Need

- ❏ Rags
- ❏ Light oil
- ❏ Wire brush
- ❏ File

Here are some basic tool-maintenance steps:
- **Clean tools**—Occasionally wipe tools clean of grime, and remove dirt and buildup from handles. Wipe eye goggles clean, shake out respirator filters, and clean where respirators touch your face. Use a wire brush to scour dirt

from plier jaws and rasp teeth. Clean grit away from a power drill chuck so the grit does not fly off during the next job. Wipe steel portions of tools with rags moistened in light oil.
- **Tune tools**—Tighten the blades of hacksaws and coping saws. File the tip of a flathead screw driver so it is straight and has no burs.
- **Sharpen tools**—Saw teeth blunt after much use and make sawing more tiresome. Ask a hardware store if it can sharpen the saw for you. Do the same occasionally for your chisels and planes. Drill bits blunt, too, and can be professionally sharpened, but it might be less bother merely to replace them with new ones.

To do list

- ❏ Plan your shopping trip.
- ❏ Make a list of necessary tools, parts, or supplies.
- ❏ Take along worn/broken parts, if appropriate.

Surviving the Home Repair Store

In the old days, you went to the hardware store and talked with the man who walked the aisles. You showed him a faucet part, and he led you directly to the kind of washer it needed. He knew hardware backward and forward and could even give you directions on how to make a repair. If there is still a hardware store near you like this, support it as long as you can.

But in many areas, these small hardware stores have been supplanted by large, warehouse-type home improvement stores. These stores are huge, with extensive lawn and garden centers, and sell everything from kitchen cabinets and dehumidifiers to smaller items such as finishing nails and faucet washers. Most of the employees are helpful to the extent that they know where items are displayed, but they have not worked in the construction or repair trades and are not particularly knowledgeable about how systems go together or are properly repaired.

Here are some tips for surviving the home improvement store experience and getting the most value from your trip:

- **Try to shop when others aren't**—This means staying away whenever possible on Saturday and Sunday. Try to plan your projects in advance, and shop Monday through Friday when other people are at work.

> **tip** Many hardware chains and home improvement stores have web sites that will allow you to browse through their catalogs and find items you are thinking about buying before you visit the store. This could save you time if you are looking for a specific item or price. Some websites also have store or dealer locators for your area, and may also include a section where you can find helpful hints on projects you are working on.

CHAPTER 1 Getting Ready

- **Before you leave for the home improvement store, make a list of all you intend to purchase**—I try to have my list in a little notebook I keep in my shirt pocket. I have all the items on the left, with plenty of empty space beside each one to the right. If an item on your list is a part from a larger assembly—say a filter from an air conditioner—write down the manufacturer and model number of the appliance as best you can determine them. Take a pencil.
- **Take any small, worn parts you are replacing**—This way, you can match them against items in the store. Take a tape measure, as well.
- **Try to park close to the exit you will use**—You can better haul or, if the items are in a cart, push heavy purchases to your car. Wear comfortable walking shoes and clothing you don't mind smudging.
- **When you walk into the store, look for a map or directory near the entrance**—It should tell you the general location of items you want to buy. Alternatively, go to Information or Customer Service or, if these have waiting lines, to someone roving who looks knowledgeable. Ask the store employee where you can find each item on your list. Just name them and he will respond with the aisle number; have your list handy, and write the number down to the right of the named item. Make any other notes the employee volunteers; often an employee will say something like "lower right" or "to the left of the door locks." If your list is small, the employee might be able to walk with you and show you exactly where the items are. With a list of aisles for your items you can walk from one end of the store to the other, stopping where your merchandise is displayed. You should be able to make one pass of the store—end to end—without having to wander back over territory you've already covered.

> **note** Even though you should always take along a list of items you want to purchase at the home improvement center, when you shop, keep an open mind. These gigantic stores carry a wide variety of items that might be useful for your project. When you find an item you are interested in, look at the area around it because you might see something that is a better one, or something that is going to make your work easier, or something related that will help with a similar repair you have in mind for two months later.

- **If you can't find an item that the first employee has said is in a certain aisle, flag down someone in that department**—Take her to that location and say what it is you are looking for. If the two of you can't find it, have the employee call management. If that doesn't help, likely you will have to go to a specialty store (plumbing, wallpapering, electrical, and so on).

> **note** Don't buy more than you need. Store aisles are filled with gadgets and solutions, but you generally only need one to deal with a problem. If an item is very low priced (cheap), it might be a short-term solution at best. Avoid these cheap gadgets unless you can use them for stop-gap measures that you will fix more permanently later.

- **If you are buying heavy material, tell an employee you want to pull your car up to the front of the store and have help in loading it**—The store can provide persons to help with the loading, and even rope for tying material to a car top or plastic or paper to protect car trunks or seats. Many can provide forklifts for especially heavy materials.

Pro's Tip

Remember, too, that you don't always have to shop at a huge warehouse-type home improvement store. You can also shop where plumbers, electricians, tile setters, and other professionals shop. Generally, these stores, though sometimes called *wholesalers* in the *Yellow Pages*, are happy enough to see nonprofessionals. You can often locate the harder-to-find replacement parts here and get higher-quality or longer-lasting supplies. You will also receive more detailed advice on repairs. Look for more information on such stores in the chapters of Part II, "Essential Home Repairs, Area by Area."

Things You'll Need

- ❑ Small notepad and writing device
- ❑ Worn/broken parts

Summary

In this chapter, you learned how to put together a basic (and even a not-so-basic) toolkit for use with most basic home repairs. You also learned some important tips for storing and maintaining your tools, to keep them in great shape and working safely and efficiently. In the next chapter, we talk about putting together a maintenance plan for your home. You'll soon be putting your new toolkit to work!

Preparing a Maintenance Plan

Do you want to hold your repairs to a minimum? Then you have to face the uncomfortable fact that you should put in some time inspecting parts of your home and engaging in some preventative maintenance. Every part, every coat of paint, every window sash yields to the unwavering pressure of time.

"A stitch in time saves nine" goes the old expression. It has just as much validity today as in centuries past: If you do a little bit of maintenance now, you save a greater repair some time in the future. While you are doing the work of maintenance, you very well might believe that you are not saving yourself time at all, but very likely you will be.

We need list only a few aspects of the home that, if not accorded proper maintenance, turn into costly—even catastrophic—repairs later:

- Leaving outdoor decks unstained or uncoated can lead to such rot in the boards that they all must be replaced.
- Not maintaining window glazing can lead to rot of the wood holding the glass in place, causing the whole window to need replacement.
- Not replacing a 20¢ washer in a faucet can lead to the complete failure of the faucet.
- Not cleaning gutters can lead to water leaking into the walls and interior of the home, causing rotting of the home's siding.

In this chapter:

* Learn how to create a maintenance plan that keeps your home running smoothly, from day to day and season to season.
* Discover some important home maintenance tasks for apartment dwellers.
* Understand when to tackle it yourself and when to call in the pros.

Every home should have its repair-prone components examined regularly. You might not like maintenance, but you sure aren't going to like making a repair that you know was preventable. In this chapter, you learn how to create a working maintenance plan that will help you keep tabs on your home's upkeep. Some maintenance tasks are on-going, and others come and go with the seasons; in this chapter, you learn how to schedule both types of maintenance chores. And, apartment dwellers reading this chapter will discover how to save themselves a lot of time and frustration by performing a few simple maintenance tasks. Finally, this chapter offers some guidance on when you should tackle home maintenance chores on your own and when you should call in professional help.

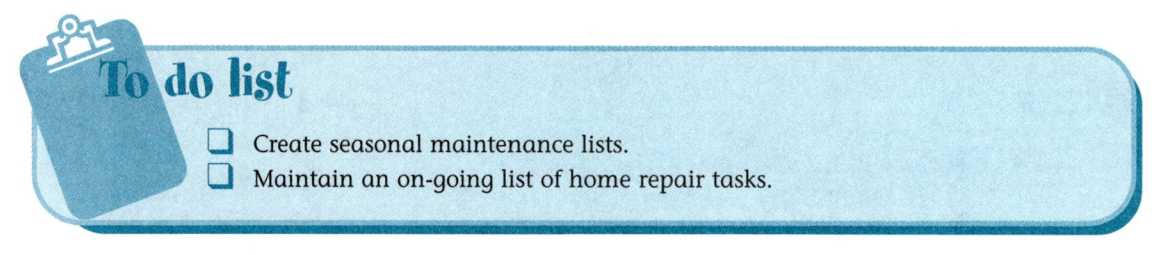

To do list

- ❑ Create seasonal maintenance lists.
- ❑ Maintain an on-going list of home repair tasks.

Creating a Home Maintenance Plan

A good home maintenance plan requires some planning, and an important part of creating a maintenance plan is listing the tasks you must perform to inspect and maintain your home. There are two good ways of approaching this plan. One is to make a list of inspections and chores by season of the year. The other is to make a list of chores for any time of year. As you learn in the following sections, both are important and both prevent larger and more expensive work down the line.

Now, where do you put a list? It does no good if you put it in a drawer and forget about it or can't find it when you need it. In January, I make notes on the calendars I look at most frequently. I might make a note in the month of January, for example, that says, "Look at the winter maintenance list"; and in March, I might note, "Look at the spring maintenance list." I don't have to keep the whole list there, just a reminder to consult it, because I need something to kick-start me. If you regularly look at a calendar on a computer, that might be the place for such reminders.

Similarly, the lists can be on paper, in a notebook, or in a computer—anywhere that's handy. You just have to know where it is and have a good reminder to consult it at the right time.

Listing Seasonal Maintenance Tasks

Some home maintenance tasks are appropriate for specific times of year. Your seasonal maintenance lists give you a maintenance blueprint for working through the right tasks at the right time. Although every home is unique, here are some suggestions for seasonal maintenance repair lists.

Autumn Maintenance List

In the fall, make inspections as follows and do appropriate repairs:

- ❏ **Windows**—Check panes and replace any that are cracked. Press sashes to see whether they move; if they do, air will get in. Shift the *stop bead*, the piece of trim that holds the sash in place, closer to the sash. Examine glazing and replace any that is damaged. Check around the window trim for missing caulk. Check weatherstripping. Check caulking around storm windows. (For more information on repairing and weatherstripping windows, see Chapter 4, "Doors and Windows.")
- ❏ **Doors**—Check weatherstripping. If, after visual inspection, you're still uncertain where air might be leaking in around a door (or a window), wait for a breezy, chilly day and move your hand around the perimeter, sensing for cold air. (For more information about weatherstripping around doors, see Chapter 4.)
- ❏ **Gutters**—Clean out gutters after the last foliage has fallen from the trees. Actually, you might have to clear gutters several times during the fall. (See Chapter 8, "Outdoor Repairs and Maintenance.")
- ❏ **Fireplace and vents**—Use binoculars to check the tops of chimneys and vents to make sure foliage or birds' nests are not blocking them.
- ❏ **Safety equipment**—Test all smoke detectors and carbon monoxide testers; insert fresh batteries. Get the instructions for testing your water heater's pressure and temperature relief valves; then test them.
- ❏ **Chimney**—If you use a chimney or wood stove for wood fires, make sure neither has a build-up of creosote in the chimney or flue.

The general rule is that a chimney or flue needs to be cleaned after each cord of wood burned. Call a chimney sweep for this work.

- ❏ **Heating system**—Check your heating system or have a professional check it for you. For a forced-air system with ducts that also serve a central air conditioning system, set the registers for warm air by opening them wider on lower floors and restricting them on upper floors. For a radiator system, check that radiator valves are open to the degree you want.
- ❏ **Decks**—Coat deck boards once every two or three years with a stain that contains ultraviolet light inhibitors (see "Stain a Deck" in Chapter 8). Examine and touch up paint on railings.

A Winter Maintenance List

In the winter, make the following inspections and appropriate repairs:

- ❏ **Toilets**—Take the tops off toilet tanks and watch as you make a practice flush. Make adjustments if the water level rises too high. Look for developing cracks in the tank. Feel under the toilet tank around the inlet valve for leaks and around the supply valve for leaks. Feel around the toilet base for leaks; do the same at showers and under sinks.

- ❑ **Faucets**—Check for leaks.
- ❑ **Floors and walls**—Look for and repair cracks.

Spring Maintenance
In the spring, check the following and make appropriate repairs:

- ❑ **Basement**—On a day when rain falls on snow that's still on the ground, the ground becomes its most saturated. Walk around the basement looking for water leaks.
- ❑ **Gutters**—Clear gutters again to prepare them for spring storms.
- ❑ **Windows**—Clean and repair screens.
- ❑ **Air conditioning**—Clean the filters. If the ducts are also used for a forced-air heating system and you adjusted the registers in the fall, readjust them now to deliver more cool air to the upper floors—the cool air will work its way downstairs and cool this area also.
- ❑ **Exterior**—Walk around the home to look for winter damage to the paint or siding. With binoculars, look for damage to the roof shingles and flashing. Examine windows and window trim from the outside. Examine the foundation's surface above ground for cracks. Check that the soil near the foundation slopes away from the foundation.

    Check that downspouts are not cracked or dislodged from gutters. Check that splash blocks and extension tubes are in place and clear. If tree limbs or bushes are touching the roof, gutters, or siding, cut them back.

> **tip** The best seasons for exterior painting are spring and fall when temperatures are moderate.

Summer Maintenance Tasks
In the summer, make the following inspections and repairs as necessary:

- ❑ **Exterior**—Take a walk around the home and check for insect infestation. Look for termite tunnels extending from the ground up the foundation masonry to the level of the first floor. Check for wasp nests under porch roofs and look for signs of mold and mildew.
- ❑ **Basement**—Look for signs of mold and mildew. If you find some, clean it with a chlorine solution (read the directions on a liquid chlorine bottle). Correct the source of moisture—this might be leaks in the basement walls. If there are no running leaks, dehumidifiers might solve the problem, but note that dehumidifiers use electricity and even though they dry the air in a basement, they also warm it.

Anytime List of Repairs and Maintenance Tasks

The seasonal list is important because it requires you to get prepared for the demands of the weather and season just ahead. Over the course of a year, it forces you to examine most of the major systems of a home and to see that they are functioning properly.

But some maintenance and repairs are not particularly seasonal and can be done just about any time. Rewiring lamps, upgrading plumbing fixtures, replacing cracked tiles, and the like can be done at any time of year. The trouble is, they are not as much fun as watching the big game or the clouds go by. My solution is to make an anytime list of the repairs that need doing around the home. I know that sometimes I feel like doing them and sometimes I don't. If you have all the home repairs listed for you in a central spot, when you have the urge to get them done, you can knock off half a dozen of them in order. Keep an anytime list in a prominent place, like on a refrigerator front. It'll nag you from time to time to get the tasks done, but you'll also have the satisfaction of drawing lines through completed tasks and letting such "Done!" marks stay up there a week or so.

Compiling a list of necessary home repair jobs also can make your trips to the home improvement store more efficient. You can see which jobs await and shop for all the necessary supplies at one time rather than having to run off to pick up materials every time you want to tackle a simple repair task or two.

> **note** Although you might be tempted otherwise, it's best to share the anytime repair list with your spouse. Your partner very likely has a set of ideas about which tasks need doing and might even want to help tackle some of them. Check the list before you head for the home improvement or hardware store, and be sure to buy supplies for all jobs.

Maintaining an Apartment

Apartments and rental properties are different from homes because the landlord is generally responsible for most major repairs and maintenance tasks. Thus a broken toilet, a flickering chandelier, or a faulty radiator typically is fixed by the landlord.

But apartment dwellers need to do some maintenance. This will make their homes more pleasant to live in and can save them from damage or loss. Apartment dwellers should make seasonal rounds of the apartment, looking for any developing trouble. Here are some sound home maintenance task ideas for those living in a rental:

- ❏ **Bathrooms**—Look for developing cracks in toilet tanks. If a tank bursts, the inlet valve will likely run until someone shuts off the supply valve, meaning a major flood is possible. Look for drips beneath sinks and toilets. Although the landlord might be responsible for fixes, if drips persist, the flooring can rot (even if under linoleum or tile), leading to insect infestation. Examine tile for gaps in grout; if water gets behind grout, it can lead to rot in floors and walls.
- ❏ **Windows and doors**—Feel around windows and doors on cold, blustery days. If you sense cold air, have the fault corrected because your heating bills will rise otherwise. Make sure caulking on the exterior is sound; if it is not, wood rot can result.

- **Kitchens**—Look for leaks under the sink and dishwasher. Call the gas company or landlord *immediately* if you detect the odor of natural gas. Keep the stove area free of grease, which attracts insects.
- **Repairs**—Be on the lookout for repairs or improvements you might enjoy making, such as painting, wallpapering, installing new plumbing fixtures, and the like. You might be able to get the landlord to lower his rent charge if you make these repairs, and you'll definitely make your living space more pleasant, comfortable, and efficient.

FINDING, CONTRACTING WITH, AND MANAGING TRADESMEN

Finding good repairmen can be difficult. When you need a good repairman, one of your best resources is your neighbors. Ask them whom they have been happy with. If you see a contractor's sign in a neighbor's yard, call that person and ask if they are satisfied with the contractor's performance. Failing such neighborhood references, check with the local chamber of commerce. You can also ask at lumberyards, plumbing supply stores, and the like whom they recommend as good and reliable. You might also note tradesmen's trucks. Are they clean? Do they have the address and phone number painted on the side? You can call remodeling contractors and ask whom they use for such jobs as tile setting, electrical work, and so on; contractors will give you such names when they know they are not going to be using these people for a while. Do not deal with persons who appear at the door and say they noticed your chimney flashing was cracked or some other fault and offer to fix it. Say thank you and have someone else look into it.

For small jobs, you are not likely to need an elaborate contract, but you should be careful to spell out and agree upon all essential details of the work to be performed. At the very least, find out in advance what the hourly charge is and set an estimate of how long the work is going to take. Get an estimate for the cost of materials. If the job is going to take more than half a day, write up an agreement on paper; if it's for more than a few hundred dollars, get a formal contract. An agreement or contract should specify the lump sum amount or hourly rate, who pays for materials plus a price range for materials, a start and stop time or date for the work, the fact that the repairman gives you warranty papers for parts, and who is responsible for cleanup.

Don't overmanage your repair workers; they should mainly be left to themselves. They work more efficiently that way, and if you talk to them too much or look over their shoulders they'll end up taking longer and charging you more money. But you should walk them to the trouble and explain exactly what you expect of them, and they should explain exactly what they can do and about how long it will take. Before a tradesman comes over, remove any jewelry, wallets, or other valuables in the area where the person will be working—temptation is best kept far away. Before a tradesman leaves, examine the work to see if it meets your standards. If there is something you do not understand, ask. And ask how long the repair person guarantees the work.

Calling In the Pros

No one does everything, not even professional handymen. Everyone has his limitations. From time to time, you will want to—or need to—call a professional. The following are probably good times for that:

- **Don't do any task that feels dangerous or that requires important safety skills you are certain you do not have**—If you are not familiar with working on roofs, don't. If you feel off balance working high on a ladder, don't work on one. Call a pro for any job for which you would feel unsafe or off balance. (For more on ladders and ladder safety, see Chapter 8.)

- **Don't tackle jobs that require a permit from the city and completion according to the city's building code**—For example, creating a new electrical circuit, say for a basement work area, requires a permit from the city (or county, if outside the city limits). The code might also require that the task be done by a licensed electrician, or it might allow you to perform the job only after you take a written test on your knowledge of residential electrical systems. Building a room addition or making substantial structural changes to your home typically requires a building permit. If you think you are about to tackle a job that is covered by your jurisdiction's building code, call the building department.

- **Don't take on a job if the work needs to be completed quickly and you don't have the skill or time**—Even though you might have to take emergency stop-gap measures, call a professional to fix dire emergencies. A burst pipe or a leak in the basement needs to be repaired quickly to limit damage or restore convenience to the family. This isn't the time to feel your way through an unfamiliar task.

- **Don't try to do repairs that require extensive use of special tools**—Professionals have expensive tools that help them make the work faster and more accurate. You can buy such tools, but if you are not going to be using them often, they probably are not worth the money. Door installers have drill guides and routers to make accurate holes for locks and mortises for hinges. You can do the work without such tools, but the task takes longer and mistakes can be difficult (and expensive) to patch up. If you have several doors to work on, buy the tools or call a pro. If you have one door, call a pro or plan on taking extra time to carefully do the work with the tools at hand.

- **Don't take on a task that requires highly specialized skills you haven't the time or interest to learn**—Given time and practice, you can master most skills, but if the work is going to be done only once, it might not be worth your trouble. An example is large and intricate wallpapering. If you'll be doing this only once in the home where you live, you'll have most of the headaches of being a novice without the later benefit of being experienced.

- **Be reluctant to go it alone on tasks that require extra hands**—Some jobs require—or go much smoother and faster—with more than one person. Working with large sheets of drywall is one example. If you do not have a willing helper, hire one or call in the pros.

Summary

No one likes to hear it, but an ounce of prevention is worth a pound of cure. With your seasonal list, keep a sharp eye out for areas that might one day need extensive help. If you see some paint peeling, scrape it and paint the area now; moisture getting under the paint will only make for more peeling paint later. Keep air conditioning filters clean to keep the motor from becoming overworked and wearing out. And if you pay attention to your anytime list, you'll keep on top of small jobs around the house that will make your home more pleasant to live in, rather than letting problems build until many tasks scream for attention all at once.

Of course, trouble is going to crop up from time to time. But you have the tools to deal with much of it. And the information you need for using your tools and making those repairs is in the six chapters that follow, beginning with Chapter 3, "Walls and Floors."

Part II

Essential Home Repairs, Area by Area

3	Walls and Floors	29
4	Doors and Windows	61
5	Plumbing	89
6	Simple Electrical Repairs	125
7	Painting and Wallpapering	149
8	Outdoor Repairs and Maintenance	185
A	References and Resources	211

3

Walls and Floors

We don't often think about the walls around us and the floors beneath our feet. But sometimes these important structural elements of our home call out for attention. Walls need to support pictures or heavy shelves, and they take a number of hits from moving furniture, vigorously propelled toys, and the everyday bumps of a busy household. Floors hold up well to the traffic we put on them, but years of scuffing feet, dropped objects, scraping furniture, and more can splinter wood or cut through resilient flooring.

Fortunately, most work on walls and floors is fairly straightforward. You don't need specialized knowledge to repair these surfaces, and for the most part, damage to walls and floors is remedied with the tools and materials you have at home or that are readily available in home improvement stores. One nice thing about repair work on walls and floors is that the improvements are visible right away. They rid eye sores to make the planes of wall and floor once again smooth and lovely—and out of mind.

In this chapter, you learn some basic techniques for repairing damage to a number of wall surfaces, including plaster, drywall, wood paneling, and ceramic tile. The chapter also talks about basic repairs to wood, resilient, and ceramic-tiled floors.

In this chapter:

* Learn basic repair techniques for plaster, drywall, and ceramic tile walls.
* Learn how to repair wooden floors and how to repair and replace resilient floor surfaces.

Repair Your Home In No Time

To do list

- ❏ Determine whether your home's walls are made of plaster or drywall and determine, where necessary, the material of the wall studs.
- ❏ Learn how to choose the correct fasteners for your wall type and the task at hand.
- ❏ Learn basic plaster repair techniques.
- ❏ Learn how to repair scrapes, dents, and larger damage to drywall.
- ❏ Clean and repair grout and replace broken tiles in ceramic wall surfaces.

Repairing Walls

Walls do not take up much of our attention, but we actually work with them quite a bit, especially right after moving into a house or apartment. We hang things on them, including posters, picture frames, hooks, mirrors, shelves, and more. Although many of these items are lightweight, some are quite heavy and require specific types of fasteners and hanging supports. To ensure that what we hang is going to stay where we put it, we have to understand something of the walls themselves and of the hardware used to do the actual supporting.

And walls occasionally need repair. Dents, scrapes, and bumps need to be smoothed over; cracks and holes need to be filled; and grout and ceramic tiles need to be replaced. In this section, you learn how to deal with these minor home repair issues. You also learn about the basic makeup of plaster, drywall, and other common wall surfaces and how to use the right tools and techniques for their repair.

Working with Wall Surfaces

Although most modern homes today are built with drywall, most homeowners at some point need to repair other types of wall surfaces. These types include plaster, wood paneling, ceramic tile, and masonry. In the following sections, you learn a bit about the makeup of each of these wall surfaces and some of the issues you'll face when working with them.

TOOLS AND MATERIALS FOR WORKING WITH WALL SURFACES

The tools and materials you use when working with wall surfaces vary, depending on the type of surface and the task you're performing. Each of the repair techniques you learn in this chapter is preceded by a list of the tools and materials you'll need for that specific task. Here is a description, however, of some of the common items you'll use when repairing wall surfaces or installing fasteners within them:

- **Joint compound**—Available in 1- and 5-gallon containers for room-size jobs (or even larger), joint compound spreads over drywall joints, corners, holes, and blemishes. Spackling compound, which is similar and dries quickly, comes in containers of 8 oz. and 32 oz. for small repairs. You can also use these compounds for repairing cracks and fissures in plaster.
- **Self-adhesive fiberglass mesh tape**—Handy for several kinds of jobs, this type of mesh tape, with joint compound, covers the narrow gaps between panels of drywall. It also bridges damage in drywall to make repairs that are strong and practically invisible.
- **Jab saw**—Also called a *small drywall saw* or *keyhole saw*, a jab saw is meant for short sawing cuts of drywall, either already installed or in preparation. The saw's rough teeth are meant to easily cut the gypsum and paper. When the drywall is already installed, the point of a jab saw can press through the drywall to begin a cut. When the drywall is on a workbench or being prepared for installation, the jab saw can make short, shaping cuts.
- **Grout saw**—This is a small, tough-toothed instrument that you pull along grout joints to loosen old grout in ceramic tile walls.
- **Grout float**—Essentially a rectangular sponge backed with wood and a wooden handle, a grout float presses fresh grout into joints between tiles and wipes off excess as it moves along. If you are doing lots of grouting, this makes the job cleaner and quicker.
- **Cold chisel**—Designed for very hard objects, a cold chisel and hammer can break up ceramic tile on a wall or floor.
- **Glass cutter**—Drawing its cutting blade across a glazed tile helps mark a damaged tile with a spot at which a drill bit can gain a grip.
- **Special drill bits**—Spade bits drill holes wider than twist bits, from 3/8" to 1 1/4". Carbide-tipped bits can drill into masonry and ceramic tile, and ceramic tile bits can drill through hardened tile. Buy them at home improvement or tile stores.
- **Drill attachment drivers for screws**—Some drills come with attachments that grip screws so the twisting action of the drill can screw them into place. If yours does not, see if one can be attached to it. If you are often working with drywall panels, it is helpful to have an attachment for screws, and such attachments come in handy for many other jobs, too.

Drywall Basics

Until the middle of the last century, nearly all wall surfaces in homes were made of plaster, a gypsum or a lime/cement mixture that is spread over strips of wood called *lath*. To save time, and thus labor charges, the building industry developed *drywall*. These are panels of plaster-like material dried between layers of thick paper, generally 4' by 8' in size and about 1/2" thick. Drywall sheets are nailed or screwed to wood or metal studs and go up much more quickly than plaster/lath combinations, thus enabling builders to finish walls far more quickly than with the old method of plastering.

Where panels meet, the narrow gaps are called *seams* or *joints* and are covered with a paper or mesh tape, which is then covered with a mastic called *joint compound*. The compound is sanded smooth with the surface of the wallboard and, when painted along with the rest of the wall, the seams are virtually undetectable.

Most drywall in homes is 1/2" thick. Most builders use waterproof, 5/8" thick drywall in bathrooms, though. Drywall might be thicker or installed in double layers where building codes call for special protection against fire. Builders also might use thicker drywall on ceilings to stop the spread of flame to an upper floor or on a wall separating an attached garage from a home to slow the spread of fires beginning in the garage.

Drywall is criticized for being thin and having a thin ring to it, and it does not support heavy weights except when fasteners enter studs behind. But its virtue to the homeowner is that it is relatively easy to repair and does not chip or crack as readily as plaster.

Hanging objects on drywall requires special fasteners, due to the limited thickness of the drywall panels and the hollow space behind them. When working with drywall, you also have to be aware that you might hit wood or metal studs behind the drywall panels.

Plaster

Plaster is the former king of home walls. In early construction, plaster was spread over the stones or logs that made a home. Builders long ago discovered, however, that they could save money by building homes with studs—that is, milled 2-by-4s that were erected 16" or so apart to be covered over with wall material. To accommodate the plaster, wooden lath strips running horizontally were first nailed to the vertical studs. Each piece of lath was about 1/4" thick and about 1 1/2" wide; gaps between pieces of lath averaged about 1/2".

This arrangement was standard in homes from the mid-nineteenth century to mid-twentieth century. Beginning in the first part of the twentieth century, plaster was spread over gypsum wallboard nailed to studs. In modern homes, when plaster is used, it is spread over a metal mesh fastened to studs.

Plaster is still considered a superior wall. It has a solid, thick feeling to it. But it also tends to chip and develop cracks more easily than does drywall.

When putting fasteners into plaster walls, you have to contend with a tough, occasionally brittle material prone to cracking or chipping, as well as the uncertainty of striking either lath or the gaps between lath strips.

Wood Paneling

Wood has been used for centuries as a wall material. In the eighteenth century, many a country manor's library were covered with Georgian wooden paneling, crafted as finely as cabinetry. In America, wood was so plentiful east of the Mississippi that vertical wood boards composed the paneling. Today, these thick panels have been imitated with thinner plywood panels, often covered with an artificial wood-grain surface and scored with manufactured vertical grooves.

Like plaster and wallboard, wood paneling is backed up with vertical wooden studs.

Masonry

Bricks, concrete, concrete block, cinder block, and stone are used to construct masonry walls. There is no mystery to how walls of these are made. For brick, stone, and block walls, the units are stacked on top of one another until the wall is finished. In the case of poured concrete walls, liquid concrete is poured into forms; after the concrete hardens, the forms are removed.

Ceramic Tile

Ceramic tile walls are commonly used in bathrooms and often do not extend all the way to the ceiling; instead the tiles rise only to about head height. Ceramic tile walls are made by adhering individual tiles to a backing of plaster or drywall to make a tough, impervious surface. The tiles themselves are very durable, but the grout between tiles has to be inspected often and occasionally replenished.

Choosing and Using Wall Fasteners

The method you use for attaching a picture, bookcase, display case, or other item to a wall depends on the wall surface type and the weight of the object you're hanging. The best chance for success depends on matching the correct fastener to the task.

As you learn in the next sections, heavy objects must be hung from wall studs or with special fasteners. Light objects are easier. A small nail hammered in at a slant works well for light picture frames hung on plaster, drywall, and most good-quality wood paneling. Heavier frames require picture hooks, and the heavier the frame, the larger the picture hook required. Especially heavy frames should be hung with two heavy-duty picture hooks nailed to the wall about a foot apart and at the same height above the floor.

Before you hammer a nail or drill a hole into plaster that you suspect is prone to crumbling or cracking (that is, if you see crumbling or cracks nearby), press a 1" piece of transparent tape over the area. Drill through the center of the tape, which adds cohesive strength to the plaster beneath it.

Locating Wall Studs

Heavy objects, such as book or display cases, should be fastened into wood studs behind drywall, plaster, or paneling whenever possible. Use a stud finder to find the studs. Stud finders use either a magnet to detect the metal screws or nails holding the drywall or lathe to the studs or wave technology to detect a stud's bulk. As you move a stud finder along a wall, indicators tell you where the studs are.

Studs typically are located at 16" intervals, so when you've located one stud, you should be able to locate others simply by measuring. In older homes especially, the 16" is only approximate, and older homes (more than 100 years old) likely have studs closer to 2" wide than 1 1/2" wide (the modern standard).

When you have located a stud, you can determine if it is wood or metal by drilling toward it with a twist bit. The sound and feel of hitting the stud might tell you if it is wood or metal. If not, when you continue, with metal, the drilling suddenly becomes easier because the stud is hollow; with wood the drilling does not become easier and when you withdraw the twist bit, the grooves show traces of sawdust.

Nails or screws can go into the studs to support weighty objects. If the studs in your home are not wood but sheet metal (which is thin enough to cut with tin snips), you can use Type S drywall screws rather than nails. These have a sharp point and, while twisting from the energy of a power drill, create their own hole in the metal stud. If you have trouble getting the screw to penetrate the stud, drill a hole through the plaster or drywall, dimple the metal stud with a *center punch* (a tool with a hardened sharp point for making such marks), and then use a twist bit to drill a hole half the diameter of the thickness of the screw you intend to use. Then the screw should fasten to the stud.

Studs are doubled to the left and right of doors and windows, thus doubling your surface for nails and screws to grip wood—in metal stud walls, there are doubled studs also, but generally the inside ones are wood. The frames above doors and windows have additional wood support, as well. The wood members here are called *headers* and are normally made of 2-by-6s or 2-by-8s on edge. Headers extend up from the top of windows and doors 5"–7", although often a good portion of this is covered by the window or door's trim.

Using Fasteners That Don't Require Studs

If you're hanging relatively heavy objects on a hollow drywall or plaster wall, in a location not along a stud, you cannot resort to mere nails and picture hooks; you need special fasteners.

If the object is of moderate weight, use plastic shields and appropriate self-tapping screws that screw into them. Plastic shields and screws to fit are sold at home improvement stores either separately or combined in packages. For heavier objects, use lag anchors (which are similar to plastic shields but are made of steel), Molly bolts, or toggle bolts, as shown in Figure 3.1. Molly bolts (also called *hollow wall anchors*) and toggle bolts are made especially for hollow walls. These bolts penetrate the wall and then a portion of them expands to grip the wall from behind.

FIGURE 3.1
From left to right: Plastic shields, Molly bolts, toggle bolts, and lag anchors are some of the fasteners that can hold heavy objects to different wall constructions in homes.

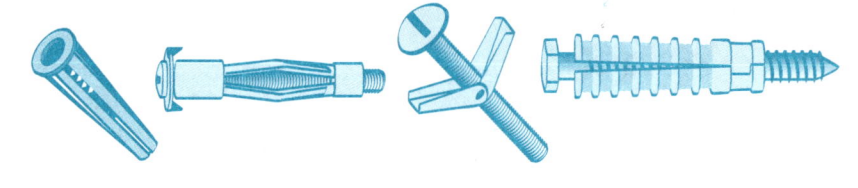

Molly bolts are made of two pieces, a threaded bolt and a metal sleeve. To install a Molly bolt, you first drill a hole in the drywall using a twist bit. You then slip the Molly bolt through the hole until its front collar grips the wall surface. You then turn the bolt head with a screwdriver, making sure the collar does not turn. As the bolt turns, it draws the sleeve projection against the back of the wall. The bolt can then be removed and set through a loop or hole of the object to be hung. Molly bolts have to be sized to the exact thickness of the wall and thus are better suited to use in drywall, rather than plaster (which often varies in thickness and is backed by lathwork).

A toggle bolt locks into a wall using two hinged arms that spring out from the end of the bolt after the bolt is inserted in the wall. To install a toggle bolt, you first drill a hole in the drywall, using a twist bit, just as you do with a Molly bolt. The toggle bolt, however, has to be placed through the object to be hung *before* the toggle portion is pushed into the hole. After you insert the toggle into the drilled hole, the two arms along the bolt threads spring open—so long as the hinged end is far enough down the bolt threads. Then you have to pull back slightly on the bolt head, or what it is connected to, to make the arms grip the back of the wall while you turn the bolt to move the bolt head closer to the surface of the wall.

Using Fasteners for Masonry Walls

Hanging items from brick, stone, and other types of masonry walls requires special tools and materials. *Masonry nails* (with twisted shafts) and *cut nails* can penetrate and grip the mortar between bricks, concrete block, or cinder block. Various kinds of anchors (or what are similar and are called *expansion shields*) work on all forms of masonry. To use them, you have to use a carbide-tipped drill bit to make holes of precisely the diameter of the anchors and then tap them in with a hammer. When screws are turned into them, the anchors expand to firmly grip the surrounding masonry. Toggle bolts and Molly bolts can work on concrete block or cinder block if they are long enough.

Repairing Plaster

Plaster can be damaged in a number of ways. When a house settles with age, the plaster sometimes cracks. These cracks can develop into rather wide fissures. Plaster can also be damaged when struck by tools, furniture being moved, and so on. Plaster can even develop cracks owing to vibration nearby, as from heavy traffic on a neighboring highway. And plaster can be damaged if water penetrates it following a roof or plumbing leak.

But all these problems have solutions, although some plaster cracks and fissures can recur. Sometimes this recurring damage is seasonal—cracks open each winter in the same place, for example, as a result of the wood behind the plaster contracting because of lower humidity. Or it can be due to nearby vibrations, which open old cracks or start new ones nearby. In this section of the chapter, you learn how to fix damaged plaster and identify its cause.

Things You'll Need

- ❑ Water squirt bottle
- ❑ 6" wide joint compound knife and putty knife
- ❑ Spackling compound or joint compound
- ❑ Medium-grit sandpaper and sanding block

Fixing a Hairline Crack

Hairline cracks are annoying but not too difficult to fix. Follow these steps:

1. Squirt the area of the crack with water from a water spray bottle. Try to get some of the moisture into the crack.
2. Put spackling compound or joint compound on the 6" joint compound knife. Then use that knife or a putty knife, depending on how much of the surrounding wall you want to cover, to transfer some spackling compound to the crack and adjacent plaster.
3. As best you can, force the spackling compound into the crack. Scrape with the knife to make the joint compound thinnest at its edges.
4. Wait for the spackling compound to dry for at least an hour. Lightly sand the spackling compound. Wipe away the dust and cover the patch with a coat of primer paint.

Filling a Wider Crack

Some plaster cracks are wider and deeper than hairline ones; you can actually look into them. These require somewhat stronger methods.

Things You'll Need

- ❏ Can opener or old flat-head screwdriver
- ❏ Water spray bottle
- ❏ Joint compound or spackling compound
- ❏ Putty knife and joint compound knife
- ❏ Light sandpaper and sanding block

With your tools and materials at hand, follow these steps:

1. Where the crack is wide enough, undercut it so that the crack is wider *under* the surface than it is on the surface itself (see Figure 3.2). A good tool for this is the pointed end of an old can opener, but a small, old, flat-head screwdriver will do. At the same time, remove any plaster that is loose or crumbling.
2. Remove grit from the crack. Brush it out with an old paintbrush or blow it out.
3. Spray water into the crack.
4. With a 6" joint compound knife or putty knife, work joint compound into the crack. Force it in so that it spreads into the undercut areas.
5. Wait a few hours for the joint compound to dry. Sand the patch smooth.
6. Brush on a paint primer before painting over it with the wall color.

FIGURE 3.2
Make the crack wider beneath the surface than at the surface. This holds the patching material in place.

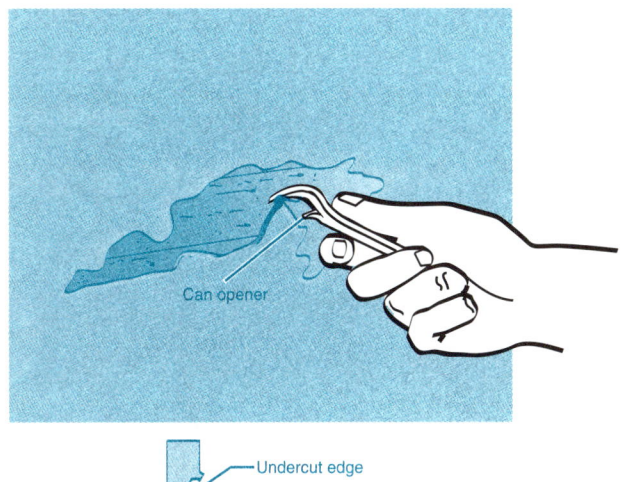

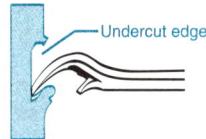

Can opener

Undercut edge

Patching a Recurring Crack
Some cracks return repeatedly owing to seasonal expansion and contractions in the walls or to outside vibrations from heavy traffic.

Things You'll Need

- ❑ Joint compound
- ❑ Joint compound knife
- ❑ Fiberglass mesh tape
- ❑ Medium- and fine-grit sandpaper and sanding block

Here's how to patch these cracks and help prevent them from recurring:
1. Follow steps 1 and 2 of "Fixing a Wider Crack."
2. Apply self-adhesive fiberglass mesh tape to the crack. If the crack curves, use short lengths of tape that do not overlap rather than making one longer piece bend with the crack; overlapping or bending the tape makes bulges at the turns.
3. With a 6" joint compound knife, press joint compound into the tape (see Figure 3.3). Make the joint compound as smooth and flat as possible. Finish by drawing the knife along the outside edges of the joint compound to make the joint compound thinnest here. Wait for this coating to dry.
4. Spread another coat of joint compound over the first. Use a blade wider than 6" if you have one. Taper the edges as in step 3. Wait for this coat to dry.

5. Use medium-grit sandpaper to sand the patch smooth, taking care not to sand down to the level of the mesh tape. Switch to fine grit for the last passes.
6. Dust off the patch using a soft brush. Coat with a paint primer.

FIGURE 3.3
Press joint compound into the self-adhesive tape already applied to the crack. Do not let the mesh kink, fold, or double up.

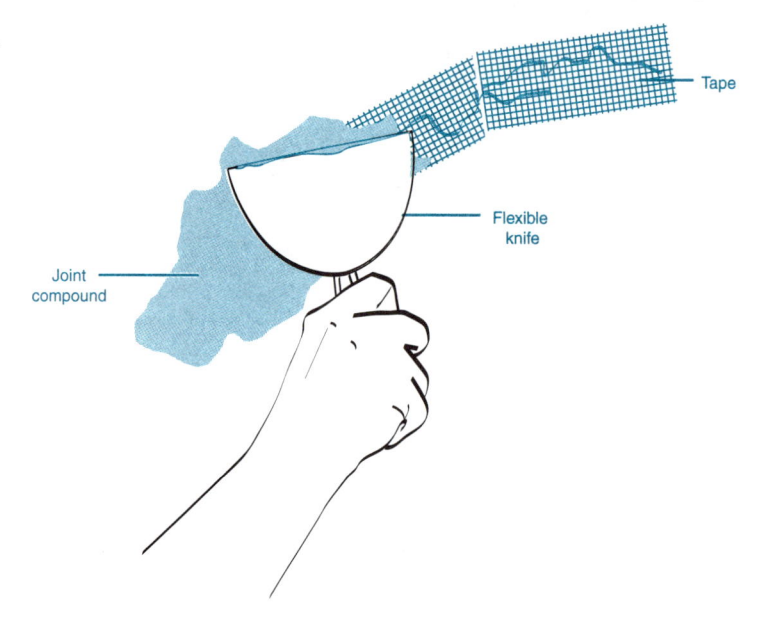

- Tape
- Flexible knife
- Joint compound

Patching a Hole in Plaster

Plaster doesn't always fail in cracks. Sometimes whole sections are damaged. But a section of drywall and a bit of effort can make a patch no one can detect in your plaster wall.

Things You'll Need

- ❏ Hammer and cold chisel
- ❏ Dust mask, eye protection, and a hardhat
- ❏ Tape measure or carpenter's rule
- ❏ Scrap of drywall sized to fit
- ❏ Utility knife or jab (drywall) saw
- ❏ 6" joint compound knife
- ❏ Sandpaper and sanding block

1. Wear eye protection and a dust mask. If you are working on a ceiling, wear a hardhat, too. Remove all loose and damaged plaster with a hammer and cold chisel. As best you can, make the opening in the plaster a rectangle.
2. Measure the depth of the sound plaster around the edges of the opening. With a utility knife or jab saw, cut a piece of drywall that is this thickness or a bit less.

3. Fasten the drywall patch to the backing material behind the plaster, as shown in Figure 3.4.
4. If the gap between the drywall edges and the sound plaster edges are more than 1/4" wide, cover the gaps with self-adhesive fiberglass mesh tape.
5. Spread joint compound across the drywall and gaps around it. Allow the joint compound to dry.

    If possible, use a joint compound knife that is longer than the patch is wide. That way, both ends of the knife can rest on sound plaster as the knife is drawn across the moist joint compound. Knives come as long as 12". If you are going to be doing a lot of patching or a lot of drywall work, buying a long knife is worth the cost.
6. Use medium-grit sandpaper to smooth the joint compound. Apply another coating and let it dry.
7. Sand the joint compound. Remove dust and coat the patch with primer paint.

If, when removing the damaged plaster, you find that the lath is itself too damaged to support a piece of drywall, remove plaster all the way back to the studs on either side. Use screws to attach the drywall patch through the damaged lath and into the studs.

If you find no lath at this location and the area of damaged plaster is small, use the technique for repairing a hole in drywall.

Sometimes a small area of plaster is sound but merely loosened from the lath behind, making a small bulge in the wall or ceiling. Eventually this bulging plaster will fall away completely. You can avoid this by reattaching the bulge to its backing with a screw and thin plastic washer. Fasten a flathead screw through the washer to the lath behind the plaster, using the screw head and washer to draw the plaster back to the lath, as shown in Figure 3.5. Try to carefully fasten the screw so that its head and the washer are slightly below the level of the surrounding plaster. Cover the screw head and washer with layers of joint compound, and then sand it smooth. This kind of repair works for both ceilings and walls.

> **tip** A good way to measure the depth of the plaster is to use the extending end of a folding rule. Touch the end of the rule to the edge of the hole. Extend the extending portion into the hole to touch whatever is backing the plaster—that is, the lath or plaster board. With a thumb, hold the extending end immobile in the end of the folding rule and remove from the hole. The extending end's gradations will show you the depth of the plaster.

> **tip** If you're attaching a patch to plaster that's backed by wood lath, screw the drywall to the lath—do not use nails because hammering loosens more plaster. If it is gypsum board, use glue or screws. If it is metal lath, score or remove a portion of the patch's back paper. Spread joint compound on the back of the patch and a liberal amount to the metal lath so some oozes through to the back; then press the patch into place.

FIGURE 3.4
Make sure the patch of drywall is no higher than the plaster around it. Screw the patch of drywall to the lath, or attach it using the type of fastener appropriate to the plaster backing.

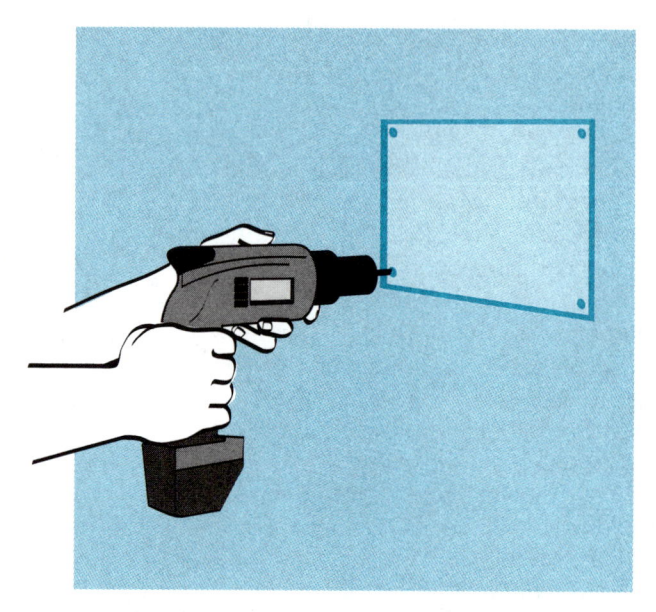

FIGURE 3.5
Use one hand to press the plaster against its support and the other hand to drive the screw through the washer and plaster.

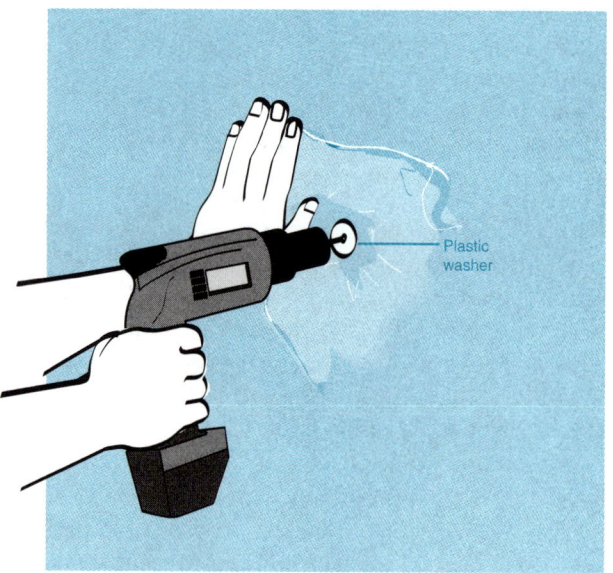

Plastic washer

Patching Drywall

Drywall can be more easily damaged than plaster. Doorknobs have been known to make holes in drywall when doors are opened with some force. But drywall has the virtue of being fairly inexpensive and quick to fix. The repair is sometimes gooey, though, and the dried joint compound becomes dusty when sanded. Wear old clothes and, when sanding, use a dust mask.

In this section, we treat drywall ailments from simple to more complex.

CHAPTER 3   Walls and Floors   41

Things You'll Need

- ☐ Joint compound
- ☐ 5" joint compound knife

Repairing Scrapes and Dents

Everyone has small damage to drywall at sometime. But these are fixed rather quickly and, once painted over, the repair is not visible. Follow these steps:

1. With a utility knife, cut away any torn or damaged paper and any loose drywall material underneath.
2. Spread joint compound into the area of the depression. Wipe joint compound fairly clean of the area surrounding the damage. Wait for the joint compound to dry.
3. Sand the repair, and wipe away the dust. Coat with a primer before you paint the repair with the color of the wall.

Pro's Tip

If the depression is large and deep enough, the first coat of joint compound might shrink as it dries and end up slightly below the level of the surrounding wall. If you want to avoid a second coating of joint compound, attempt to make the first coating bulge out slightly from the surrounding wall. As it dries, the bulge shrinks down closer to the level of the surrounding wall. A light sanding levels it.

Repairing Larger Drywall Damage

The best method for repairing a hole in drywall depends on the hole's size. A hole less than 1" across can be repaired by treating it like a large plaster crack—that is, covering it over with a piece of self-adhesive fiberglass tape and then applying joint compound to the tape and surrounding area.

Things You'll Need

- ☐ Rubber gloves
- ☐ 6" joint compound knife
- ☐ Joint compound
- ☐ Sandpaper and sanding block
- ☐ Screen mesh, small stick, and string

To repair a hole that's about as large as an electrical receptacle, you can use two methods. Here's the first:

1. Cut the hole to the shape of a rectangle; then bevel the edges outward for about 3/4".
2. Cut a piece of drywall to fit, and cut complementary bevels along its own edges.

3. Coat the beveled edges of both the wall and the patch with joint compound; then press the patch into place.
4. Smooth the excess joint compound, allow it to dry, and then sand it.

Another method for filling these larger holes in drywall is as follows:
1. Remove the torn paper and damaged drywall.
2. Cut a piece of wire mesh or heavy window screening that is 1" larger than the hole in all dimensions.
3. Loop a string through the middle of the mesh, as shown in Figure 3.6. About an inch and a half from the mesh, loop the other end of the string around a small stick or pencil.

FIGURE 3.6
Push the wire mesh through the wall and pull it back toward you so the coated edges press against the back of the drywall.

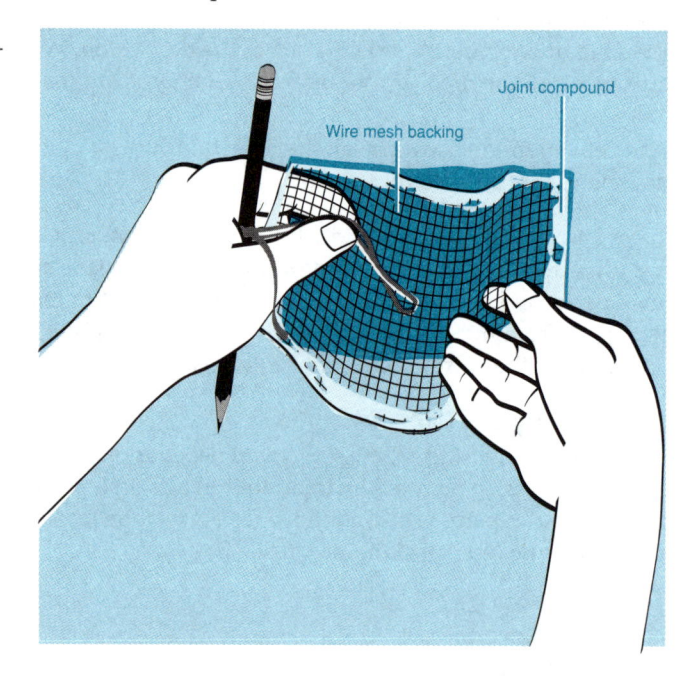

4. Coat the edges of the mesh with joint compound; bend it slightly; and work it through the hole. With your fingers, spread the mesh out behind the hole and pull forward slightly on the pencil; this presses the mesh edges against the back side of the drywall around the hole.
5. Twist the small stick as shown in Figure 3.7, thus shortening the string, until the stick is pressing against the outside of the drywall.
6. With a joint compound knife or putty knife, apply a thin coat of joint compound to the mesh—it should press through the mesh but not more than about 1/8" thick. Allow this coating to dry.
7. Cut the string near the top of the coating. Moisten the first coating, and apply another coating on top of the first. Do not make it thicker than 1/4". Allow it to dry and repeat until the coating is the same level as the surrounding wall. When it is dry, sand it smooth.

CHAPTER 3   **Walls and Floors**   **43**

8. Wipe away dust and coat with paint primer.

FIGURE 3.7
Twist the stick or pencil to shorten the string. Keep twisting until the stick presses firmly against the drywall surrounding the hole.

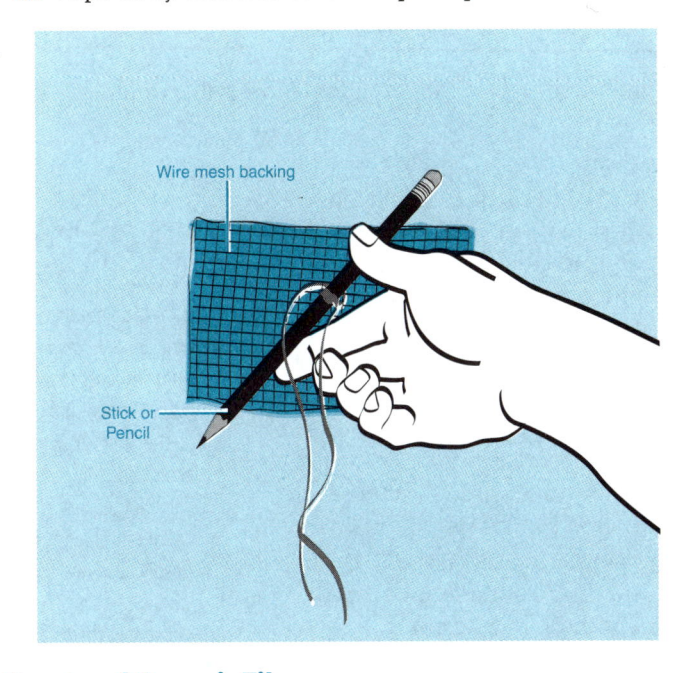

Working with Grout and Ceramic Tile

As I mentioned earlier, ceramic tiles are quite durable and might never need to be replaced. But grouting can crack, mildew, shrink, and fall out. The following sections explain how to perform routine grout maintenance and repair tasks that will keep your ceramic walls in great shape.

Cleaning Grout

Grout absorbs water, and with it any staining agent in the water, including minerals. Over time, these can stain the grout. Mildew is another culprit, leaving darkish spots on the grout. But caught in time, grout stains can be scoured away.

Things You'll Need

- ☐ Chlorine bleach
- ☐ Plastic container
- ☐ Hard-bristle toothbrush
- ☐ Rubber gloves
- ☐ Protective apron or expendable cleaning clothes
- ☐ Eye protection

Repair Your Home In No Time

1. Ventilate the room you are about to work in.
2. In the plastic container, mix a solution of 10 parts water to 1 part chlorine bleach.
3. Scrub the stains with the solution. Rinse with water.

Repairing Grout

If the grout is badly cracked or missing in places, the best recourse is to remove most of it and set new grout between the tiles. If the tiles are in a bathroom, the job is of greater urgency—cracked and missing grout allow water to reach behind the tile and deteriorate the wall material.

Choose cement-based grout rather than epoxy-based. If the joints are less than 1/4" wide, choose plain unsanded grout; if more than 1/4" wide, choose sanded grout.

Grout comes in many colors. A darker one shows less staining, so it might be a better choice for you than a white one.

If you are grouting a large area—for example, the wall of a shower—buy a grout float, essentially a long and wide sponge attached to a backing and handle. You can use a grout float to press grout into the joints and do the wiping as well.

> **caution** Although this is a weak solution of chlorine bleach, do not breathe chlorine fumes for long. In addition, wear eye protection to guard against splashes. And you might want to wear rubber gloves and old clothes—your skin might be sensitive to the chlorine and it can permanently stain your clothes.
> Never mix chlorine bleach with ammonia; deadly gases are produced. In fact, never let chlorine be mixed with any other sort of household chemical or cleaner.

Things You'll Need

- ❑ Dropcloth
- ❑ Cement-based grout
- ❑ Small plastic container for holding the grout mixture
- ❑ Rubber gloves
- ❑ Grout saw, old can opener, or similar item
- ❑ Popsicle stick
- ❑ Sponge or grout float
- ❑ Clean cloth

With your materials ready, follow these steps:

1. If you are working in a bathtub area, close the drain and lay a dropcloth in the bottom of the tub.
2. Use a grout saw to scrape out old grout, or choose another tool that better matches the thickness of the grout joint. Other tools that can do the job include the point of an old can opener, an old flat-head screwdriver, a nail, and a putty knife. Use an old toothbrush to brush out dust and loose grout.

CHAPTER 3 Walls and Floors   45

3. Mix grout with *cold* water according to the manufacturer's instructions in an amount you can deal with in 30 minutes or less. Work on about 4 square feet at a time.
4. If you are grouting around only a tile or two, work the grout into the joints with a finger (protected by the rubber glove). If the joints are narrow and the grout is not going in well, thin the mixture with drops of water. For thick joints, use a stiffer mixture. For corners, press in grout with your finger or a Popsicle stick or similar instrument.
5. Use a clean damp sponge to wipe diagonally across the tile and grout joints, as shown in Figure 3.8. Take care not to wipe out the grout but rather leave it just below the surface of the tile. Look for gaps and air bubbles; fill any that you see and wipe again. Rinse the sponge to keep it clean of grout build-up.
6. Let the grout dry for 15 minutes. Wipe off the haze on the tile with a clean cloth.
7. Do not dispose of any leftover grout down a drain; it hardens in drain pipes and blocks flow.

FIGURE 3.8
Wipe grout into the cracks with a clean damp sponge. Rinse the sponge to keep it free of grout build-up.

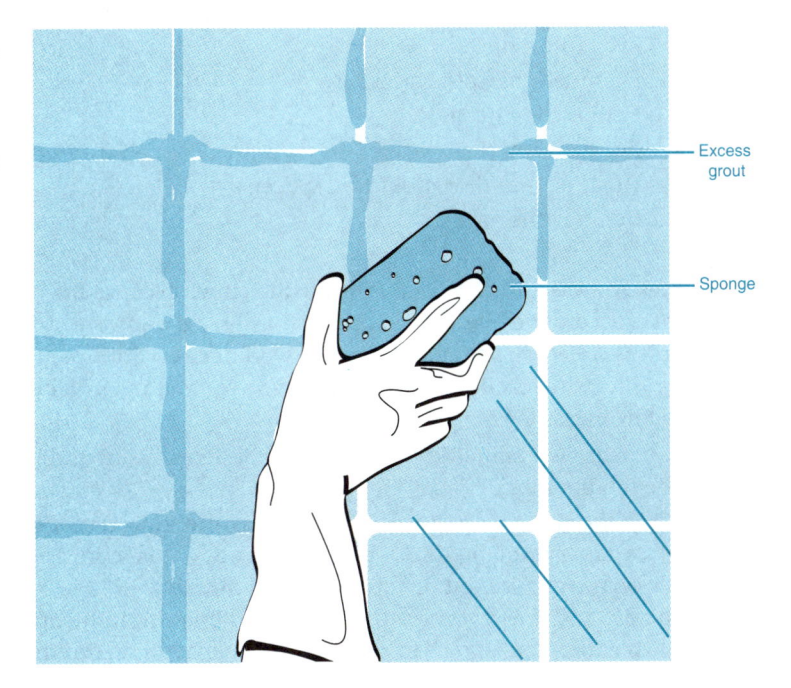

Excess grout

Sponge

Pro's Tip

You can buy and apply grout sealer, which helps keep the grout from staining and absorbing water. Read the manufacturer's instructions—they might recommend that new grout cure for up to a month before being treated with a sealer. Wipe grout sealer on with a sponge, wait for several minutes according to instructions, and wipe it off. Grout sealer can be cleaned with soap and water.

Short Cut: If the grout is merely hopelessly soil-stained but otherwise intact, you can spare yourself replacing it by staining it instead. Grout stains are sold in home improvement stores. Essentially they are paints, but they come in a variety of colors and cover blotchy stains. If you use one, clean the grout, rinse it well, and let it dry for a day. Apply the stain with a small brush, wipe away the excess, and then clean up with soap and water. The stain might make the grout look great, but it is really cosmetic and you might have to reapply the stain every year or so.

Replacing a Tile

Things You'll Need

- ❑ Putty knife
- ❑ Dropcloth and rags
- ❑ Glass cutter or masking tape
- ❑ Drill with ceramic-tile bit or carbide-tipped masonry bit
- ❑ Eye protection
- ❑ Hammer and cold chisel
- ❑ Ceramic tile mastic
- ❑ Replacement tile
- ❑ Toothpicks and/or grout-line spacers
- ❑ Ceramic tile grout

Sometimes you want to replace a ceramic tile either because the tile is damaged or you want a decorative one in its place. You will need adhesive to fasten the tile in place. This is called *mastic* and, if you are working in a bathroom, you should use Type 1 mastic, which is the water-resistant variety. With your tools and materials ready, follow these steps:

1. If you are working in a bathtub area, close the drain and lay a dropcloth in the tub bottom.
2. If the tile is not loose, score it corner to corner and corner to corner with a glass cutter (making an *X*), taking care not to touch neighboring tiles. Using a ceramic-tile drill bit or carbide-tipped masonry drill bit, drill a hole through the tile at the point where the two scored lines meet. If you do not have a glass cutter, make an *X* of masking tape at the center of the tile and drill through the middle of the *X*.
3. Apply masking tape to the edges of surrounding tiles to protect them.
4. Wear eye protection. With a hammer and cold chisel, chip at the tile from the center (see Figure 3.9). Work toward the edges.
5. Clean away all grout and mastic where the tile was—a putty knife is a good tool to use. If you gouge the wall material, fill the depression with joint compound and let it thoroughly dry.

CHAPTER 3   **Walls and Floors**   47

6. Wearing rubber gloves, use a putty knife to spread mastic on the back of the tile to within 1/4" of its edges.
7. Press the tile into place, wiggling it slightly to spread the mastic. Press a piece of 2-by-4 longer than the tile across the tile surface, leveling the new tile with its neighbors. Check the corners and wipe away any mastic that has oozed into the empty grout joints.
8. If the tile slides downward, raise it again and keep it in place with broken toothpicks slipped into the grout joints perpendicular to the wall; these can be pulled out later. If the grout joints are wide, you might be able to buy spacers for them at a tile store—the spacers keep the grout joint the proper width and remain in the joint under new grout.
9. Wait for the mastic to dry for a day. If you have used toothpicks as spacers, pull them out. Then apply grout (see "Repairing Grout").

FIGURE 3.9
Wear eye protection. Use a hammer and cold chisel to chip out the old tile, beginning at the middle and working toward the edges.

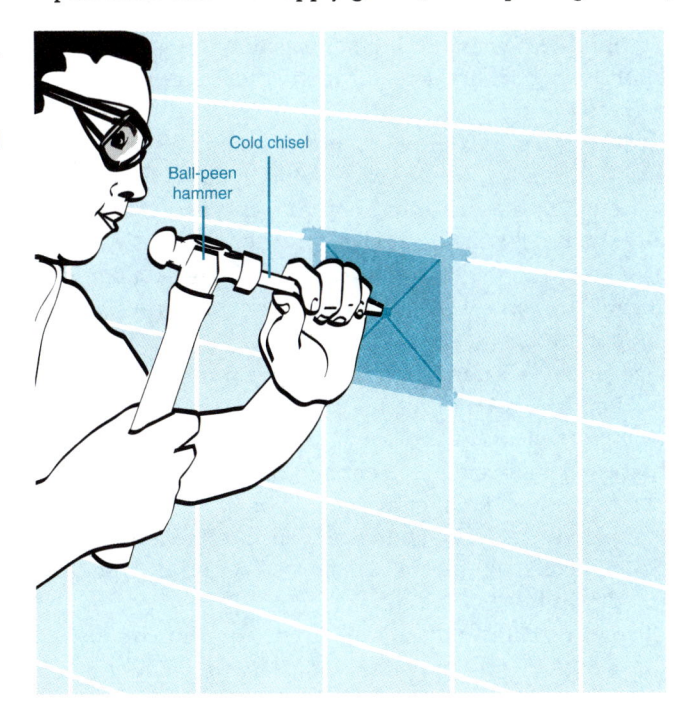

Things You'll Need

- Learn to repair splintered hardwood flooring or repair/replace a floorboard.
- Learn to repair holes, dents, or scratches in resilient flooring; reseal flooring edges; and repair or replace resilient tiles or sheet flooring.

Repairing Floors

Floors have to put up with a lot, and it's not surprising that occasionally cracks or missing portions appear. These can be a hazard to you and your guests, so the quicker you fix the damage, the better.

Wood floor repairs mainly call for skills with carpentry tools and glue. Resilient flooring repairs can be even simpler, requiring not much more than a sharp utility knife and the proper adhesive. No matter what the type of flooring, you might do well to have a knee pad (mentioned in Chapter 1, "Getting Ready") because even a resilient flooring can feel hard to knees after a few minutes.

The following sections explain how to handle a number of common repairs for both wood and resilient flooring. As always, I'll give you a list of necessary tools and materials with each set of repair instructions, but the following descriptions explain how you'll be using these tools and materials in the repairs:

- **Pry bar**—This small prying bar is good for prying up pieces of damaged flooring. Pry bars are good for many other uses as well, including prying open stuck windows.
- **Carpenter's wood glue**—Although common white glue is good for many wood-on-wood joints, yellow carpenter's glue is formulated specially for wood and comes in interior and exterior types—the latter is better for resistance to moisture. Both white and yellow glue require that you apply pressure to the glued pieces, so the glue will work into the wood's pores.
- **Rubber gloves**—Sturdy rubber gloves protect your skin from chemicals in floor adhesives.
- **Knee pads or kneeling pad**—Why torture your knees by kneeling on a hard floor surface? A little knee protection will make your worktime seem much more pleasant.
- **Mastic**—Adhesive for resilient flooring is spread with a putty knife or a notched trowel. The adhesive should be matched to the type of flooring and the underlayment, the boards on which resilient and tile flooring is laid. A flooring dealer will be able to tell you the correct type of mastic for the kind of work you have in mind.
- **Toothed or notched trowel**—These come in various widths and are always used by flooring professionals to spread adhesives. Notched trowels are a step above putty knives for the amateur because they allow for a more even distribution of adhesive to the subsurface and wood, tile, or resilient flooring pressed to the subsurface. Notched trowels are available with metal blades, but plastic disposable ones are available for a dollar or less.

Repairing Hardwood Floors

Because wood is made of grain running in a single direction, it is not uncommon for wood to splinter. Dropped objects, high heels, pushed chair legs, and more can prompt a part of a floorboard to dislodge from the grain below. Such splinters for a time remain attached at one end to the floorboard, but later they can become

CHAPTER 3   Walls and Floors   49

detached entirely; they should be refastened in the first stage. But even if wholly detached, they can be glued back into place so long as they are preserved generally in tact.

Repairing Splinters
If a floorboard begins to splinter, repair it sooner rather than later.

Things You'll Need
- Utility knife
- Carpenter's wood glue
- Waxed paper and flat heavy object
- Damp cloth or paper towel

1. Use the blade point of a utility knife to pry up the portion of the splinter that is unattached to the grain below.
2. Squeeze some wood glue under the splinter.
3. Press the splinter back down, and wipe the area with a damp, not soaking, cloth or paper towel—the glue is water-based.
4. Place waxed paper over the repair and a heavy object over both. Leave the weight and the waxed paper overnight.
5. The next day, remove the weight and paper and lightly sand the repair.

tip Check your wood floors regularly to find splinters and other damage in need of repair. Splinters are much easier to repair when they have just begun to form, rather than after they've detached and become lost (or wedged in someone's bare foot!).

tip If the splinter has come completely off the floor, try to find it and set it aside. Use an old toothbrush to clean all dirt and grit out of the hollowed space left by the splinter; then determine that the splinter fits correctly back in the space. Place a bit of glue on the back of the splinter and into the hollowed space. Then follow steps 3–5 of the instructions for repairing a splinter.

Pro's Tip

Keep wood glue handy; it saves trouble when a splinter comes up from a wooden floor to have the glue around for a quick fix.

Repairing a Floorboard
If a whole section of floorboard is ruined, it can be replaced. Unfortunately, floorboards do not come up easily; they are designed and installed to stay in place. Floorboards connect using tongue-and-groove joints; one edge has a groove and the other a tongue so that the floorboards lock together when joined side by side. When a floorboard becomes irreparably damaged, however, you can cut out and replace the damaged sections.

The following instructions assume a subfloor beneath the finished flooring pieces. In the rare instance you drill your first hole and do not find a subfloor, remove the piece of wood at your drawn lines. Then with a flashlight and tape measure, probe until you find the location of the joists on either side of the removed piece. Remove flooring back to the middle of these joists and cut a piece to fill this exact space. See the Pro's Tip following the instructions for more information.

Things You'll Need

- Utility knife
- Drill and a 1/2" spade bit
- Old wood chisel and hammer
- Pry bar
- Replacement board
- Miter box and saw
- Several 2 1/2" finishing nails (if no subflooring)
- Nail set
- Colored wax wood repair stick

1. Draw straight lines across the board on either end of the damage. The lines must be at least 6" apart and no closer than 1" to the damage. If one line is to be within 16" of the end of the floorboard, just remove all of the floorboard from the damage to the end.
2. Wear eye protection. Drill along the lines all the way through the floorboard to the subfloor so that each drilled hole just touches the damaged side of the line and its neighboring hole.
3. Use a hammer and old but sharpened chisel to cut down along the drawn lines, as shown in Figure 3.10.

FIGURE 3.10
Use a sharp wood chisel to cut down through the floorboard along the marked lines, being sure the beveled side of the chisel faces in toward the damaged area.

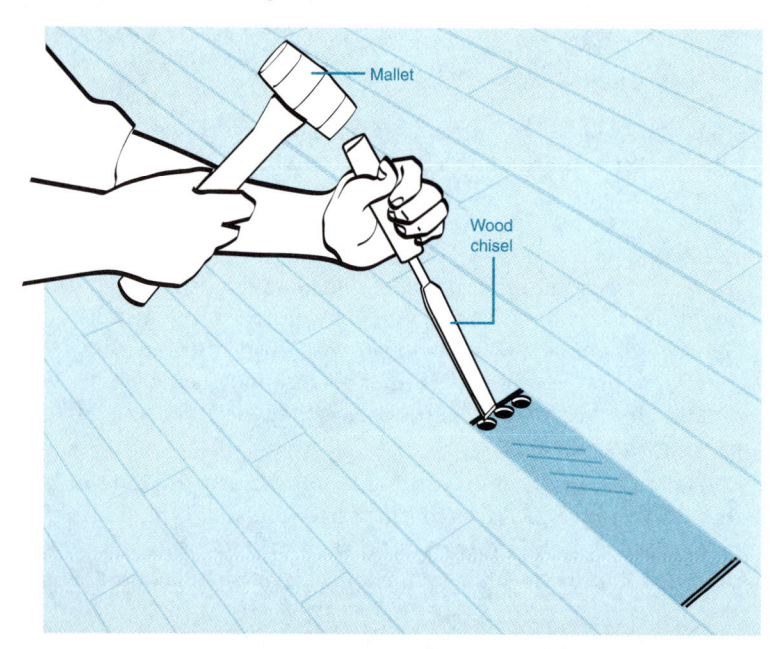

CHAPTER 3 Walls and Floors   51

4. Use the hammer and chisel to make lengthwise cuts along the damaged floorboard from one set of drilled holes to the other. This should splinter the floorboard enough to allow you to remove the pieces. If the pieces do not come out easily, use a pry bar to pry them out.
5. Clear out all the damaged piece, being sure to also remove the tongue that is set in the groove of the adjacent floorboard and the damaged wood from around the tongue of the floorboard on the opposite side. Vacuum out the small pieces.
6. Measure the length of the opening and cut a replacement piece to fit. Use a miter box and back saw if available to ensure a straight cut on each end.
7. Clamp the replacement piece upside down to a workbench. To fit the replacement board in place, you need to remove the bottom lip of the grooved side. Use a straightedge and utility knife to score along a line where the lower lip of the groove meets the main portion of the replacement floorboard.
8. With a hammer and chisel, make starter cuts on the scored line all along the replacement floorboard's length. Then go back and make deeper cuts until the lower lip of the groove falls off.
9. Apply glue to the tongue and groove of the replacement board and to its bottom. Slip the tongue of the replacement board into the groove of the adjacent floorboard and lower the groove portion onto the tongue of the board on the opposite side (see Figure 3.11). If the replacement board does not want to go in, place a small block of wood on top of the floorboard and tap it with a hammer to force the replacement board into position.
10. Wipe away excess glue with a damp cloth or paper towel.

FIGURE 3.11
Insert the replacement piece at an angle so its tongue slides into the groove of the adjacent floorboard. Let the other side fall into place—this works because you have cut away the lower lip of the replacement board groove.

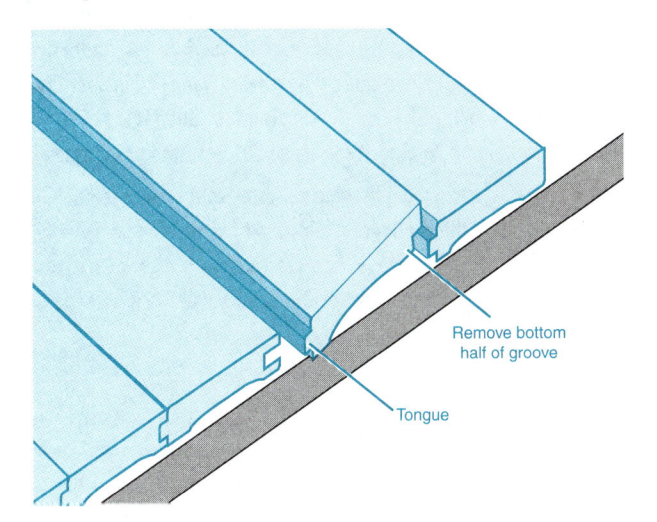

Remove bottom half of groove
Tongue

Pro's Tip

If your flooring does not have a subfloor, you cannot make your repair cuts anywhere you want; you need to be sure your replacement floorboard extends over two flooring joists, so you can nail the new piece into the joists. Replace the damaged floorboard from the end nearest the damage (the end of a board will always be over the middle of a joist) to a line 16" (or 32" or 48") away, depending on the extent of damage and the spacing of your floor joists. This line should align with the center of a 1 1/2" wide floor joist below.

For this kind of repair you need 2 1/2" finishing nails as well as glue. Following step 10 of the preceding list, nail through the replacement board, using two nails for each joist. Use a *nail set* (a small punch used with a hammer to sink nail heads) to set the nail heads below the wood's surface. Fill the depression above the sunken nail head with a wax stick that approximates the color of the wood flooring—such sticks are sold for furniture repair.

Repairing Resilient Flooring

Resilient flooring is of two types: tile and sheet flooring. Tiles go down as individual units, whereas sheet flooring goes down in room-sized sheets. Early resilient floorings were made of linoleum (a linseed oil/wood fiber/felt composition) and asphalt (used for tiles). Modern resilient flooring—both tile and sheet—are much more likely to be pure vinyl or vinyl-composites, although linoleum and asphalt remain available (and are once again popular choices).

Although resilient flooring is tough, its surface can be cut, burned, or otherwise marred. In addition, the adhesive holding it down can fail. Tiles can curl up at the corners, and sheet flooring can bubble up.

TAKE CARE WHEN REPLACING ASBESTOS FLOORING

You need to be take special note of the fact that any resilient flooring—and adhesive—installed before 1986 could have asbestos in it. Asbestos can cause lung disease if inhaled in quantity. There is little danger that asbestos will be released into the air if the flooring is intact. But if it is deteriorating, or if you scrape, sand, or chip at asbestos-containing flooring, it can release asbestos fibers into the air.

If you want to put new flooring into a room that has asbestos-containing materials, it is often best to lay new flooring over the old or have the old flooring removed by professionals specially licensed for asbestos-removing work. To learn more about asbestos in flooring and how to deal with it, contact your local building department or go to the U. S. Environmental Protection Agency website (www.epa.gov) and click Asbestos in Your Home.

Most homeowners or professional flooring installers save extra tiles or scraps of resilient flooring whenever they install a new floor covering. That's a good way to ensure that you'll have matching material to repair future damage. But you can buy replacement tiles and sheet flooring sections from flooring stores. Remember that existing flooring can look different from what it did when new, owing to wax build-up, long exposure to sunlight, and foot traffic.

When preparing to repair damage to any resilient flooring, be sure to have the proper adhesive for your flooring type. Go to a flooring dealer and describe as best

CHAPTER 3   **Walls and Floors**   53

you can the kind of flooring you have and its likely age. Salespeople there can recommend an appropriate adhesive and, for large repairs, tools for applying it.

Repairing a Hole, Dent, or Scratch

Often resilient flooring damage is small and needs only touch-up work. The following repair can work on vinyl and linoleum.

Things You'll Need

- Utility knife
- Piece of matching tile
- Piece of paper and a shallow container
- Clear fingernail polish
- Putty knife

1. Use a knife to trim around the damaged area, cutting back to undamaged material. Clean out the space.
2. Place strips of masking tape around the edges of the hole to protect the undamaged flooring surrounding the damaged area.
3. Take a matching piece of flooring—old or new—and bend it into an arc over a piece of paper or cardboard, with the top surface of the flooring facing outward. Scrape this surface with a knife and catch the powder-like scrapings on a sheet of paper (see Figure 3.12). Pour the powder into a shallow container.
4. Apply clear fingernail polish one drop at a time to the powdered scrapings to make a thick paste. With a putty knife, work the paste into the damaged area.

FIGURE 3.12
Fold a spare piece of flooring good side out and scrape at it with a knife blade. Catch the scrapings on a piece of paper.

Shavings

5. Spread a top coat of fingernail polish over the repair and let it dry.
6. Remove the masking tape. Smooth the patch with fine steel wool.
7. Apply one more coat of fingernail polish and let the repair dry.

Resealing a Sheet Flooring Edge

In large rooms, more than one section of sheet flooring can be used. They meet at seams. If the edges of the flooring become loose at the seams, you can glue them down again, following these steps.

Things You'll Need

- ❏ Putty knife
- ❏ Knife
- ❏ Rubber gloves
- ❏ Sheet flooring adhesive recommended for your kind of flooring and underlayment type, and solvent for this kind of adhesive
- ❏ Several cloths
- ❏ Straight board
- ❏ Heavy weight

1. With a putty knife, lift up the loosened edge. With a knife, scrape away old adhesive from the underlayment (supporting wood base) and underside of the sheet flooring.
2. Wearing rubber gloves, raise the loose edge with a putty knife and, with another putty knife, spread the adhesive onto the underlayment.
3. The adhesive needs to set for a short period of time before being pressed in place, as recommended on the adhesive can's label. Wait the appropriate amount of time and then press the loose edge down. Wipe up oozing adhesive with a damp cloth.
4. Place a clean cloth along the repaired edge. Lay a flat board on the cloth and a weight (such as a full paint can) on the board. Leave these in place until the adhesive dries (check for the duration on the adhesive can's label).

caution Take note of the asbestos warning in the sidebar titled "Take Care when Replacing Asbestos Flooring."

caution Some floor adhesives give off volatile compounds. When you work with them, ventilate the room and turn off all nearby pilot lights.

CHAPTER 3   Walls and Floors

If scraping at the adhesive is not doing the job, you can buy commercial floor cleaner from a flooring dealer. Tell the dealer what kind of floor you have and the color of your old adhesive. You can apply the cleaner undiluted with an old toothbrush, wipe up the residue with a cloth, and then throw away the cloth. Let the area dry before going to step 2 in the preceding list of steps.

Deflating a Blister

Occasionally, sheet flooring loosens away from the underlayment and thus forms a sort of blister in mid-floor. You can reseal the blistered area to make the flooring smooth again.

Things You'll Need

- ❏ Utility knife
- ❏ Metal straight edge
- ❏ Sheet flooring adhesive recommended for your kind of sheet flooring

1. Using a metal straight edge (such as one from a combination square) and a utility knife, make a straight cut all the way through the center of the blister of the sheet flooring from one end of it to the other.
2. Press the edges flat. If they overlap, trim a portion of one away until there is no overlap.
3. Glue down both edges, using the same procedure as in the section "Resealing a Sheet Flooring Edge."

If you have a number of blisters that are smaller than 3 square inches or such small blisters reoccur in your floor, you can buy a tool used by professionals to repair these areas. This tool is a type of syringe with a metal needle for injecting flooring adhesive underneath the surface of resilient flooring. You insert the needle into the sheet flooring blister (best at a dark line or pattern) and squeeze adhesive into place. Follow the manufacturer's instructions for the amount of adhesive, but generally use 1/4 oz. of adhesive for every square inch of blister. Wipe up oozing adhesive and then cover it with a cloth and heavy weight.

Replacing a Tile

Sometimes the damage is so bad you want to replace a whole tile, or several tiles. To do so, follow these steps.

Things You'll Need

- ❏ Work gloves
- ❏ Utility knife or linoleum knife
- ❏ Heat gun or hair dryer; or an iron and old towel
- ❏ White paper

- ❏ Replacement tiles
- ❏ Appropriate adhesive for the tile material and putty knife or trowel for spreading the adhesive
- ❏ Rags and solvent appropriate for the adhesive
- ❏ Two boards, longer than the width of the tile
- ❏ Heavy weights

1. Wearing work gloves, make a cut all the way through the tile from top to bottom about 1" from one edge.
2. Turn the heat gun on at the low setting and move it up and down along the cut to soften the tile and the adhesive below it. If you do not have a heat gun, cut the tile through with two diagonal cuts corner to corner. Then place an old towel at the center and use an iron set on low on top of the towel.
3. Remove the source of heat and work a putty knife into the cut. Peel back the tile and apply more heat as needed. Pry up all parts of the tile.
4. Test the adhesive that is left on the underlayment by rubbing white paper on it. If the stain is a dark brown, the adhesive might contain asbestos. See the caution in the sidebar "Take Care when Replacing Asbestos Flooring."
5. If the adhesive is a non-asbestos-containing kind, use the putty knife to scrape up as much as possible. If you see any protruding nail heads, use a hammer and nail set to set them flush—or slightly under—the top surface of the underlayment.
6. If the tile is the self-adhesive type, set the replacement tile into the cleaned space now.
   If not, wear rubber gloves and spread on the underlayment an adhesive appropriate for the tile. Use a notched trowel if you have one. Follow the manufacturer's instructions for allowing the adhesive to set up. Avoid getting adhesive on the tops of adjacent tiles; if you do, wipe it away quickly.
7. Hold one edge of the replacement tile against one edge of a tile bordering the repair and carefully allow the replacement tile to drop into place, as shown in Figure 3.13. Press down along the edges of the tile to seal it in place.
8. Lay two boards—longer than the new tile—across the new tile. Place weights on the boards and leave them for as long as the manufacturer says the adhesive needs to dry.

Pro's Tip

If you cannot find a replica tile at a store, consider taking one from a closet or from under a refrigerator if the floor is in a kitchen. You can replace the one you have taken from this hidden area with another of the same thickness—no one is likely to see the mismatch.

Repairing Sheet Flooring

Replacing a section of damaged sheet flooring is similar to replacing a resilient floor tile (refer to "Replacing a Tile"). The difference is that you in effect create your own replacement tile.

CHAPTER 3   **Walls and Floors**   57

FIGURE 3.13
Position one edge of the replacement tile along the edge of one adjacent to the prepared opening. Let the tile fall into place.

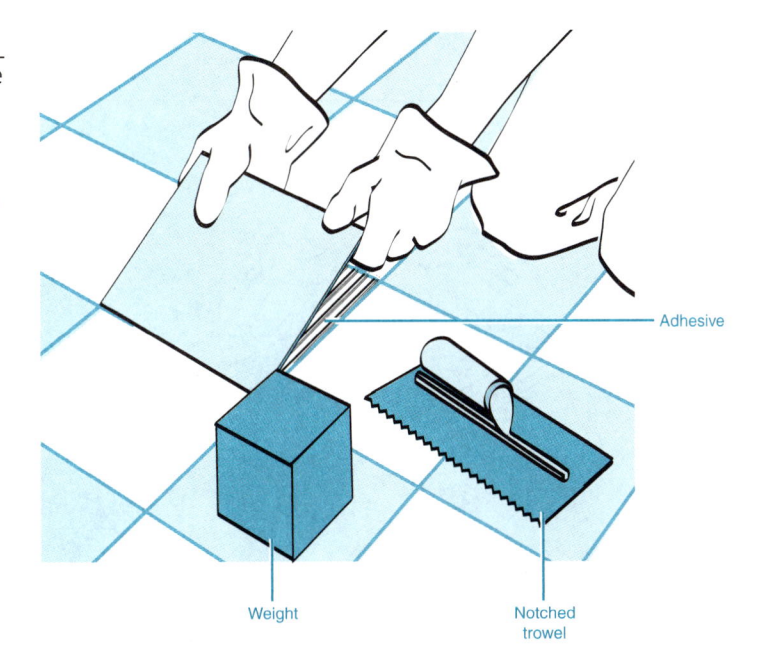

Adhesive

Weight

Notched trowel

Use adhesive recommended by the manufacturer of the sheet flooring. Ventilate the workspace and wear rubber gloves to protect your skin from adhesive.

Things You'll Need

- ❏ Cloth
- ❏ A section of replacement flooring
- ❏ Utility knife
- ❏ Masking tape
- ❏ Rubber gloves
- ❏ Adhesive recommended by the sheet flooring manufacturer
- ❏ Notched trowel and putty knife
- ❏ Piece of plywood
- ❏ Weights

1. Cut a piece of replacement flooring larger than the area of the damage, but larger than a 9"-x-9" tile.
2. Exactly align the pattern of the replacement piece to the sheet flooring below and use masking tape to tape the replacement piece to the flooring.
3. Use a sharp utility knife to cut through the replacement piece and into the flooring below (see Figure 3.14), cutting along pattern lines as much as you can, while still cutting beyond the area of damage in the original flooring. Cut all the way through the flooring beneath the replacement piece until you feel underlayment.

FIGURE 3.14
When the replacement flooring is aligned and taped over the damaged flooring below, carefully cut through both pieces. This creates a replacement piece exactly matched to the flooring below that you will be removing

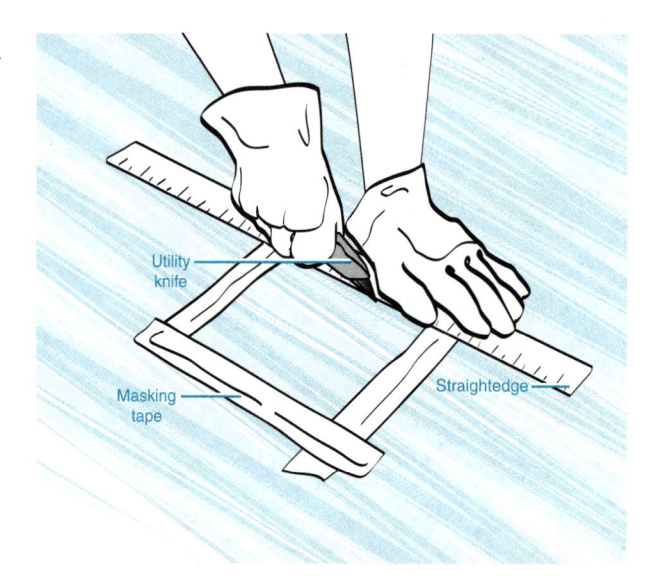

4. Carefully remove the replacement piece and masking tape. Remove the section of sheet flooring within the four cuts you have made. If the section of sheet flooring seems firmly attached to the underlayment, try using the point of the utility knife blade to probe between the top of the sheet flooring and its manufactured backing (sheet flooring comes in layers of lamination). If the damage is limited to the top lamination and you can remove this top layer from the manufactured backing, proceed to steps 5 and 6. If the sheet flooring comes up whole from the underlayment, proceed to step 7.
5. If the top seems to be coming up and the damage does not go all the way to the underlayment, pull the top of the damaged section all the way up, thus delaminating it and leaving its backing firmly attached to the underlayment.
6. Delaminate the replacement piece by using adhesive to glue the bottom of the replacement flooring to an old piece of plywood. When the adhesive is set, use a utility knife to lift the top of the flooring off its backing. Proceed to step 8.
7. Clean away all the old adhesive from the underlayment.
8. Wear rubber gloves. Then, preferably with a notched trowel, spread adhesive into the area for the replacement piece. Allow the adhesive to set up according to the manufacturer's instructions.
9. Lower the replacement piece into position. Wipe away any oozing adhesive with a damp cloth.
10. Place a cloth over the patch and a flat piece of plywood over the cloth. Place a weight on the plywood until the adhesive is dry according to the manufacturer's instructions.

Summary

In this chapter we patched up walls and floors, two elements of a home that take their bumps and knocks. Fortunately, with some inexpensive materials and some clever techniques, the blemishes to walls and floors are fairly easily fixed. Plaster and drywall patching has the virtue of being barely noticeable when done. Working on tile walls is trickier, but the result usually looks great.

Wood floor problems normally yield to some carpentry techniques and glue. We discussed those techniques in this chapter, and we also covered tricks for making resilient flooring look like new again.

Next up are doors and windows. Unlike walls and floors, these elements of a home *move*. That can make them trickier to work on, but most of the solutions to their problems are straightforward and don't take up a lot of time.

4

Doors and Windows

Doors and windows provide the gateways between our homes and the outside world. They welcome those who enter our homes, let light in while letting us see outside, and protect us from the elements. Good-fitting and functional doors and windows are absolutely vital to making our homes pleasant and livable.

But like any mechanism that moves, doors and windows are susceptible to various ailments. Sometimes their parts wear so that portions rub where they should not rub or leave gaps that are unsightly and allow in rain water or cold air. Window glass breaks, weatherstripping cracks, and door locks wear or simply look old and need replacing.

In this chapter you learn how to fix common problems with many types of doors and windows. By doing so, you'll keep wind and rain water outside where they belong and make your home more secure and more attractive. Believe it or not, all this will help you sleep better at night, too.

In this chapter:

* Understand the construction of common types of windows.
* Learn common window repair techniques.
* Learn to repair doors, door latches, and door screens.

To do list

- [ ] Free a stuck window.
- [ ] Repair or install weatherstripping.
- [ ] Fix a broken window pane.
- [ ] Fix a screen.

Making Basic Window Repairs

Windows are normally static and do their jobs just fine. But when something goes awry with your windows, you want to be ready to fix it. A window with a broken pane lets in outside weather and insects. A window that is meant to open on a muggy day but won't is an aggravation. A screen that has a hole in it is not much of a screen at all.

Consequently, being ready and skilled for window and screen work so you can make repairs quickly will keep you and everyone else in your home that much happier. Generally, the work requires small hand tools in your basic toolkit, although some screen work requires a specialty tool called a *spline roller*. And the work is usually not dangerous. However, you do have to be careful when handling glass so you don't cut yourself. And you need to check before scraping paint around windows that the paint does not contain lead. I discuss how this is done in a section that addresses scraping paint.

As in previous chapters, all procedures I describe in this book are preceded by their own list of necessary tools and supplies. But here's a description of some of the tools you'll use when making the repairs described in this chapter:

- **Pry bar**—A flat piece of steel for prying, a pry bar can also remove nails if the nail head is above the wood surface.
- **Nail set**—A hardened steel, pointed cylinder that is used to sink the heads of finish nails slightly below the surface of a piece of wood; by filling in the depression above the nail head, you cover any evidence of the nail and leave the surface smooth.
- **Glazier's points**—Small pointed pieces of steel that are pressed into window sashes and muntins to hold panes of glass in place.
- **Glazing compound**—Glazing compound is a putty-like substance spread onto the edges of window panes to waterproof and hold the panes to the sash.
- **Replacement screening**—Window screens are typically made of fiberglass, plastic, aluminum, steel, or copper wire.
- **Shims**—These narrow strips of wood, also called *cedar shakes*, are sold in home improvement and lumber yards and can be used for making fine adjustments to the thickness of door and window jambs.
- **Spline roller**—This special tool rolls the edges of new screening into the groove of a screen's metal frame and then rolls a vinyl spline on top to keep the screen edges in place.
- **Screen bead**—This is a type of thin wooden molding applied to wood screen frames to cover the screen edges.
- **Tin snips**—These are heavy scissors for cutting thin metal.

Understanding the Anatomies of Double-Hung, Casement, and Sliding Windows

To work efficiently and correctly on windows, you should know how the parts go together to make a functioning unit. And if you know the names of the parts, you'll

CHAPTER 4 Doors and Windows

more readily be able to follow repair instructions. Some windows are simple. Picture windows, for example, are merely glass in a frame with no moving parts. But some windows are complex and have a gaggle of parts, a few with exotic names.

Double-hung windows, the most common type in American homes, consist of two sashes (framed window panes) set in a surrounding frame (see Figure 4.1). Both sashes can move up or down to open the window, although most homeowners tend to raise the lower sash and leave the upper sash in place (in many homes the upper sash has been painted shut and never moves at all). The two sashes can move past one another and, when closed, touch at their *meeting rail*, which is the upper part of the lower sash and the lower part of the upper sash.

FIGURE 4.1
A double-hung window is an assemblage of precise parts so that sashes can move up or down for the passage of air into the home. Double-hung windows used to be made entirely of wood (and glass) but now can be wood covered in vinyl or aluminum, all vinyl, or all aluminum. But no matter what the material, the operation is the same and the names of parts identical.

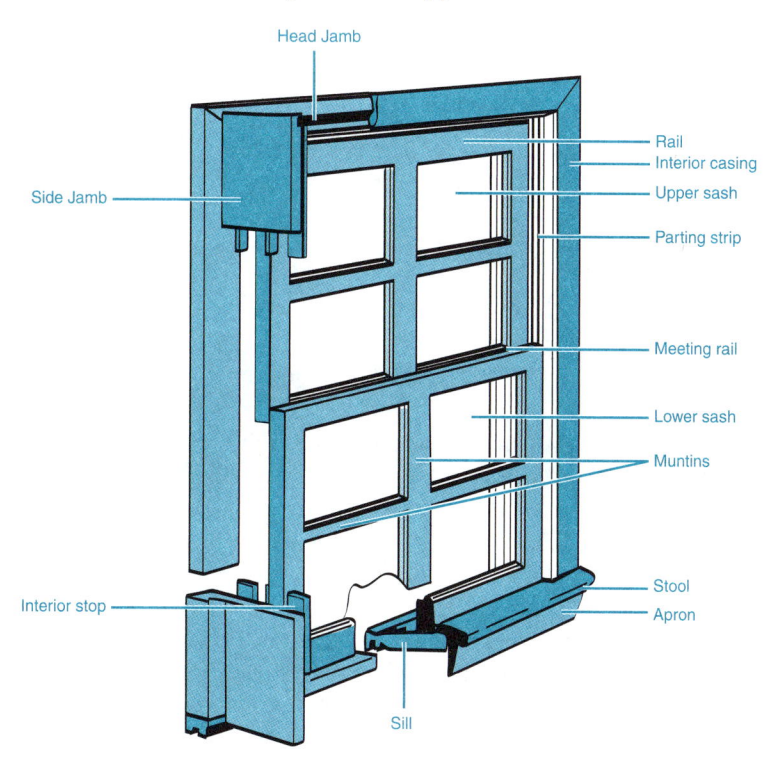

Panes of glass are held in place by slender pieces of wood called *muntins*. Each muntin is precisely milled on the inside face and cut to hold the glass on the outside face. This cut is called a *rabbet*.

The channels in which the sashes move are defined by the jambs and by two strips of wood, one called the *parting strip* and the other called the *blind stop*, or simply *stop*.

Sliding and casement windows are simpler than double-hung ones. A *sliding* window resembles a double-hung window turned on its side. Two sashes slide horizontally past one another, but there is only one pane in a sash. These windows typically have sashes set with rollers to help the sliding movement, but these rollers usually offer no trouble.

A *casement* window hinges on one edge and a crank pushes the opposite edge open. Typically, casement windows have only a single pane as well, and the cranks normally last for decades.

Freeing a Stuck Window

Windows commonly become painted shut—that is, the sash won't budge because coats of paint have solidified between the sash and the window frame. The first form of remedy for this problem is to break this paint bond.

Avoid this problem in the future by opening the window after you have painted the sash and frame. Close the window when the paint is mostly dry.

Things You'll Need

- [ ] Utility knife
- [ ] Putty knife
- [ ] Wide joint compound knife
- [ ] Pry bar or crow bar
- [ ] Touch-up paint, brush, and rags

1. Use a utility knife to slice through paint between the sash and the frame. Do this wherever you see a paint bond, including (for double-hung windows) where sashes meet.
2. If the sash is still stuck, check the outside and break any paint bonds there. If the sash will not move, work a putty knife blade into the cracks between the sash and frame and try again.
3. If the sash remains stuck, on the outside of the window and near one corner of the sash, force two wide putty knives between the bottom of the sash and the window sill. Work a pry bar or crow bar end between the blades, which helps protect the wood from being marred. Use a hammer to tap the end of the pry bar or crow bar if necessary to force the other end under the sash. Then press down on the pry bar or crow bar. Do the same at the other lower corner.
4. Touch up paint or stain, as necessary.

If you are working on an old stuck window for the first time, be sure the window is unlocked. Then look for any nails, bolts, or screws holding it shut—they might have been put there for security or to stop the sash from rattling. Unscrew bolts and screws. For finish nails, use a hammer and nail set to hammer the nail entirely through the sash into the frame.

CHAPTER 4 Doors and Windows 65

Nails and screws can be hidden by layers of paint. If the steps in the section "Freeing a Stuck Window" fail, the window frame will have to be dismantled to free the sash. You might want a professional to do this job for you.

Improving Sash Movement

Window sashes are meant to fit closely to their frames. This close fit keeps the rain and wind out but often makes the sash difficult to move. Over time, wooden window frames and stops can swell and bow, causing the window to bind. Years of paint build-up adds to the problem. But you can make sashes move more easily in a few steps.

Things You'll Need

- ☐ Rag
- ☐ Old wood chisel
- ☐ Sandpaper
- ☐ Narrow block of wood, approximately 6" long
- ☐ Hammer
- ☐ Block of paraffin

1. Raise the sash (or if you are working with an upper sash, lower it). Examine the channel in which the sash moves and determine the best way to clean it while removing the least amount of material:

   If dirt build-up seems to be the problem, clean the sash channels with a damp cloth and then dry the channels.

   If paint build-up is the culprit, use sandpaper to cut it back; for especially thick portions, use an old wood chisel.

2. If the window frame has moved out of alignment, place a narrow wooden block in the sash channel and, with a hammer, tap the block against the frame, budging the frame outward (see Figure 4.2). This can make the sash move more easily.

3. You can also tap the block against the parting strip and against the window stop to move those pieces back into alignment (see "Understanding the Anatomy of a Window," earlier in this chapter).

4. To finish your repair and keep the sash operating smoothly, raise it to expose the channel and rub a block of paraffin up and down in the channel. Rub paraffin on the sash sides of the parting

> **note** If the frame moves out of alignment again, you can screw them through the frame into wooden wall members behind to hold the frame in place. To hold a parting strip or window stop in place, use finishing nails; then use a nail set and hammer to countersink the nail heads, fill in the depressions with wood putty, and paint over the repair.

strip and window stop as well. (If you plan to paint inside the channel, paint first and then apply the paraffin after the paint is dry.) You can also use spray-on silicone lubricant.

FIGURE 4.2
You can sometimes make a sash move more freely by tapping the surrounding frame outward. If this helps but the problem recurs, tap the frame back into position and fasten there with screws or nails.

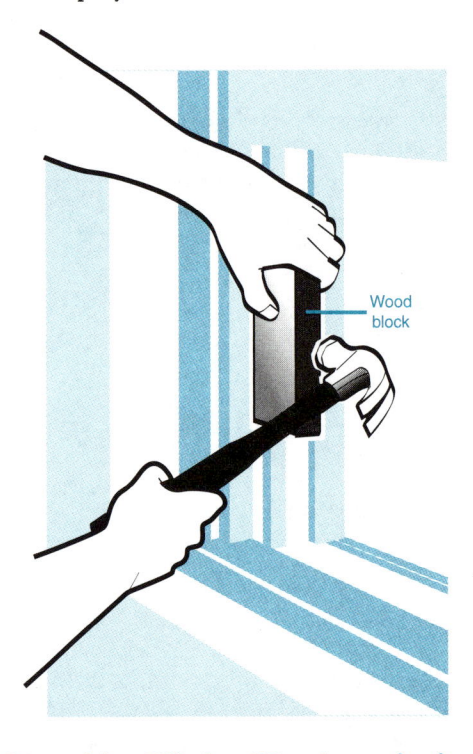

Wood block

Installing and Repairing Window Weatherstripping

Air leaking around window sashes is a nuisance and money-waster. It makes a room feel drafty and makes the heating or cooling system work harder than it should, driving up energy bills. You can check for air infiltration by placing your hand near sash edges and window frames on a cold, windy day; you also can hold a tissue or lit match nearby—if either of these flutters, air is coming in.

Window weatherstripping comes in several varieties:

- **Spring metal weatherstripping**—This is nailed to one window element and presses against the adjacent element to block air flow. This kind of weatherstripping is useful on windows where the sash is loose within the window jamb.
- **Self-adhesive foam stripping**—This is good on the bottom of a sash that does not fit well against its sill, and it is not visible from the inside when the window is closed.
- **Tubular flexible gaskets (made of vinyl or foam)**—These can work well but can be unsightly when installed on the room side of a sash.

If the window has weatherstripping, look it over. If the weatherstripping is cracked, cut, brittle, or crushed, it is no longer doing its job. Measure the perimeter of the window. Write it down and even make a quick sketch of the window on the same paper. Take these with you to the home improvement or window store. Try to consider what kind of stripping will work best for your window before you go to the store, but keep an open mind because products change (and, generally, improve).

If the weatherstripping is spring metal—that is, a metal strip meant to press from its nailed side to the piece opposite to stop air flow—it can sometimes be bent back into a position where it is effective again.

Casement windows and sliding windows have their own kind of weatherstripping, which can be harder to come by. Call ahead to home improvement stores or window repair shops; if they don't keep it in stock, the weatherstripping might have to be ordered.

Generally, you can remove poor weatherstripping by prying it away from the window channels, jambs, and sashes using an old flathead screwdriver. Then, you simply replace the old stripping with new stripping material. Most weatherstripping comes with its own tacks or is self-adhesive.

> **caution** If you are working in a house built before 1978, your window frames and jams might be coated with lead paint. Before scraping or sanding the paint around the window, buy a test kit at a home improvement store. These cost less than $10 and work by wiping a dampened wick from the kit through a scratch in the paint—lead in the paint turns the wick a specified color.
>
> If you find that the paint does contain lead, do not create dust. Contact your local building department. It can give you instructions for removing lead paint yourself or hiring someone to do it for you.
>
> You can leave lead paint in place, although covering it with a fresh coat of recently manufactured paint is a good idea. If the sash is moving up and down in a channel painted with lead paint, you should remove the paint or install jamb liners that separate the sash from the channel's paint, although you might have to buy new sashes to do this.

Things You'll Need

- ❑ Small hammer
- ❑ Tape measure or carpenter's rule
- ❑ Pencil and paper
- ❑ Replacement stripping
- ❑ Needle-nose pliers
- ❑ Tin snips or heavy scissors
- ❑ Weatherstripping

To install new weatherstripping, proceed as follows:

1. Measure the lengths of the sides of the window that need weatherstripping; then purchase replacement stripping.

2. Cut the weatherstripping to fit the sides of the window where it will be installed. Cut spring metal stripping with tin snips; cut other kinds with heavy scissors.
3. Spring metal can be tacked to the jamb in a window channel if the sash is loose. Raise the sash and cut a piece that extends from the sill to a couple inches above the highest point that the lower sash reaches.
4. Slip the top of the spring metal up in the channel between the jamb and the sash. Tack the spring metal to the jamb, tacked edge toward the inside of the home as shown in Figure 4.3.

FIGURE 4.3
Raise the sash and slide the top of the weatherstripping a couple of inches up into the channel between the bottom of the sash and the window jamb. Nail the weatherstripping in place so that the nailed edge is toward the inside of the house. You might need a nail set to make the nails go flush to the weatherstripping.

Test the movement of the sash. If it works well enough, place another strip of spring metal in the channel on the other side of the window.
5. You can also tack spring metal along the bottom of the sash, nailed edge toward the inside of the house.
6. Other types of weatherstripping are also tacked in place, either along the bottom of the bottom sash or to the jamb just inside the sash but close enough to block air movement. Some, however, are self-adhering; you peel off protective paper and press the weatherstripping in place.

Pro's Tip
The tacks for weather stripping are generally small, short, and difficult to hold between two fingers while striking at with a hammer. Try holding a tack with needle-nose pliers until you get it started in the wood.

CHAPTER 4   Doors and Windows   69

Removing a Broken Window Pane

Everyone faces it sooner or later: a cracked or broken window pane. In most cases, you can remove the damaged pieces and put in new without removing the sash.

When you remove old putty or glazing compound, you have to watch out for metal *glazier's points*, small metal pieces that were pressed into both the sash and muntins to hold the glass in place.

Things You'll Need

- Masking tape
- Sheets of newspaper
- Heavy leather gloves
- Eye protection
- Regular pliers and needle-noise pliers
- Old wood chisel and fine sandpaper
- Linseed oil

1. Wear heavy leather gloves and eye protectors. Tape a sheet of newspaper to the window stool and lay newspaper on the floor beneath both inside and outside of the window.
2. Work from the outside if you can. Grip a piece of glass firmly and wiggle it free of the glazing compound and glazier's points along the glass edge. Small pieces you can grip and pull carefully with a pair of regular pliers. If the glass is merely cracked but not broken and you want to replace it, you must break it. From inside the house, push the glass gently outward with the head of a hammer until the glass breaks. Then proceed as outlined previously.
3. Remove the old glazing compound and the glazier's points. Use an old wood chisel or putty knife on the glazing compound, watching for glazier's points, which you can remove with needle-nose pliers. You can save old glazier's points if they are in good shape, but new ones are inexpensive.

   You can soften glazing compound with a heat gun or hair dryer. Alternatively, you can brush it with linseed oil or lacquer thinner and then wait 30 minutes.
4. Clean the rabbet of all traces of the old glazing compound either by scraping it well or sanding. Remove the dust and fragments and then brush the cleaned wood with linseed oil. The linseed oil will keep the wood from drawing too much oil out of the new glazing compound when it is installed and thus making it brittle.

Installing a New Pane

Buy a new pane from a home improvement, hardware, or glass store. Tell glass cutters there the exact dimensions of the opening and the type of glass that was there previously. If the window is in an area that's exceptionally exposed to mishap, you might want to install tempered glass or laminated glass. Glass cutters should make the new pane about 1/8" smaller all around than the dimensions you have given.

Handle the glass carefully on the way home. Lay it flat in your car on old towels. Have delivered any pane you cannot lay flat in your car.

Things You'll Need

- Putty knife
- Glazing compound
- Heavy leather gloves
- Replacement pane of glass
- Glazier's points
- Small container of water
- Damp cloth
- Paint to match the sash and a single-edge razor blade

1. Roll some glazing compound between the palms of your hands to make long rolls about 3/8" thick. Working from the outside, press these into the rabbet all along the rabbet's length.
2. Wearing heavy leather gloves, lift the new pane and press it gently into the glazing compound that is in the rabbet.
3. Press glazier's points into the wood of the rabbet every 4", as shown in Figure 4.4. Most people use a putty knife for this, but there is a special tool for pressing glazier's points, a kind of bent steel blade that keeps your fingers away from the glass. Press downward toward the wood and not toward the glass, which you could crack.
4. Roll more glazing compound rolls. Make these about 5/8" thick. Press each firmly in the rabbet covering the glazier's points.
5. Press and smooth the glazing compound with the putty knife, dragging one face along the wood and corner on the glass. Be sure to keep the top edge of the glazing compound even with the top edge of the rabbet on the other side of the glass, as shown in Figure 4.5. If the glazing compound rises higher than this, it will be visible from the other side of the window; if it's lower, it will not hold the glass firmly in place. If the blade of the putty knife becomes sticky, dip it in water.
6. Use a damp cloth to wipe off excess glazing compound.
7. Let the glazing compound cure according to the manufacturer's label, generally several days.
8. Paint the glazing compound the color of the window sash. Allow paint to just cover the edge of the glazing compound where it meets the glass, making a waterproof seal. If there is excess paint on the glass after you're finished, wait until it is dry and then scrape it away with a single-edge razor, taking care

CHAPTER 4 Doors and Windows

not to harm the area where the paint covers the edge of the glazing compound.

FIGURE 4.4
Set the glazier's points alongside the window pane and press lightly into the wood. Finish pressing the points into the wood with a putty knife. Take care not to press against the pane itself.

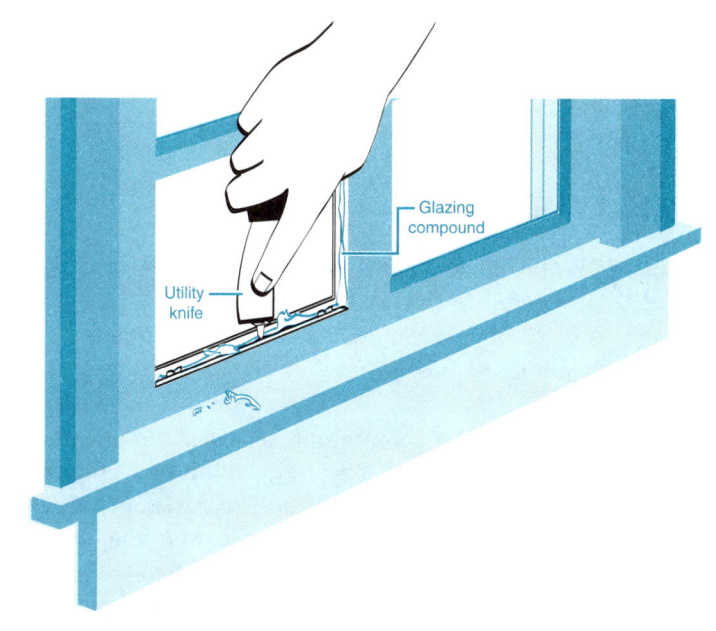

FIGURE 4.5
Place rolls of glazing compound in the rabbet. Smooth it with a putty knife, the top edge of the knife on a level with the top of the rabbet on the other side of the window pane.

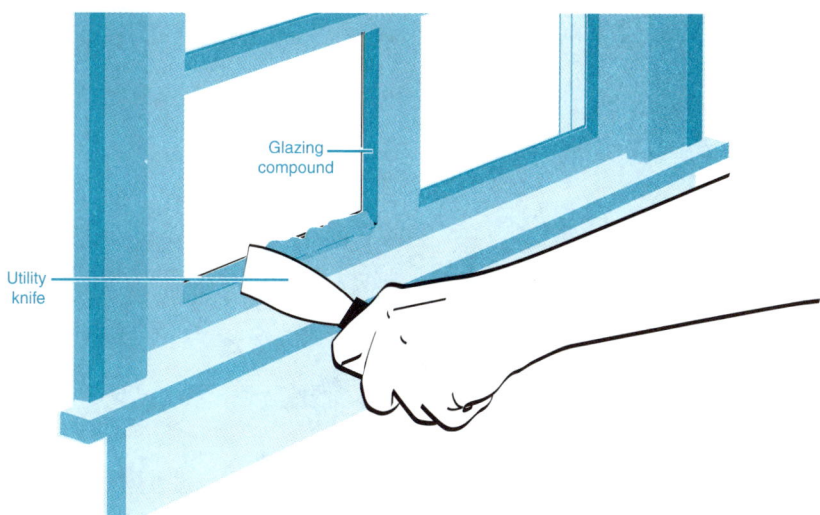

Making Small Wire Screen Repairs

Screens are very nice in good weather, but they are vulnerable to pokes and jabs. Small damage can be repaired, although the larger the area of damage, the more noticeable its repair will be. When you think a large repair might be unsightly, consider replacing the screen, as described in "Replacing a Screen in a Wooden Frame" or "Replacing a Screen in a Metal Frame."

Metal-wire screens are relatively easy to repair. Very small pokes often do not break the thread of the screen, or the breaks are very minor. The repair for such a mishap might be no more than using a small nail to nudge the threads back in place. Even if broken, if the ends can be made to align, the fix is barely noticeable and the screen will still do the job of stopping insects. Where you need to make a larger repair, use the procedure described here.

Things You'll Need

- Silicone glue or epoxy glue for small tears
- Heavy-duty scissors or tin snips
- A patch of matching wire screening for larger repairs
- Small needle-nose pliers

1. Move the broken aluminum threads back into line. If the ends are close, dab on a little epoxy glue or silicone glue; this binds the ends together.
2. For larger repairs, use tin snips or heavy scissors to cut the hole square. Cut a piece of matching screen an inch wider than the hole on all sides. Unravel 1/4" of the patch all the way around. Bend the unraveled section down 90°.
3. Fit the patch onto the area around the hole by working the protruding unraveled sections through the good screening around the hole (see Figure 4.6). Bend the protruding sections back, binding the patch to the larger screen.

FIGURE 4.6
Hold the patch over the area of the hole and work the unraveled threads of the patch through the areas of undamaged screening.

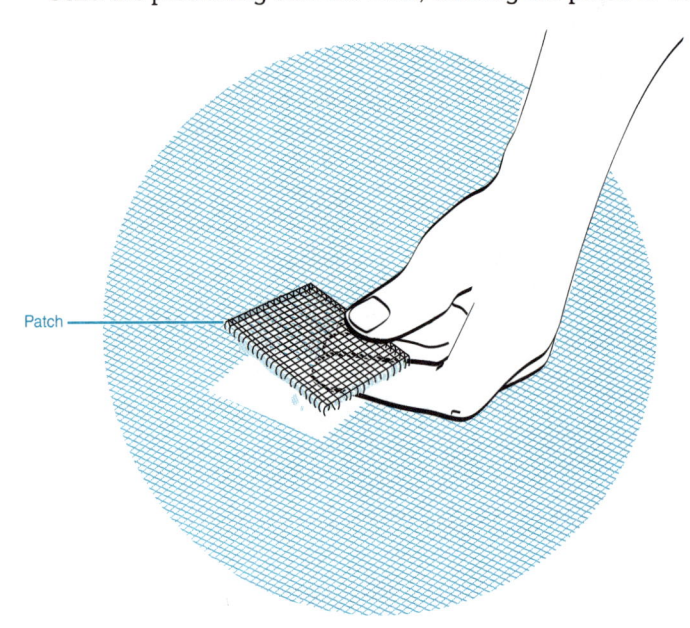

Patch

CHAPTER 4   Doors and Windows

Making Small Fiberglass Screen Repairs

Fiberglass screening requires different methods from those used on metal-wire screening, but the time and effort required for the repairs are about the same. For very small tears, apply dabs of Super Glue or epoxy; the glue can sometimes bridge the gap between the torn ends and thus effect the repair. Clear nail polish might even work here. For larger damage, follow this procedure.

Things You'll Need

- ❏ Protective gloves
- ❏ Super Glue or epoxy glue
- ❏ Replacement piece of fiberglass screening

1. Cut the damage to a square or rectangular shape.
2. Cut a piece of matching screening an inch wider than the hole on all sides.
3. Coat the edges of the patch with Super Glue or epoxy glue and press it in place.

Replacing a Screen on a Wooden Frame

When the damage is large or when you are not particularly pleased with the looks of patches, you might prefer to replace the whole screen in its frame. Use the following procedure to replace a screen on a wooden frame.

Things You'll Need

- ❏ Stapler
- ❏ Small hammer and old wood chisel
- ❏ Replacement screen, either aluminum or fiberglass
- ❏ Utility knife and nippers
- ❏ A section of 1"×4", cut 2" longer than the width of the replacement screen
- ❏ Screen bead and small nails

1. With an old wood chisel, pry up the screen bead that covers the edges of the old screen. The old screen bead might break as you pry it up. If it does not, you can use it again; if it does, have some replacement on hand.
2. Use nippers to extract the staples holding the screen to the wooden frame. Throw away the old screen.
3. Cut new screen several inches wider than the opening it will fill and 8" longer. Clamp the frame on a workbench and lay the screen on the frame. Staple one end of the screen in place.

4. At the opposite end of the frame, staple the end of the screen to a piece of 1"×4", with one side lodged against the end of the frame and one side slightly raised above the workbench, as shown in Figure 4.7. Lower the raised end of the board, thus stretching the screen.
5. Staple the second end of the screen to the frame. Staple the sides of the screen to the sides of the frame.
6. Replace the screen bead to its old position, or nail new screen bead where the old had been.
7. Use a utility knife to cut excess screen protruding from the screen bead.

FIGURE 4.7
Staple the second end of the new screen to a raised board touching the end of the screen frame. When you depress the board, the screen is stretched. Staple the end of the screen to the frame.

Staple the second end of the new screen to the far edge of the raised board touching the end of the screen frame.

Pro's Tip

If you are placing screen on a screen door rather than just a window frame, there is another way to stretch the screen. Lay the door on planks supported by two sawhorses. Clamp the middle of the door to the planks. At the top of the door slide a board 3/4" thick between the door and the planks, and do the same at the bottom of the door, as shown in Figure 4.8.

Staple the screen to the top of the door and to the bottom of the door. Unclamp the door, stretching the screen. Then staple the sides and cover with screen bead.

Replacing a Screen on a Metal Frame

Replacing a screen on a metal frame is in some respects easier than replacing one on a wooden frame. But it does require a special tool called a *spline roller*, available in home improvement stores.

CHAPTER 4   **Doors and Windows**   75

FIGURE 4.8
Clamp a door to planks on two sawhorses. Elevate both ends of a screen door with pieces of 3/4" boards. Staple the screen to both ends, and release the clamps to stretch the screen.

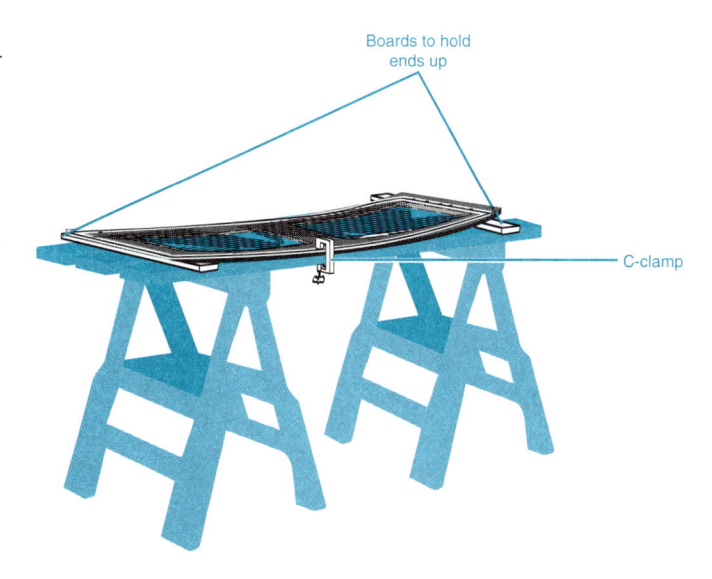

Boards to hold ends up

C-clamp

Things You'll Need

- ❏ Spline roller
- ❏ Flat-head screwdriver
- ❏ Replacement screening, either aluminum or fiberglass
- ❏ Replacement spline, if necessary

1. Pry out the spline with a screwdriver. If the spline is still flexible, you can reuse it; if it is brittle, replace it with new spline you can buy in a home improvement or window repair store.
2. Cut new screening to fit across the frame in all directions. Lay the screen on the frame.
3. If your screening is fiberglass, proceed to step 5.
4. If your screening is aluminum, use the convex wheel of the spline roller to press the screen into the groove along one long edge.
5. Use the concave wheel of the spline roller to press in a length of spline over this portion of the screen, as shown in Figure 4.9.
6. Make a preliminary 45° cut of the screen at the corner. Cut the spline at the corner.
7. Pull the screen taught and roll the opposite edge into its groove, binding it with the spline. Cut the spline at the corner.
8. Work the sides of the screen into their grooves using the spline roller.
9. Trim away excess screen with a utility knife.

tip If the frame wants to warp while you are rolling in spline, place it on a piece of plywood, set four wooden blocks touching the four outer sides of the frame, and screw the blocks to the plywood, holding the frame rigid.

FIGURE 4.9
Use a spline roller to press a spline onto the new screen and secure it in the frame's groove

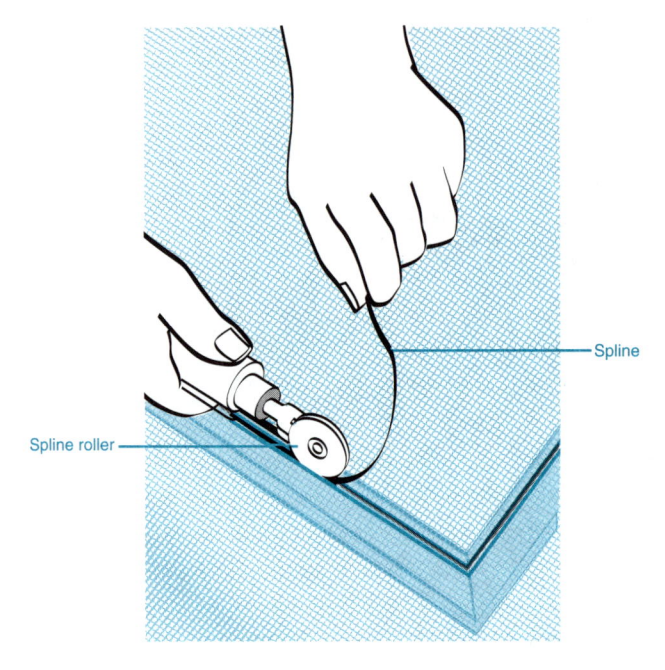

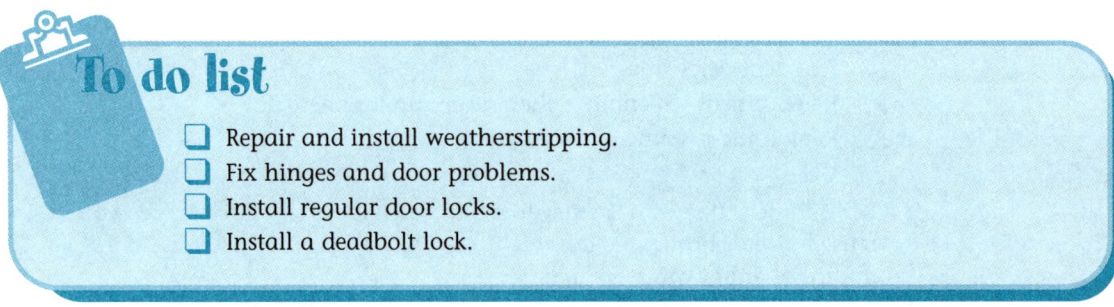

Spline

Spline roller

To do list

- ☐ Repair and install weatherstripping.
- ☐ Fix hinges and door problems.
- ☐ Install regular door locks.
- ☐ Install a deadbolt lock.

Repairing Doors and Door Latches

Doors are essential to homes, and generally they work well year after year. But they are finely tuned mechanisms, and anything finely tuned can get out of kilter.

A door fits into a door frame. Ideally, the gap between the door's edge and the three sides of the frame is identical all around. Occasionally, this gap in one place or another is too narrow or two wide. Both faults can be corrected.

Other ailments can plague doors also. The latch might not catch properly in the strike plate that is screwed to the doorjamb. But here some filing or adjustment of the strike plate can solve the problem. And moving a strip of wood called the *stop* can make a couple of door ailments disappear.

Doors occasionally need new locks. The job is not difficult when the locks are merely replacing older ones in the same holes already drilled in the door. The job is more difficult if you want to add a higher measure of security to the door by installing a

CHAPTER 4 Doors and Windows

deadbolt lock above the main door lock. This requires precise drilling of large holes in the door but is not beyond the ability of homeowners.

Of course, a major function of a door is to keep out the weather. When a door fails to do this as well as it should, lack or failure of the weatherstripping is normally the culprit.

As always, each set of instructions in this section includes its own list of necessary materials and supplies. But here are some general descriptions of special tools and equipment you'll use when repairing doors:

- **Weatherstripping**—Made of metal, foam, or elastomers, weatherstripping keeps rain and outside air outside, lowering your energy bills and saving you maintenance time.
- **Cylinder locks**—Most locks on interior doors and many on exterior doors are cylinder locks. They can be replaced with new ones bought at a home improvement store or locksmith's shop.
- **Deadbolt lock**—More secure against entry than a cylinder lock, deadbolt locks can be installed on doors higher up than the cylinder locks.

Installing or Repairing Weatherstripping

Generally the largest cracks of a home leading to the outside are the ones around the exterior doors. Most homes compensate for this with weatherstripping. If the weatherstripping on one of your doors has become too compressed, torn, or crumpled to do its job, buy replacements. You might be able to match the existing weatherstripping and patch in some new pieces after removing old and damaged areas. Otherwise, merely take out all the old stripping and replace it with new.

Weatherstripping for doors comes in two main varieties: One type is used to protect the area between the bottom of the door and the threshold, and another type is used along the door's edges. Threshold weatherstripping called *sweeps* have metal frames that attach to the bottom of the door with flexible material below. When the door is closed, the flexible material presses against the door's threshold to seal the gap and block air infiltration. Other types of threshold weatherstripping can be wholly or partly attached to the threshold.

Weatherstripping for the door's sides can be spring metal, self-sticking foam, plastic tubing, strips of felt, or any other material that compresses when the door is closed to block air. All varieties of weatherstripping are available in home improvement stores, and most types come with their own fasteners and can be cut and adjusted to the proper angle or width.

Things You'll Need

- ❑ Nail nippers
- ❑ Putty knife or wood chisel
- ❑ Replacement weatherstripping and fasteners
- ❑ Heavy-duty scissors, tin snips, hacksaw, or other cutting tool

1. Remove old weatherstripping with a putty knife or old wood chisel. Use nippers to extract old nails left behind.
2. Measure for and cut the new weatherstripping.
3. Place one strip at a time along the door edge or door frame according to manufacturer's instructions, driving nails or screws only partway into the door or door frame.
4. Close the door, and adjust the position of the weatherstripping to seal the gaps while allowing the door to seat firmly.
5. Drive the nails or screws in all the way.

Fixing a Loose Hinge

When a door fails to close properly or binds against some portion of its frame, the problem is likely one of three things, from most to least likely:

- A loose hinge
- A warped door
- A skewed frame (resulting from house settlement)

A warped door and house settlement are severe problems. The latter definitely calls for professionals; the former often does.

But a loose hinge is fairly easily set right. Step back and look at the gap around the door. If the gap widens along the door's top leading away from the hinge and tapers to zero opposite the top hinge, the top hinge is likely loose. Open the door and see if you can press its forward top edge back against the top hinge. If the door moves toward the hinge, the hinge needs tightening. A bottom hinge can become loose, also, though not as often; it is fixed in the same way.

Things You'll Need

- ❏ Screwdrivers
- ❏ Replacement screws, two that are 1 1/2" long
- ❏ Wood glue and narrow dowels or slivers of wood

1. Examine the screws of the hinge. If you find any that are loose, tighten them.
2. If, in attempting to tighten one or more hinge screws you find that they continue to turn and cannot be tightened, the screw's hole is no longer able to adequately grip the screw's threads. Twist out the loose screw and replace it with one that is 1 1/2" long; the extended length will screw into "fresh" wood and hold the hinge in place.

The preceding technique works best for the screw holes that are farthest from the hinge's *barrel*, the stacked cylinders that hold the hinge pin. Long screws placed in the holes closest to the barrel might not twist into wood studs just behind the frame but rather into drywall or plaster. In this case, follow these steps:

1. Place a dab of wood glue on a short piece of narrow dowel or on a sliver of wood that fills most of the old screw hole.
2. Press it into the hole and use your fingers to snap it off level with the hinge surface.
3. Reinsert the old screw.

If a door binds only during the humid season of the year, the problem is likely not a loose hinge but rather not enough paint. Humidity is swelling the door, and in the non-humid season the door shrinks enough so that the problem disappears. Here the remedy is painting the door thoroughly on both sides as well as its four edges. Do this during a period of low humidity—that is, when the weather is cool and dry.

Shimming a Hinge

If the screws of the hinges are tight but the door binds at the top or bottom of the latch side, the problem might be a hinge that is set too deeply into the door jamb. You can remedy this situation by using a cardboard shim behind the hinge. The cardboard shim has the effect of moving the hinge forward, thus slightly tilting back the portion of the door edge opposite the other hinge, eliminating the binding.

Things You'll Need

- ❑ Screwdrivers
- ❑ Wooden shims
- ❑ Piece of cardboard

1. Open the door. Place two shims beneath the bottom of the door to hold it in place and to keep it from sagging.
2. Loosen the jamb-side screws of the hinge that is *not* across from where the door binds.
3. Cut a shim of cardboard the size of the hinge and with cutouts that will allow the shim to slip behind the hinge leaf, moving past the hinge screws, to fit into the depression—the mortise—behind the hinge (see Figure 4.10).
4. Tighten the screws again. Remove the wooden shims from beneath the door bottom and test the door's movement.

If the door binds all along the latch side, do not plane along that edge. If you do not remove the latch, you leave a bulge around it. Even if you remove the latch before planing in this area, you have shortened the required precise distances between the holes for the latch mechanism and the door's edge.

Instead, take the door out of the jamb. Remove the hinge leafs from the door edge. Secure the door on the floor hinge-edge upward and then plane evenly along this edge. With a sharp wood chisel, carefully deepen the hinge mortises as needed. Reinsert the hinges and rehang the door in the jamb.

FIGURE 4.10
Slip a cardboard shim behind the hinge while the screws are loose but still in place.

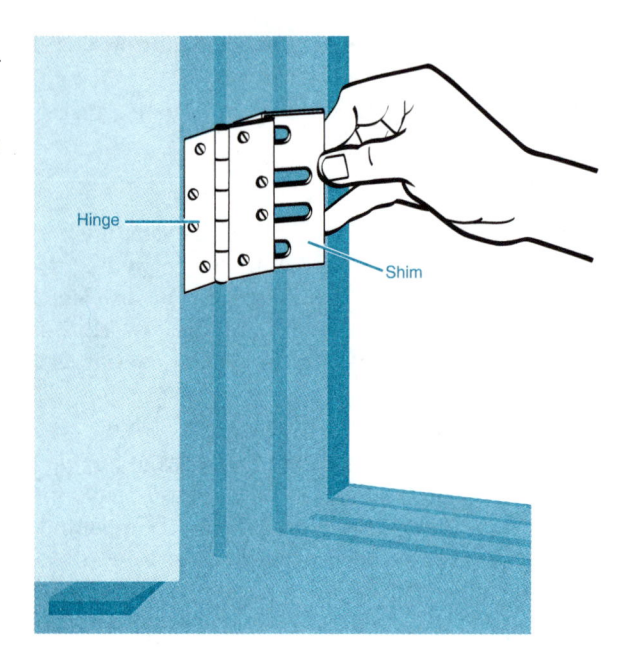

Hinge

Shim

Things You'll Need

- ❑ Screwdrivers
- ❑ Fine metal file
- ❑ Sharp wood chisel

Repairing a Door Latch by Filing the Strike Plate

Over time a house can settle—that is, lower slightly into the ground, and often not evenly. This movement is very small and generally not noticeable, but it can shift a door jamb just enough that a latch bolt no longer aligns with the opening in the *strike plate*, the small frame of metal that is screwed to the door jamb.

To file the strike plate and fix the door latch, follow these steps:

1. Open the door. On the door's outside, kneel down so your eye is at latch level. Draw the door toward you, watching the level of the latch and the hole of the strike plate.
2. See if the top of the latch is higher than the top of the hole or the bottom of the latch lower than the bottom of the hole. If so, make a mental note of the distance.
3. Remove the strike plate from the door jamb by removing its screws. Secure the strike plate in a vise and, with a fine file, file away metal to enlarge the strike plate's hole.

4. Hold the strike plate back in its original place to see if wood has to be removed behind the area where you filed off the metal. If so, use a wood chisel to carefully remove the excess wood.
5. Reattach the strike plate and see if the latch now fits entirely into the hole.

Repairing a Door Latch by Repositioning a Door Stop

Occasionally, a latch does not fit into a strike plate's hole because it cannot move far enough in the direction the door is closing. Here the problem can be a warped door, a poorly positioned doorstop, a poorly positioned strike plate, or a combination of these.

Things You'll Need

- Putty knife
- Hammer and nail set

1. Standing at the outside of the door, pull it closed gently and see how it meets the piece of wood, called a *stop*, running up the frame and across the frame top. Every inch of this door edge should meet every inch of the stop at the same time. If it does not, the door is warped or the stop is not properly aligned.
2. If you suspect the door is warped, open it and eye it along its edge, examining especially the area that touches the stop in advance of other areas. If you have a straight edge 40" long that you trust, hold it to the door across the suspected area. If the door is warped, a professional might be able to straighten it for you. But it might be more worthwhile discarding the door and buying another.
3. If the door is not warped (or even if it is; see the following Short Cut), you might be able to move the stop to conform to the door's shape. For older door jambs, the stop was fastened with small finishing nails after the frame was in place. In newer, "pre-hung" doors, the stop is often an integral part of the door jamb and not removable.
4. If you think the stop is removable (although likely you will not be able to see the nails, which are hidden by filler and paint), work a putty knife or old wood chisel between the stop and the jamb on the door side and pry the stop away from the jamb.
5. Likely you will not have to remove the entire stop, just that portion from the floor through the problem area or from the top of the jamb through the problem area. When you see where the nails holding the stop are, hammer them all the way through the stop using a nail set. This frees the stop in that area.

6. Close the door and renail the stop to conform to the alignment of the door. The door and the stop are in alignment when you can insert and pull a single playing card down the gap touching both sides but without binding anywhere.

   Note that shifting the door stop can also be a repair for a warped door. If the warp is not severe, by shifting the stop, you merely conform to the door's shape. The door will close and no one will notice that it is warped. This saves the time and expense of a new door or of straightening a warped door.

7. If the door does not seem warped or the stop misaligned but the door still does not latch, move the strike plate slightly toward the room into which the door swings. Remove the strike plate screws. Fill the screw holes with glue-covered lengths of dowel or wood scrap you have whittled.

8. Hold the strike plate to its new location, shifted toward the room enough so the door's latch will set into it. Mark the screw holes with a pencil and make pilot holes for the screws. Fasten the strike plate into the new location with the old screws.

9. Fill any gap left by the shifted strike plate with wood filler. Sand and paint the wood filler when it is dried.

Recognizing Types of Door Locks

Before World War II, most doors used locks whose mechanisms were built in to thin rectangular metal boxes. These were set into the thickness of the door and were called mortise locks. Mortise locks still grace many exterior doors, especially front doors, but in other parts of the home, most locks have their mechanisms built in to the knobs and the cylindrical space drilled through the door allowing the two knobs to attach. Collectively these are called cylinder locks and fall into three categories: passage, privacy, and entrance locks. Dead bolts, which are security exterior locks, are somewhat different.

These days most interior door locks are either passage locks or privacy locks. A *passage* lock has two round knobs but no locking mechanism on either side and cannot be locked. A *privacy* lock—most often used for a bathroom or bedroom—has a push button on the knob of one side; the other knob has only a small hole, needed for unlocking the door in an emergency.

An *entrance* lock is similar to a privacy lock. The push button on the interior side locks the lock when the button is pushed in. The exterior knob has a slot for a key, which locks or unlocks the lock.

Each of these three types—passage lock, privacy lock, and entrance lock—installs along the same principles. A deadbolt, which can measurably add to the security of a door locked only with an entrance lock, installs above the lock with knobs and along the same principles but without so large a cylindrical hole for its mechanism.

Installing a Cylinder Lock

You might want to replace a cylinder lock because it has been damaged or simply because you want something newer looking. The task is not difficult so long as you pay attention to detail. A replacement is really a matter of disengaging the old lock from the door and then installing the new lock and its parts in exact opposite sequence.

Buy a replacement lock that is going to fit the thickness of your door and the location of the holes drilled in the door for your old lock. (If you are replacing one passage, privacy, or entrance lock for another, this is generally not a problem.)

If you want to install a lock into a door that has not been drilled for one, the task is much like installing a deadbolt lock. See "Installing a Deadbolt Lock," later in this chapter.

Things You'll Need

- [ ] Flat-head and Phillips-head screwdrivers
- [ ] A replacement lock

1. For an entrance lock, go to the inside side of the door. Look on the shaft between the knob and the door for a small tab sticking through a small hole in the shaft. Press on the tab with a flat-head screwdriver until the tab is below the surface of the shaft. You should now be able to pull off the knob. For a passage or privacy lock, you might instead have to look for two screws in the body of the lock fitted against the door. Remove these screws.
2. For an entrance lock, now look for a spring clip protruding slightly through the circular plate (called a *rose*) fitted against the door. With a flat-head screwdriver, push the spring clip toward the center of the rose and pull the rose off the door. Now you should see a thicker mounting plate that has two screws. Remove these screws.
3. The two halves of the lock—whether entrance, passage, or privacy—should now come apart. Pull each from its side of the door and lay them aside.
4. What remains in the cylindrical hole in the door is the projection of the latch mechanism. Unscrew two screws at the edge of the door that hold the latch plate in place. Pull the latch mechanism out of the door.
5. If you are going to replace the strike plate—and most locksets include a new one—remove the two screws that hold it in place and pry it from its mortise in the doorjamb.
6. Lock sets come with their own installation instructions. Because the holes are already in place, installation is merely a matter of assembling the new lock in the reverse order as taking out the old, but read and follow the manufacturer's instructions, which generally follow steps 7–11.
7. Screw the new strike plate into the place of the old strike plate.
8. Insert the latch mechanism into the hole drilled in the edge of the door (make sure the beveled edge of the latch is facing the curved portion of the strike plate). Screw the latch plate in place.
9. Insert one half of the lock into the cylindrical hole (this could be the interior side or the exterior side depending on the type of lock). An entrance lock

likely here engages protrusions of the latch mechanism; a passage or privacy lock might not.

10. Insert the other half. An entrance lock at this point may call only for a mounting plate to be set against the door and two long screws set through the plate into the body of the lock set into place in step 9. Passage and privacy locks engage the latch mechanism with posts and bars.

11. Insert screws for passage and privacy locks. For entrance locks, snap on the interior rose over the spring clip and then press on the interior knob until its slot clicks into place over the knob catch.

FIGURE 4.11
An entrance lock has various mechanisms to keep it together. These are a slot and knob catch, a spring clip, and two screws from one side to the other. A latch mechanism comes in from the side.

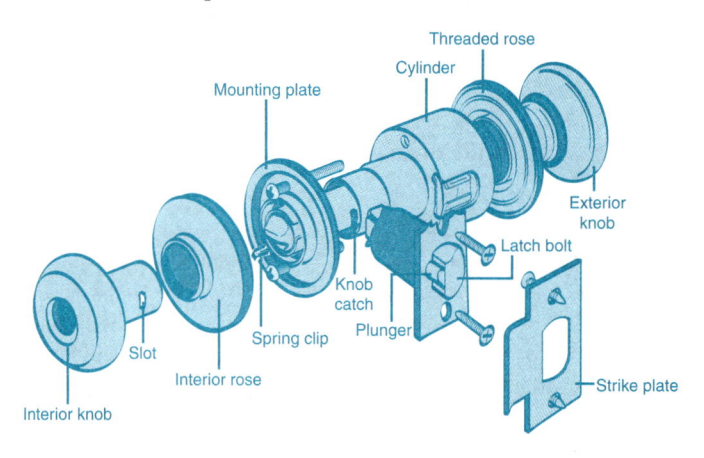

Pro's Tip: A new latch plate and strike plate might not line up exactly with the mortises in the door edge and jamb. But you can make these lock pieces fit by using a sharp utility knife to trim away any excess wood. If the screw holes do not align fill them with dowels or whittled wood and glue. If some of the mortise has to be filled, cut a piece of wood to fit and glue it in place. Or use wood filler. Wait for the repair to dry and then sand and paint it.

Installing a Deadbolt Lock

A door with only an entrance lock is not as secure as it could be. The latch of an entrance lock, even with a plunger next to the latch and meant to hold the latch in place when the door is closed, is still vulnerable. You can increase the security of your door by placing a deadbolt above the entrance lock.

A deadbolt lock has a keyed cylinder on the outside and either a keyed cylinder inside or a thumb turn. A keyed cylinder inside is preferred when the door has glass—if an intruder broke the glass and reached through with his hand he still could not turn the deadbolt without having the key.

A *deadbolt* is so-called because once the bolt is extended into the doorjamb it cannot be pried back into its unlocked position. The bolt itself is made with hardened steel to resist the efforts of sawing.

Installing a deadbolt requires a paper template that comes with a new deadbolt lock. The template is aligned with the edge of the door and shows the location of holes to be drilled. One large hole is required through the door from face to face. A smaller one for the bolt is required into the edge of the door running to the first hole. In addition, a hole is required in the doorjamb for the strike plate or strike box.

Installing a passage, privacy, or entrance cylinder lock in a door without predrilled holes is similar to the following procedure for a deadbolt lock. You use a template on the door, mark the location of holes, and drill accurately. Then you install the lock as described in "Installing a Cylinder Lock."

Locks come with their own installation instructions, but generally following these steps.

Things You'll Need

- [ ] Utility knife
- [ ] Deadbolt lock
- [ ] Drill, hole saw, and spade bit
- [ ] Flat-head and Phillips-head screwdrivers
- [ ] Wooden shims

1. Carefully align the paper template to the door edge at the height you want the deadbolt, generally about 6" above a door handle or entrance lock. Tape the template in place. If the door edge is beveled, check the instructions to see if the crease of the template should be on the "high" side of the bevel or the "low" side.
2. Use an awl or a nail through the template hole centers to mark where the centers of the main hole and bolt hole are to be as shown in Figure 4.12.
3. Remove the template from the door and close the door or wedge it tight. Use a drill with a hole saw bit of the diameter called for by the lock manufacturer to begin drilling a hole for the deadbolt through the door. Be careful to hold the drill level and at a right angle to the door. When the center bit of the hole saw emerges from the opposite side of the door, stop and back the hole saw out of the door. Go around to the other side, place the center bit in the hole it just emerged from, and complete sawing the large hole from the second face.
4. If the door was shut, open it and wedge it tightly in place with wooden shims beneath the bottom. With a spade bit of the diameter called for in the instructions, drill the hole for the bolt into the edge of the door until this second hole meets the first. Drill perpendicular to the door edge and straight into the door; deviation here will cause problems later.
5. Insert the bolt into its hole in the edge of the door. Hold the faceplate against the door edge and use a utility knife blade tip to mark its perimeter. Remove the faceplate and, with a sharp wood chisel, cut a depression (called a *mortise*) within the marked perimeter the thickness of the faceplate metal.

Replace the bolt mechanism into the hole, mark the screw holes, drill pilot holes for the screws, and use the screws to fasten the faceplate to the door.

6. Insert the two parts of the deadbolt into place as shown in Figure 4.13. Generally, the outside portion goes into place first, a turning bar extending from it needing to pass through a hole in the bolt mechanism now protruding into the large hole in the door. The interior portion is then put into place, linking with the exterior portion according to the manufacturer's instructions. Insert and tighten screws through the inside portion to fasten the two parts together, thus firmly attaching them to the door.

7. With the door open, turn the key or thumb turn to make the bolt extend all the way out. Lightly coat its face with a crayon or dark chalk. Retract the bolt, close the door and extend the bolt again against the doorjamb, marking the jamb with the bolt end's coating.

8. At the marked location on the jamb, drill a hole for the bolt using a width and depth called for by the manufacturer.

9. Place the strike plate over the hole for the bolt and mark its perimeter. Cut a mortise for it there. Mark its screw holes, drill pilot holes for the screws, and then screw the strike plate into place.

FIGURE 4.12
Tape the lock's template to the edge of the door and mark through the center points to the wood below. These show the centers of where the holes must be drilled.

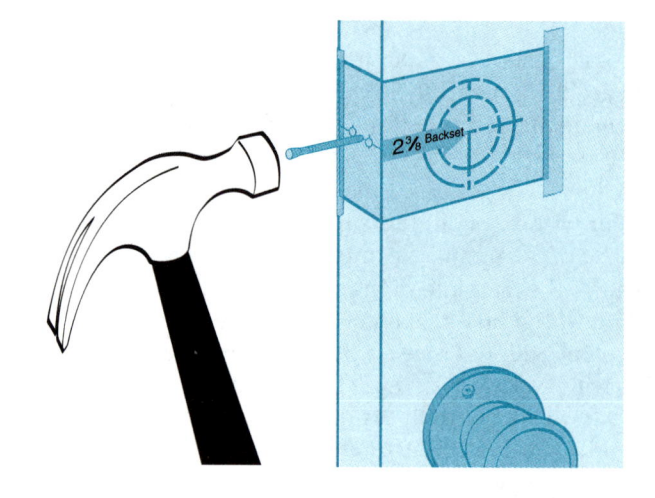

FIGURE 4.13
A deadbolt has reinforced collars that protect the key tumblers. The two halves are held together with two screws from one side to the other.

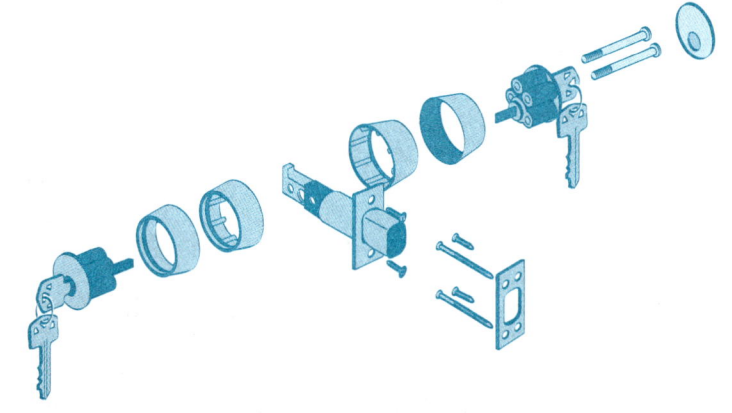

Pro's Tip: Locksmiths have tools called *drill guides* that help them drill straight and true when making holes in doors for locks. They take different configurations, and some types are available in home improvement stores or locksmiths' stores. Others might be available for hourly or daily rental from tool rental stores.

Summary

Windows and doors are mostly stationary and do their jobs as silent guardians of the home year in and year out. But they do move and have parts that wear or need maintenance or replacement. Most repairs to doors and windows require only simple hand tools, although installing a new lock requires a power drill. The key to working on doors and windows is being careful and precise because the tolerances, as between a sash and its window jamb or between a door edge and its door jamb, are very small, often around 1/16". Set aside the time you need to work with deliberation and precision.

Precise work is also required for plumbing, which is the subject of the next chapter. But much of the precision is forced on you by metal parts that fit together in only one way, so in some respects, working on plumbing is easier than some door and window repairs. No matter where you live, you will have some plumbing problems sometimes, but with the aid of the information in the following chapter, you will put most of them right in a short amount of time.

Plumbing

5

Plumbing repairs and upgrades often scare people away. But at least the simplest ones shouldn't. Moreover, nearly everyone is faced with a plumbing-type problem at one time or another, and if it's on a Sunday, no plumber is going to make a house-call unless he's paid a whole lot of money.

In addition, not all plumbing work is messy or unsanitary. The water in a toilet tank, for example, is clean. And replacing a shutoff valve should not cause any more mess than you can deal with using a paper towel.

Everyone should know how to unstop a toilet without having to call for outside help. Many of the other tasks in this chapter—stopping a faucet's leak, screwing on a water filter, replacing a toilet tank flapper—can be so simple that outside help is just too expensive to contemplate.

Even the more demanding chores—removing a sink's trap to clean it of hair or upgrading a faucet—can be readily accomplished by a homeowner with the proper tools and materials and can save a lot of money.

And even if you do not contemplate some of these repairs and improvements, you would do well to read this chapter. You will learn how the plumbing system in your home works and the steps plumbers need to take to make their fixes. This can allow you to better evaluate their charges and the quality of their work.

In this chapter:

* Learn how your plumbing system works.
* Get the tools and materials you'll need for basic plumbing repairs.
* Conquer the simple chores.
* Clear out clogs.
* Fix faucets.
* Deal with sinks.
* Take the trouble out of toilets.

Understanding Plumbing in Your Home

The plumbing in your home falls into two basic categories: supply and drain. Water from a water utility company enters a home generally below ground. The water is under pressure, as much as 50 pounds per square inch (psi). Near the point of entry, either outside or inside, the supply pipe of about 1" diameter enters a *water meter* that measures and registers how much water the home is using.

Your Water Supply and Main Shutoff Valve

The supply line then leads to a *main shutoff valve*, which is normally very close to where the supply line enters the house. This main valve might be on the inside or on the outside of the house, and it can be of the type with a handle that turns off clockwise or a ball valve with a rod-type handle that is rotated 90°. Normally, of course, the main shutoff valve is open.

But it needs to be turned to Off when you are working on a portion of the plumbing of the home that isn't controlled by its own shutoff valve or if there is a leak in the supply system.

Every homeowner should know where the main shutoff valve is located and how to turn it on and off. Find your main shutoff valve, mark it as such with a luggage tag, and learn how to use it; you might need to shut it off in an emergency as well as for a repair.

The Hot and Cold Water Lines

Supply lines might be made of copper, galvanized steel, or in some instances plastic. In some jurisdictions, plastic types are not allowed by plumbing codes.

From the main shutoff valve, the water line moves up (in pipes called *risers*) and horizontally (in pipes called *branches*) to faucets, clothes washers, dishwashers, showers, toilets, and other fixtures. One water supply pipe also runs to the hot water heater. Cold water enters through this pipe and is heated within the insulated water heater tank (the fuel being either natural gas or electricity). Hot water then runs under pressure from the water heater in its own separate risers and branches to fixtures.

Drains and Vents

Waste water is led away by the *drain-waste-vent* (DWV) system. DWV pipes might be made of plastic, cast iron, or in some cases copper. Water within the DWV system is not under pressure but flows by gravity along drainpipes to larger vertical pipes called *stacks*. The main soil stack (where all the home's waste water drains) descends to the lowest level of the home and connects to the main drain, which then runs to the city sewer or septic tank. Near the connection of the main soil stack and main drain is the plugged main cleanout. Professionals use this cleanout when large obstructions block the main drain.

Because waste water flows by gravity, the pipes have to be vented to the atmosphere; otherwise vacuum pockets would form in the pipes and prevent adequate flow.

CHAPTER 5 Plumbing   91

Therefore, pipes are connected to the drains and stacks and rise through the home roof into the atmosphere; these pipes are called *vents*.

Figure 5.1 shows a water supply and drain system like the one described here.

FIGURE 5.1
Water is supplied under pressure to fixtures and appliances in the supply system. There is always a main shutoff valve near where the water enters the home. Waste water is led away by the drain-waste-vent system, which is not under pressure but operates by gravity. Vents are an important part of the DWV system. So are the U-shaped traps, which hold water and prevent sewer gases from rising to household fixtures.

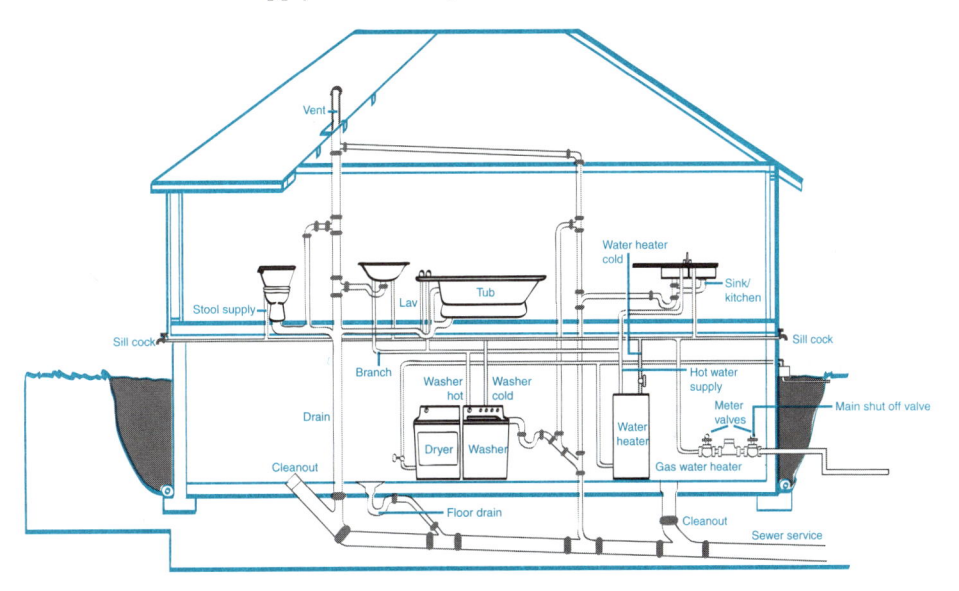

PLUMBING CODES

All jurisdictions have plumbing codes. These are written regulations that have the force of law and are meant to protect the health and safety of both individuals and the community. They govern the material supply pipes can be made of, the height a vent has to reach relative to the roof around it, the slope of a pipe leading away from a sink's trap, and much more.

Code details differ from community to community, and ones in differing regions of the country can differ markedly. In snow country, vents might have to be higher relative to the roofs around them than in warmer climates.

Generally, repairs of the type discussed in this book do not require knowledge of code provisions or inspection by building officials. But if you are uncertain about replacing one kind of pipe for another or any other sort of repair that might be covered by a code provision, call your jurisdiction's building department and ask for the plumbing code official.

In addition, every plumbing fixture—sink, toilet, washer, bathtub—has to have a trap in its waste system. A *trap* is a dip in a drain that holds the last water flowing from the fixture. The water held there acts like a seal within the drainpipe to ensure that sewer gases cannot migrate up the waste pipes to the fixtures themselves, meaning the gasses cannot pass through the water.

Basic Plumbing Tools and Materials

Plumbing fixes require basic plumbing tools, some of which you've already read about in Chapter 1, "Getting Ready." When you start to work around plumbing, you use your regular pliers, channel-lock pliers, utility knife, and more. And you'll be pulling out that bucket with its rags, as well as some sprays and lubricants. The following sections, however, discuss some of the tools you'll use specifically for basic plumbing repairs and improvements.

caution Vents of the DWV system need to be open to the atmosphere at all times. If you live in an area where leaves or birds might block the tops of vents, check them once a season. Use binoculars to examine their tops. If you see a vent top obstructed, call a roofer to clear away the trouble.

Putting Together a Basic Plumbing Toolkit

Although a wide variety of special equipment is available for household plumbing repairs, most tasks you'll tackle within your home can be completed with a basic set of plumbing tools. Here are the tools I recommend you keep handy:

- **Snake**—A snake, also called an *auger*, is a long metal cable that you feed into a clogged drain to penetrate and disperse clogs. Most homes are well served by an ordinary snake sold in home improvement stores. Some snakes come coiled in a case and with a pistol grip, and others come with only a metal handle that slides along the snake's length and is temporarily fixed in place with a thumbscrew. Professional-quality snakes are powered by electric motors and can break up clogs most homeowners can't dislodge with a regular snake.
- **Pipe wrench**—This is a tough wrench with an adjustable jaw for loosening nuts or threaded pipe. Pipe wrenches come in a variety of sizes (defined by length), but 14" is a good length for most home repairs.
- **Basin wrench**—This is a long rod with a jaw at the top and a handle at the bottom used for loosening and tightening nuts in hard-to-reach places beneath sinks.
- **Spud wrench**—This is a wide and toothless wrench for tightening and loosening large nuts, like those used between toilet tanks and bowls and beneath sink drains. You won't need a spud wrench if you don't intend to work on these types of plumbing connections.
- **Hex wrenches**—Also called Allen wrenches, these are L-shaped, hexagonal, cross-section pieces of steel for turning screws or bolts with hex-head depressions. They come in sets of various diameters.
- **Toilet and drain plungers**—Most of us are familiar with these tools, which typically are made up of a flexible rubber cup attached to the end of a wooden rod. By placing the plunger cup over a clogged drain and pumping the rod up and down, you push water or create suction that sometimes agitates a clog into breaking up. You should have two plungers. For sink drains,

CHAPTER 5   Plumbing   93

have one with a simple flat bell. For toilets, have one with a projection from the bell because it fits better to toilet drain holes.

- **Faucet handle puller**—Faucet handles are often hard to pull from the stems or assemblies that they cover, even after the screws—often covered with decorative caps or in places out of normal sight—have been loosened or removed. A plumbing supply store can sell you a faucet handle puller, a screw-down gripping device with a handle that allows you to more easily pull a faucet handle away from the stem (to learn about common faucet components, see "Stopping Drips and Repairing Faucets," later in this chapter).

FIGURE 5.2
Here are the tools you should gather in your basic home plumbing toolkit: a basic snake, pipe wrench, basin wrench, spud wrench, sink plunger, toilet plunger, and faucet handle puller.

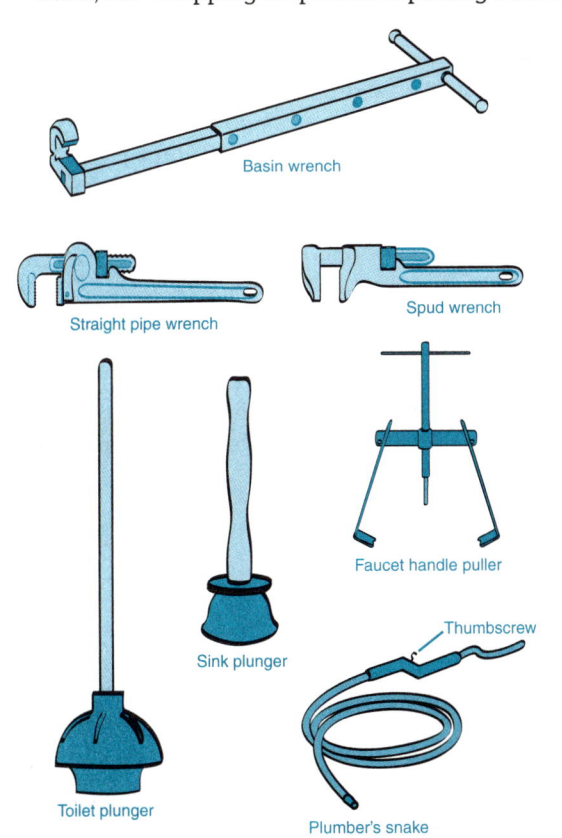

Basin wrench

Straight pipe wrench

Spud wrench

Faucet handle puller

Sink plunger

Thumbscrew

Toilet plunger

Plumber's snake

Plumbing Materials to Have on Hand

A good supply of plumbing materials will make your work easier *and* better. Most of the materials listed here are available in large home improvement stores; all are available in plumbing supply stores:

- **Pipe joint compound**—This is also called *threaded-joint sealer* and *plumber's dope*. Many plumbing joints are connected with threaded pipes and large nuts or caps. This gray joint-sealing compound is available in small tubes or larger cans. You apply the compound to any sort of pipe threads to make the threading easier and help seal the threaded connection to protect against

leaks and corrosion. Apply it evenly to the threaded area of pipes, using enough to fill just to the tops of the threads.
- **Pipe-thread tape**—This is also called *fluorocarbon tape*. This thin, flexible white tape comes in small rolls and is used much like pipe joint compound. You wind the tape one and a half times in a clockwise direction around the circumference of any sort of pipe thread. The tape makes the threading easier and helps seal the connection to protect against leaks and corrosion. Pull as you wind the tape, which then grips the threads, sinking into them and allowing the tops of the threads to show through. You can use pipe-thread tape in place of pipe joint compound.
- **Plumber's grease**—This grease comes in a small can. You apply it to the stems of plumbing valves and stem faucets to make them easier to turn.
- **Plumber's putty**—This is a kind of putty you roll by hand into long strands and place beneath faucets, sink strainers, and the like to make a waterproof seal. You can use plumber's putty on any surface except plastic.
- **Penetrating oil**—Available in small cans or in spray cans, penetrating oil works its way into threads to make it easier to loosen a nut or coupling. If you have threaded couplings that have grown rusted or corroded, you can apply this oil to help loosen them up.

In addition to the materials in the preceding list, you also need to keep some basic equipment and supplies handy. Along with the eye protection and light gloves listed in Chapter 1, you'll need these supplies for almost any plumbing job in your home:

- Bucket, rags, paper towels
- Rubber gloves

To do list

- ❏ Learn the tools you should keep in a basic plumbing toolkit.
- ❏ Gather the necessary materials and supplies for basic home plumbing repairs.
- ❏ Keep tools and materials that are especially for plumbing in a logical, easy-to-find location removed from the tools and materials for other repairs.

Shopping at a Plumber's Supply Store

Home repair stores have lots of plumbing equipment and supplies, but you are often better off going to the plumbing supply store where the local professionals shop for their own supplies and parts. These are sometimes listed as "wholesalers" in the *Yellow Pages*, but they also sell retail over the counter and take most kinds of payment (cash, credit card, and check). Of course, you'll look and sound like an amateur, but the salespeople are used to this. One advantage of shopping for plumbing parts at these professional outlets is that you can take in old parts and ask for replacements; normally they will have them. The staff at most plumbing supply stores can also tell you how to install parts and recommend any other pieces you might need to make the job go more smoothly. They can also tell you if the part you're wanting to replace is going out of style and, if so, what you should use in its place.

Pro's Tip

When you go to a plumber's supply store, take old parts with you—even washers and screws—and be prepared to answer questions. The sales agents might want to know what kinds of pipe you are connecting to (copper, plastic, and so on) or the brand and model of fixture you are working with. He might also ask about the "o.d." (outside diameter) or "i.d." (inside diameter) of the pipes in question. Measure the o.d. and i.d. as best you can with a ruler and write down the results.

Home improvement store salespeople know considerably less about individual plumbing parts and repairs, so they are not likely to be as helpful. Home repair stores, however, do carry replacement parts for common models of faucets, toilets, and so forth. In addition, their replacement part kits generally have installation instructions. The parts, however, might be manufactured to suit many plumbing arrangements and not just the one you are dealing with. This could be a problem; because they are not specifically manufactured for the fixture or connection you are working on, they might not last as long.

Prices at home improvement stores and plumbing supply companies are likely to be comparable. However, plumbing fixtures sold at home improvement stores, despite having brand names, can often be made to the specifications for that store (which wants low prices) and might not be made of the manufacturer's best materials. You might get parts and fixtures with a longer life expectancy at plumbers' supply stores than at home improvement stores.

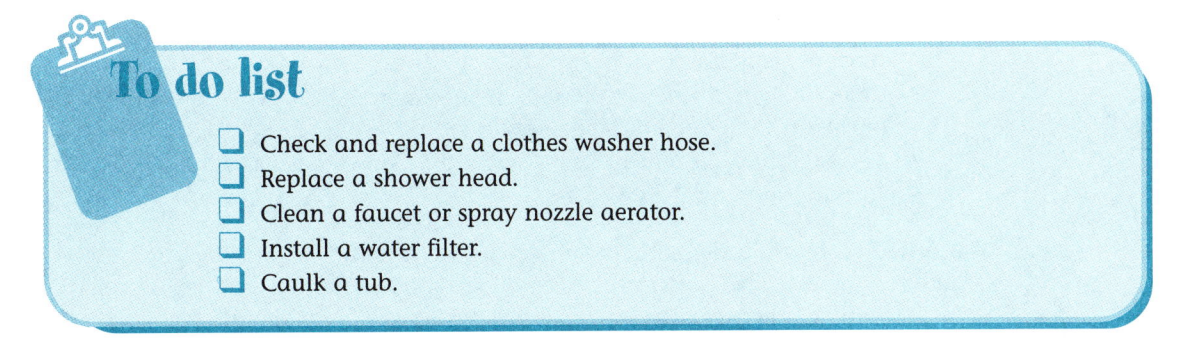

To do list

- ❏ Check and replace a clothes washer hose.
- ❏ Replace a shower head.
- ❏ Clean a faucet or spray nozzle aerator.
- ❏ Install a water filter.
- ❏ Caulk a tub.

Taking Care of Simple Plumbing Chores

Some plumbing-related jobs are pretty easy. They require no more than unscrewing parts and screwing new ones together again. Anyone should be able to do the following jobs, and generally, the tasks here do not require safety cautions. You'll save money and know the job is done right when you do it yourself.

Replacing Clothes Washer Hoses

Every six months you should examine your clothes washer supply hoses for worn, brittle, or weak spots (a hose should feel supple and strong). The water in these hoses is under pressure, and this pressure can cause the hoses to wear. If one begins to leak or ruptures, you'll have a flood. If a hose appears cracked or is brittle to the touch, replace it.

While you're at it, you should go ahead and replace the companion hose as well (all washers have two supply hoses, one for hot water and another for cold water). These hoses were probably installed at the same time. When one goes bad, the other is likely to follow soon, and a year from now you won't have to remember which hose you replaced and which one you didn't. Replacement hoses are available in home improvement stores.

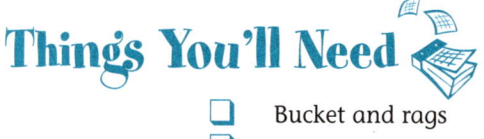

Things You'll Need

- ❏ Bucket and rags
- ❏ Regular or channel-lock pliers
- ❏ Replacement hose
- ❏ Pipe-joint compound

Follow these steps to replace a hose:

1. Turn off the shutoff valve to the hose. Unthread the hose at the shutoff valve. You might be able to use your hand alone; if not, use a pair of regular pliers or channel-lock pliers. Be careful; water will come out. Drain the hose into a bucket. Unthread the hose where it connects to the clothes washer.
2. Take the hose to a home improvement or plumbing supply store. Buy one of the same length and with the same type of connectors at the ends.
3. Coat the male threads of the shutoff valve and the washer connection with pipe-joint compound or pipe-joint tape.
4. Screw on the replacement hose at both the clothes washer and the valve.
5. Turn the supply valves back on.

Be sure to carefully match the threads when you begin to thread one part onto another. The threaded pieces need to be aligned and straight as you begin to screw them together; otherwise, the connection will be crooked, the threads will be damaged, and a leak will ensue. When a clean threaded part goes straight onto another clean threaded part, the turning should feel easy; when it goes on crooked, there will be greater resistance.

Replacing a Shower Head

Many homes have shower heads old enough to be considerably behind the styles now available in stores. Replacing an old shower head is basically a matter of unscrewing the old one and screwing on the new one.

CHAPTER 5   Plumbing   97

You do not need to shut off water supply for this job. But be careful because you will be working in at an awkward height and possibly over a very hard surface—for example, a cast iron tub.

Things You'll Need

- ❑ Pliers or adjustable wrench
- ❑ Pipe joint compound or pipe-thread tape

Take care that the tub or shower stall is dry and that you have good footing. Then follow these steps:

1. Use a wrench to loosen the shower head collar fixed to the pipe extending from the wall—it should turn counterclockwise as you face it. If the collar does not move and if the pipe wants to twist when you attempt to turn the collar, wrap the pipe near the collar with tape and hold it firmly with pliers in one hand while you try again to unscrew the shower head with another wrench in your other hand. Complete the shower head removal by hand.
2. Apply pipe joint compound or pipe-thread tape to the threads on the pipe that extends through your shower wall.
3. Making sure the two pieces are properly aligned, turn the shower head collar of the new shower head to the right (clockwise) to screw it onto the shower supply pipe and tighten the connection. Generally, tightening by hand suffices.

Pro's Tip

Professional plumbers say that amateurs commonly over-tighten. Over-tightening is hard on threads, as well as on washers, valve seats, and nuts, and can lead to leaks. Shutoff valves that are meant to be tightened by hand should be tightened firmly and no more. Valve or nuts meant to be tightened with pliers or a wrench should be tightened firmly by hand and then given no more than a full rotation more with the pliers or wrench.

tip When using pliers to loosen or tighten a part that is normally visible to the eye, either wrap the part with tape or place a couple of layers of tape over the teeth of the pliers. You can use masking tape, electrical tape, or duct tape. This practice prevents the pliers from gouging the metal or plastic.

Cleaning a Faucet or Spray Hose Nozzle Aerator

Many faucet spouts have aerators, which mix air with the water to make a more even flow. Aerators are fine mesh screens enclosed in a stainless steel body that screws onto the opening of a faucet. Kitchen sink spray hoses have similar nozzles, except that the aerator body is often plastic and not stainless steel. When the water coming out of the faucet spout looks uneven or flows to one side, the culprit is usually mineral grit caught in the aerator. You can clean it out to restore full water pressure and flow from your faucet. Figure 5.3 shows an exploded view of a faucet with a sink spray and aerator.

Repair Your Home In No Time

FIGURE 5.3

An aerator mixes water and air for a smoother flow of water. It has four parts: washer, perforated disk, screen, and body.

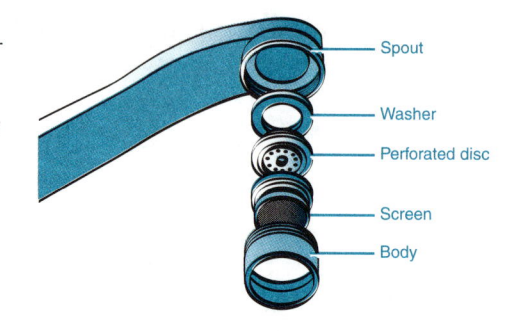

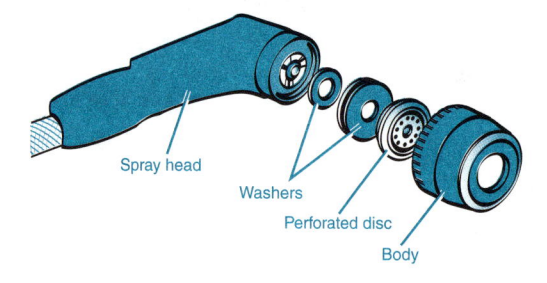

- Spout
- Washer
- Perforated disc
- Screen
- Body

- Spray head
- Washers
- Perforated disc
- Body

Things You'll Need

- ☐ Pliers
- ☐ Pipe joint compound or pipe-thread tape
- ☐ Toothpick
- ☐ Old toothbrush
- ☐ Replacement parts, as necessary

Follow these steps to remove, clean, and replace an aerator:

1. Close the sink drain; place a paper towel over it if you think you might bump the pop-up stopper to the open position. The towel will prevent any loose parts from accidentally going down the drain.
2. Because the aerator body is visible, use taped pliers to loosen it. Once loose, unthread the aerator body the remainder of the way with your fingers.
3. Lay the aerator body and any components that come loose with it in correct order on a level surface beside the sink. With your fingers, reach up into the faucet spout and remove any loose components that remain in the spout; the last piece should be a rubber washer. Likely there will be, in this order bottom to top, the aerator body, screen, perforated disk, and washer.

caution Take special care applying pressure with pliers to remove or attach a kitchen aerator. Otherwise, you might crack the plastic body.

4. Use a toothpick to clean debris from the screen and perforated disk. Grit in the perforated disk is hard to spot; look closely and test each hole with a toothpick. Flush the perforated disk and screen with water (again, be certain that you have stoppered the sink so dropped pieces can't fall down the drain). If mineral deposits are especially tough, soak the parts in vinegar.
5. If the perforated disk, screen, or washer is broken, take it to a plumber's supply store for replacements.
6. Use an old toothbrush to clean the threads of the body and faucet spout.
7. Reassemble the components in the correct order and screw the body back to the faucet.

Installing a Water Filter

Installing a water filter at a faucet is much like replacing a shower head. After the hardware is installed, the filter portion has to be changed periodically.

Things You'll Need

- ☐ Water filter kit
- ☐ Regular or channel-lock pliers
- ☐ Plumber's joint compound or pipe-thread tape

Filters come in kits with installation instructions, but these steps outline the general process:

1. Unscrew the aerator of the faucet (use the process described earlier in "Cleaning a Faucet or Spray Hose Nozzle Aerator").
2. Apply joint compound or pipe-thread tape to the male threads.
3. Screw on the water filter following the instructions that accompany the filter. Trim away any visible joint compound or tape.
4. Save the aerator in your plumbing supplies area in case you have use of it at a later time.

Caulking a Tub

The line where the bottom edge of a wall of tile meets the upper edge of a bathtub is a potential source of water leakage behind the tub and into the wall. This area might have been filled with grout at one time, but the grout can fail. In addition, caulk, having replaced the grout, can itself fail over time. Then the area should be cleaned out and filled with new caulk.

Caulking for bathtubs, or other bath or kitchen areas involving splashed water, is generally of a silicon base and clearly marked in home improvement stores. Some come in squeeze tubes; others come in cartridges meant to be used in conjunction with caulking guns. They can be smoothed with water when applied and washed off hands with soap and water.

Things You'll Need

- ☐ Rag
- ☐ Utility knife or single-edge razor
- ☐ Tube of silicon-based caulking
- ☐ Caulking gun

Follow these steps to replace failed caulking:

1. Use either a utility knife or a single-edge razor with a backing to remove the old caulk. Try to remove caulk from within the gap between the lower edge of the tile and the top of the tub, creating a depression there into which the new caulk will be pressed.

   Short Cut: Sometimes the caulk can be removed by pulling; it comes out like a string. Try to get a finger behind one end and slowly pull because this is faster than the razor method.

2. Cut the caulk tube nozzle at an angle and about as wide as the gap between tile and tub.
3. Start in a corner with the point of the nozzle touching the corner. Squeeze the caulking gun trigger and pull the caulking gun along the gap; the point of the nozzle presses the caulk into the gap and smoothes as it goes.
4. Use a moistened finger, a moistened cloth, or the back of a moistened plastic spoon to further press and smooth the caulk in place.
5. Allow the caulk 24 hours to cure. Trim away any smears with a utility knife or single-edge razor.

WORKING WITH CAULK AND CAULKING GUNS

Caulk comes in tubes or in cartridges. Tubes hold about 4 oz. and cartridges 10 oz. Buy cartridges for big jobs, but plan ahead. After you cut open the nozzle of a tube or cartridge, you need to close it again when the repair is done; otherwise, the caulk inside solidifies and becomes useless. Many tubes come with caps you can use for this purpose. For cartridges, seal the open top with plastic cut from tough plastic bags: Hold the plastic in place with rubber bands. Even with these measures, the caulk will solidify or become too congealed to apply if left unused for months; do not buy more caulk than you expect to use within six months.

To use a tube or cartridge, carefully cut the nozzle at an angle using a utility knife blade. Cut as wide an opening as you want to make the bead of caulk you are about to squeeze out; err on the small side because you can always make the opening larger.

If you are using a cartridge, pull back the plunger rod of the caulking gun and slip the cartridge into the caulking gun body. Move the plunger rod back firmly against the base of the cartridge. Rotate the cartridge until the nozzle slant is in the position you want. Pull back the trigger to move the plunger forward; caulk will be squeezed out the nozzle.

Squeeze the trigger as little as possible. Especially at the beginning of a cartridge, it is all too easy to squeeze too much. This applies pressure to caulk all through the cartridge and even when you release the trigger, caulk continues to flow out of the nozzle—more than you anticipated and can reasonably deal with.

When done with a tube or cartridge, wipe the nozzle clean and seal it as best you can.

To do list

- ❏ Learn how to adjust a pop-up stopper.
- ❏ Remove and clean the stopper.

Dealing with Sinks

Sinks rarely have problems, except at the pop-up stopper and when becoming clogged, both of which are covered in the next section. Sink stoppers can develop problems for two reasons: poor adjustment and trapped hair. If a stopper is incorrectly adjusted, it doesn't seal properly and either fails to hold water in the sink or fails to rise far enough to release the water. Hair trapped around the stopper slows water drainage.

Adjusting a Pop-Up Stopper

Figure 5.4 shows a drain and pop-up stopper with its ball and pivot rod linkage. Occasionally, pop-up stoppers need maintenance to hold water in the sink without leaking and to release the water for quick draining. If the pop-up is not performing both of these tasks adequately, you can adjust it using the steps shown here.

tip If you are working near a sink or tub with some heavy tools, place thick rags in the sink or area of the tub in case you drop a tool. Without the padding, the tool could cause the sink or tub to chip.

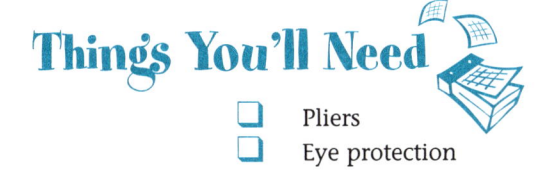

Things You'll Need

- ❏ Pliers
- ❏ Eye protection

Follow these steps to adjust a pop-up stopper:

1. To tighten a pop-up stopper's seal, look under the sink and loosen the setscrew that holds the lifter and the clevis (the flat metal rod with holes) together. In the sink, press the stopper closed, making the pivot rod under the sink rise.
2. At the sink, pull up on the lifter rod up as far as you can without its leaving the clevis and then lower it 1/4". Under the sink, tighten the setscrew again.

> **caution** When you have to look up at your work and there is corrosion on the joints you are working on, wear eye protection to guard your eyes from falling grit.

FIGURE 5.4
Most sinks now have pop-up stoppers that raise and lower by means of a lifter behind the faucet.

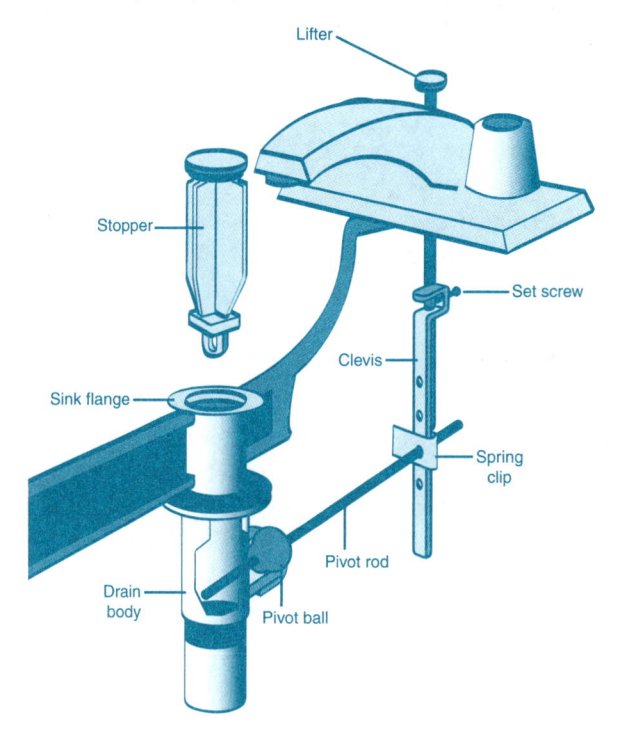

3. If the pop-up stopper is now difficult to operate, move the pivot rod to a higher hole on the clevis. To do this, pinch the two ends of the spring clip together and move it toward the wall, freeing the end of the pivot rod from the clevis.
4. Reinsert the end of the pivot rod into the next higher hole in the clevis and slip the wall-side end of the spring clip over the pivot rod's end, securing the pivot rod to the clevis.
5. Test the pop-up again. Go to increasingly higher holes if you have to.

Removing and Cleaning a Pop-Up Stopper

If a pop-up stopper is clogged with hair or water leaks from the sink owing to a deteriorated gasket around the pop-up stopper head, you need to remove the pop-up. Some pop-up stoppers simply lift out at the sink. Others can be removed by twisting and then lifting. If your pop-up stopper does not lift out this way, it is connected to a pivot rod under the sink and you must follow the next set of steps to remove it.

> **caution** If you are working under a sink, consider wearing light gloves. With large wrenches and the confined space, you are likely to strike your fingers against something hard.

When you lift out the pop-up stopper, it might come up wrapped in hair; after you clean and reinsert the pop-up, the sink might drain normally. If not, stronger measures are needed.

Things You'll Need

- ❏ Regular pliers
- ❏ Channel-lock pliers
- ❏ Bucket, rags, and paper towels
- ❏ Eye protection and light gloves

Follow these steps to remove and clean a pop-up stopper:

1. Place a bucket beneath the trap below the sink.
2. Use channel-lock pliers to loosen the retaining nut on the back side of the pipe descending from the sink. When it is all the way loosened, slide the nut back along the pivot rod.
3. Use regular pliers to pinch the ends of the spring clip at the clevis together. Then push the pivot rod away from the pipe back through the clevis. The pivot rod connects to a pivot ball, which you are likely to see. If it comes all the way free of the pipe, you might also see a gasket and washer; don't allow them to escape.
4. The pop-up stopper is now free from the pivot rod. Pull it out of the sink. Clean it, *but not in the sink* because water will flow out of the pipe where the pivot ball has been dislodged. If your problem is a leak around the pop-up stopper, remove and replace the washer at the pop-up stopper's head.
5. Reassemble the pop-up stopper assembly in reverse. Have the pop-up stopper in place when you push the pivot rod back into its proper position, thus engaging the end hole or slot at the bottom of the pop-up stopper. Thread the retaining nut on straight and tighten. Turn on the water and check for drips.

If the sink is still draining slowly, remove and clean the trap (see the next section).

Pro's Tip: If you cannot loosen a part using normal strength, try penetrating oil. Apply it near where the two parts meet and tap the parts lightly. Wait a few minutes. If this does not allow you to loosen the parts, apply more penetrating oil, tap again, and wait an hour. Still no luck? Apply a bit more and wait overnight.

Call the Pro: If the tools you have available and penetrating oil do not allow you to loosen parts, call a pro. Applying too much brute strength might wrench the pipe or devices and cause greater trouble.

Things You'll Need

- ❏ Remove and clean a sink trap.
- ❏ Learn the right way to use a plunger to unclog a toilet.
- ❏ Learn to use a plumber's snake to clear clogs.

Clearing Out Clogs

One of the most common household plumbing problems is clogs. At first, you might notice that water is draining slowly from your sink or tub, but eventually the clog becomes complete and drainage stops altogether. When that happens, you might have a messy job on your hands.

But with the right tools and materials, you should be able to readily handle these annoyances. If hair around a pop-up stopper isn't the culprit in a sink, the trap probably is, and removing and cleaning the trap takes only a few minutes. Using the right kind of plunger on a toilet can dispense of those clogs in less time than that. If the clog is so bad you need to use a snake, however, the solution might require some perspiration. After you unclog a pipe with a snake, though, you are not likely to have to return to the same task for years, as long as you take some precautions and avoid clog-prone habits (see the tip in the section "Using a Plumber's Snake to Unclog a Drain").

Removing and Cleaning a Sink Trap

When bathroom sinks drain slowly, the culprit is generally hair caught around the pop-up stopper mechanism in the pipe just below the drain (the tail piece) or built up in the trap just below the tail piece (see Figure 5.5).

note Even if your sink is not draining slowly, it is a good idea for you to know how to remove a sink trap. You might drop a ring or contact lens in the sink and watch it go down the drain. If this does happen to you, *turn off the water immediately*; otherwise, the water might flush the ring or lens out of the trap and further down into the DWV system. Then remove the trap, carefully pour its contents into a bucket, and search the bucket for the lost item.

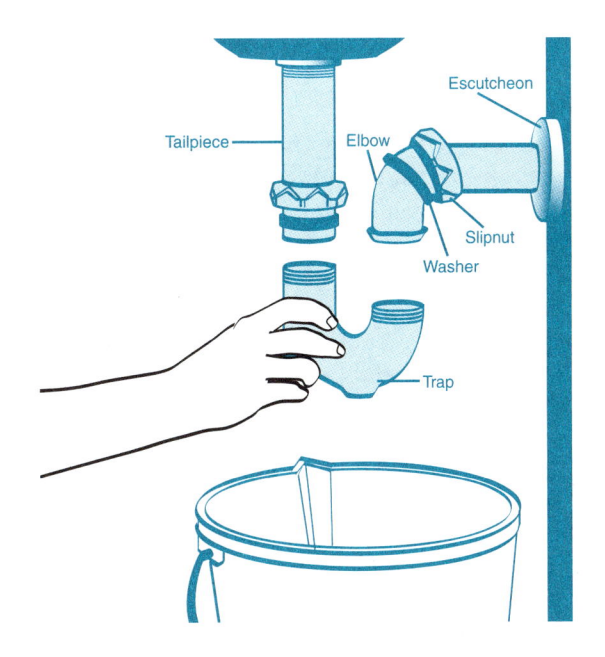

CHAPTER 5 Plumbing

FIGURE 5.5
Two slip nuts and two washers hold a trap to the tail piece (descending from the sink) and the elbow or drainpipe that goes into the wall.

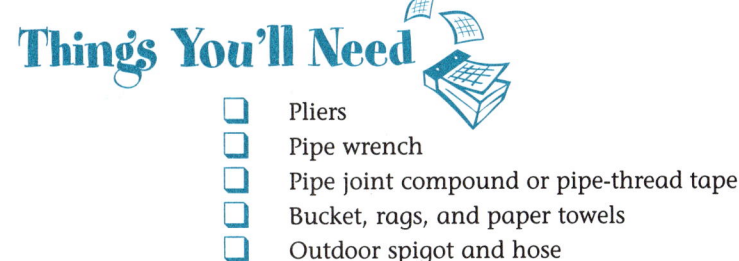

(Diagram labels: Tailpiece, Elbow, Escutcheon, Slipnut, Washer, Trap)

Things You'll Need

- ☐ Pliers
- ☐ Pipe wrench
- ☐ Pipe joint compound or pipe-thread tape
- ☐ Bucket, rags, and paper towels
- ☐ Outdoor spigot and hose

If you have removed and cleaned the pop-up stopper and still the sink drains slowly, remove and clean the trap as follows:

1. Place the bucket beneath the sink trap.
2. The trap might have a clean-out plug at the bottom; it looks like a square-headed or hex-headed nut. If you see one, use pliers to loosen and then remove it, and move on to step 3. If there is no clean-out plug, move on to step 4.
3. Standing water in the trap will come streaming out as the plug is loosened. If you are lucky, you can pull out the hair with your fingers. If you think there is more in the trap, you want to be more thorough, or there is no clean-out plug, you should remove the trap.
4. Use an adjustable wrench, pipe wrench, or channel-lock pliers to loosen the slip nuts holding the trap to 1) the *tail piece* descending from the sink and 2) the elbow leading toward the wall. If there was no clean-out plug, water begins to flow from the trap, so have the bucket in place. When the trap can

be pulled down from the tail piece, hold it upright because there will still be water in it if there was no clean-out plug. Place the trap over the bucket.

5. Tilt the trap, letting the water flow from the trap into the bucket. Look inside the trap for obstructions. Use your fingers to clean out what you can; use a hose outdoors to clean out the rest.

6. Treat threads with pipe joint compound or pipe-thread tape. Replace the trap by slipping the tail piece end up the tail piece as far as it will go.

7. Swivel the elbow end of the trap to align with the lower portion of the elbow. Slip the gasket and slip nut down the tail piece to the threads of the trap and begin to thread the slip nut onto the trap threads. Be sure they go on straight. Do the same at the elbow end.

8. Hand-tighten the slip nuts. Then give each a half turn with the wrench or pliers. Place the bucket under the trap and turn on a faucet to run water into the trap. Check for leaks. If there are any, the slip nuts either are not threaded straight or could use a bit more tightening. If the threads are crooked, loosen the slip nuts and start threading and tightening them again. If they appear to be straight, try tightening them more to stop the leak. If there is still a leak, the problem might be with the gaskets. Replace them with new ones.

> **tip** When you reinstall a trap, run it up as high as you can on the tail piece. The reason is that you want the elbow end to be high as well. This ensures that the pipe leading from the curve of the elbow to the wall remains slanted downhill. If that slant is reversed, the sink will drain slowly or not at all and create an unsanitary condition.

Using a Plunger to Unclog a Toilet

Toilets can clog entirely or only partially when water drains but drains slowly. Both problems are remedied with a toilet plunger.

Things You'll Need

- ❏ Toilet plunger
- ❏ Rubber gloves (optional, but a good idea)

Follow these steps:

1. If the water level is as high as the upper rim of the toilet, try to wait until its level is lower. Otherwise, you are likely to splash water out of the toilet onto the floor and possibly yourself.

2. Fit the circumference of the plunger bottom as tightly around the hole inside the toilet bowl as you can. Press down rapidly several times. (If the water level is high, make these first plunges gentle to hold down splashing and overflow.) Lift up on the plunger to see if the toilet is draining.

CHAPTER 5 Plumbing 107

3. Repeat the rapid strokes until the toilet drains. After it has drained, try a regular flush to see whether the obstruction has gone.

Using a Plumber's Snake to Unclog a Drain

You can use a plumber's snake to unclog both sink and tub drains.

Things You'll Need

- ❑ Regular pliers
- ❑ Plumber's snake
- ❑ Channel-lock pliers
- ❑ Bucket, rags, and paper towels
- ❑ Eye protection and light gloves

To use a snake to clear a sink drain, follow these steps:

1. Remove the pop-up stopper (see "Removing and Cleaning a Sink Trap"). Work the end of the snake down into the drain until it meets an obstruction; the first might actually be a bend in the drainpipe, not the actual clog.
2. Tighten the thumbscrew in the curved handle. Rotate the handle clockwise several times in your hands—this rotates the end of the snake because the thumbscrew fastens the handle and snake together—and press forward at the same time. When the handle gets close to the sink drain, loosen the thumbscrew and pull the handle back to a more comfortable position.
3. Tighten the thumbscrew again and repeat the rotating and pressing. Pressing the snake end around pipe bends takes some patience and practice, but stick to it; the snake eventually moves forward.
4. Occasionally pull the end of the snake out of the drain. Have a bucket ready because the snake's end is likely to have some of the obstruction snared to it when it comes into sight.
5. Repeat steps 1–4 as many times as it takes to dislodge the clog.
6. If the pop-up stopper and trap are clear, the obstruction might be in the drainpipe. Remove and clean the sink trap (see "Removing and Cleaning a Sink Trap"). Poise a bucket beneath the end of the drainpipe, feed the end of the snake into the drainpipe, pressing and twisting as you go.
7. After you have cleared an obstruction with a snake, reassemble the pipes and parts, test for leaks, and then run hot water through the system.

tip Cleaning clogs is bothersome, even nasty, work. So avoid it by preventing clogs. Have users use toilet paper to wipe hair from sinks before they leave the bathroom. Use strainers in showers and tubs and ask users to throw trapped hair into a wastebasket after each shower. Do not allow persons to place anything except toilet paper into toilets. Regularly check sink pop-up stoppers and clean them when you see hair build-up.

For a slow-draining bathtub, your best option is to snake through the overflow pipe. This way, you avoid a sharp turn just beyond the drain opening at the bottom of the tub. Follow these steps:

1. Remove the cover from the overflow opening. Remove the pop-up assembly if it operates through the overflow opening.
2. Push the snake end through the overflow opening. Rotate and press as in the directions for using a plumber's snake in a sink drain.
3. The first turn will be in the trap. The obstruction is likely here or just downstream. Press and turn the snake into these turns. Repeat until the obstruction is cleared. Run hot water through the drain.

caution Take care if you decide to use chemicals or biological additives to clear drains, and follow the directions exactly. Generally, these additives do not work well if a clog has become severe. If you have a septic tank, do not use chemicals unless the container's directions say that you can. After you have poured chemicals into a drain, do not use a snake or a plunger. There is danger that the chemicals will splash back on you.

If you have not been able to clear a clog with a snake or chemicals, then it is likely beyond your repair capabilities. Call a professional who will have a motor-driven snake.

To do list

- ❑ Learn to replace worn washers and fix worn seats in compression valve faucets.
- ❑ Repair a stem valve's packing.
- ❑ Stop leaks in a ball faucet.
- ❑ Repair a single-handle cartridge faucet.
- ❑ Fix a leaking disk faucet.
- ❑ Replace a defective faucet.
- ❑ Install new supply tubes.
- ❑ Replace shutoff valves.

Stopping Drips and Repairing Faucets

Basically there are two kinds of faucets. The older ones are called *compression faucets* (or *stem faucets*); the other type is *washerless faucets*. Compression faucets have separate handles for hot and cold water, although they might mix their water to a common spout. These faucets shut off water by screwing down a stem, which has a washer at the bottom that presses against a metal *seat*.

After long usage, the washer can become deformed and should be replaced. If a defective washer is left in place for a long time, water seeping past it can carve a depression in the seat. You also can replace or smooth a faucet seat, although both tasks are more difficult and expensive than replacing a defective washer. Faucet seats are smoothed in place with a *seat dresser*, a hand tool that, when rotated, cuts the metal slightly to eliminate irregularities. It can also be removed for replacement by a *seat wrench*, which is little more than a curved piece of steel with a shaped end for fitting into a seat's opening.

Compression faucets, shown in Figure 5.6, can also leak around the handles, having failed at the *packing*, which is compressionable material around the stem that is meant to keep water from seeping up toward the handle.

Washerless faucets generally have one handle that moves left and right for hot and cold and fore and back for pressure. These faucets fall into the categories of cartridge, ball, and disk faucets. Washerless faucets have turning or twisting mechanisms that, when turned, properly align inlet openings to openings further upstream, allowing water to pass. The inlets are accompanied by small springs and elastomer seals. When the springs or seals go bad, leaks through the spout result.

Washerless faucets can also leak around the handles or lower bodies, owing to worn O-rings, which are thin washers that act like packing, meant to keep water from seeping out of the faucet.

Plumbing fixtures, especially faucets, can have many parts. Take them apart slowly and place them in a location where you are not likely to knock into or disturb them. Lay the parts down in the order in which they were assembled, and in the direction they faced. If you think you might need to move them or otherwise disturb their order, make a sketch of the order in which they should be reassembled or take a digital picture of them as they lie in the correct order. Include all screws and washers—it's amazing how quickly you can forget how a faucet is assembled.

Things You'll Need

- ❑ Hex wrench
- ❑ Basin wrench
- ❑ Flat-head and Phillips screwdrivers
- ❑ Adjustable wrench
- ❑ Seat wrench and seat dresser
- ❑ Manufacturer's repair kits, as available
- ❑ Needle-nose and regular pliers
- ❑ Rags
- ❑ Replacement parts as needed

Repairing a Compression Valve Faucet

If the drip is from the spout and your compression faucets share a common spout, you need to determine whether the drip owes to the hot water faucet or cold water faucet. If you cannot determine this by sensing the temperature of the dripping water, turn off the shutoff valve beneath either the cold or hot water faucet and see whether the drip stops.

When you have determined which faucet is defective, proceed as follows:

1. Turn off the shutoff valve under the sink.
2. With older stem faucets, the packing nut is exposed beneath the handle. If this is the case, use an adjustable wrench to loosen the packing nut, lift out the handle-stem assembly, and move to step 4; otherwise, continue with step 3.
3. If you do not see a nut beneath the handle, the handle is covering it. Pop off or unscrew the handle's decorative cap (it might have an H or a C on it for hot and cold). You can do this with a flat-head screwdriver or, if the cap is elevated and has ridges, with a pair of pliers, taking care not to mar the ridges or the handle. Unscrew the handle screw that lies beneath the decorative cap. Lift off the handle, exposing the packing nut. Use an adjustable wrench or pliers to unscrew the packing nut, and then lift out the whole handle-stem assembly.
4. If your drip problem was at the spout, first examine the washer held to the stem bottom with a screw. If the washer is grooved from long use pressing against the valve seat below, it is no longer doing its job. Remove the screw and washer (take the old washer with you to the hardware or plumbing supply store to get the correct replacement). Replace the washer with an identical one.
5. Coat the stem threads with plumber's grease. Reinstall the handle-stem assembly, tighten down the packing nut, and replace the handle if you took it off. Turn on the shutoff valve and test the faucet.

If the faucet still drips, the culprit might be the metal seat against which the new washer is pressing. Some seats are removable and replaceable. Turn off the shutoff valve again and remove the faucet stem. Use a *seat wrench* (you can buy these in hardware stores) to remove the seat by pressing the end of the seat wrench in it and turning counterclockwise. Buy a new seat from your plumber's supply store. Press some plumber's pipe-joint compound on the new seat's exterior, press the seat onto the seat wrench end, and use the wrench to screw the new seat back into place.

If the seat cannot be removed, it can still be dressed or smoothed with a valve seat dresser available in home improvement and plumber's supply stores. After you have removed the stem from the valve, insert the smoothing end of the valve dresser down to the seat and rotate the dresser handle a couple of times. This smoothes the seat making for a better seal between it and the stem washer. Remove grit with a rag. Reassemble the faucet and turn on the water to check for leaks.

CHAPTER 5 Plumbing 111

FIGURE 5.6
All compression faucets share these features: handle screw, packing nut, stem, seat washer, and washer screw. Most drips arise because of a worn seat washer.

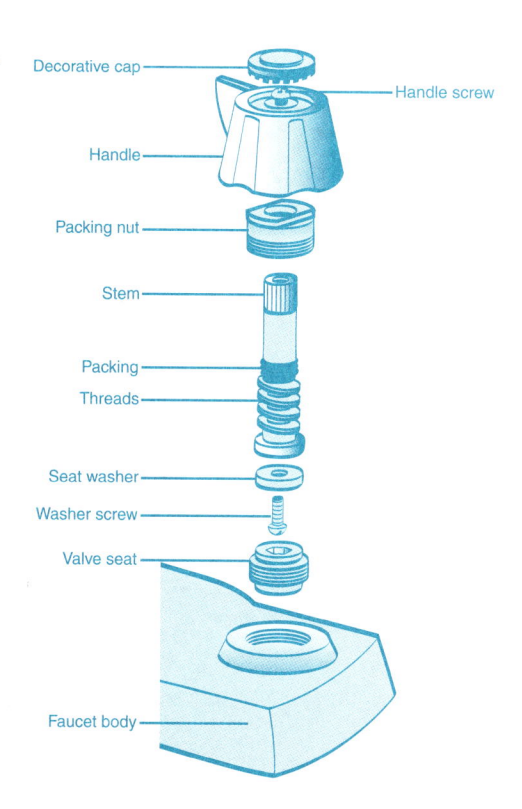

Decorative cap
Handle screw
Handle
Packing nut
Stem
Packing
Threads
Seat washer
Washer screw
Valve seat
Faucet body

Short Cut

If a new stem washer is not stopping the leak at the spout and you have determined the seat is bad, you might consider buying a new faucet. A bad seat means the faucet has gone through some rough times and might continue to give you problems.

Repairing a Stem Valve Packing Leak

Does the compression faucet leak from the handle when the handle is turned on? The culprit likely is the packing, whose job it is to keep water in the valve. Do the following:

1. Turn the shutoff valve to off. Open the faucet.
2. Loosen and remove the packing nut. (See step 3 from the previous procedure if the packing nut is covered by the handle.)
3. Take the parts to a plumbing supply store for new packing materials.
4. Reinstall them in the proper order.

Pro's Tip

If they are not there already, consider installing shutoff valves for every faucet and toilet in your home. Shutoff valves allow you to keep water on elsewhere in your home when you are working on only one fixture (see "Replacing Shutoff Valves").

Repairing a Ball Faucet

A ball faucet, shown in Figure 5.7, can leak in any of three places depending on its defect: If the leak is from the spout, the culprit is probably one of the inlet seals or springs; if the leak is at the handle, the problem is likely a loose adjusting ring on the cap or a worn cam seal; and if the leak is below the spout, one of the O-rings is bad or the ball itself is.

With your repair kit and other tools handy, follow these steps:

1. Turn off the shutoff valve to the faucet. Close and cover the drain.

> **tip**
> Your faucet might have a repair kit. Look for it in a home improvement store by the faucet manufacturer's name and model name. If there is such a repair kit for your model, buy it; it has the proper parts and often a hex wrench or other tool to help with disassembly and assembly. If no such repair kit exists, you need to take the worn parts from your current faucet to the hardware store and buy replacements.

FIGURE 5.7
A ball faucet relies on a ball that contains openings for water flow. Above it is a cam assembly and above that an adjusting ring.

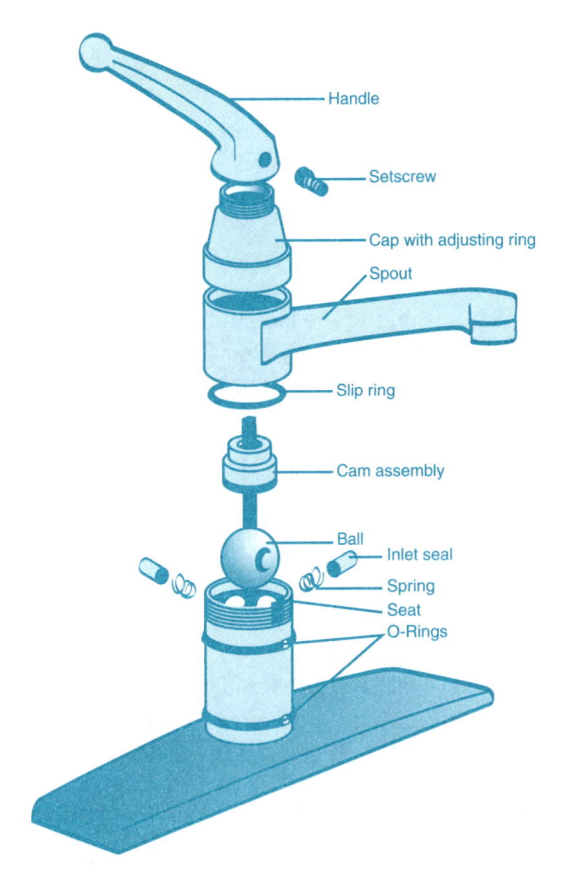

2. Use a hex wrench to loosen the setscrew on the underside of the handle. Pull the handle up and off.

3. If you suspect a loose adjusting ring, it is now exposed—it is the ring on top of the cap and has slots in it. Tighten it by rotating it clockwise using a flathead screwdriver in one of its slots or a special wrench that comes in the manufacturer's repair kit. Test to see if the leak has stopped. If it has not, turn off the shutoff valve again and drain the faucet.
4. Use taped pliers to unscrew the cap, exposing the cam and cam washer. Lift out this cam assembly, taking care to notice any projections on it that fit into slots in the faucet body. Those projections will have to go into those same slots when you reassemble the parts.
5. Lift out the ball. Now you will see the two inlet seals; they resemble dark washers. Remove them and the springs below using needle-nose pliers. Replace them with new springs and seals.
6. Below the portion of the sleeve holding the ball is a portion holding one or more O-rings. If they appear damaged, cut them away with a utility knife. Slide new ones into place; a little soapy water might make the installation easier.
7. Reassemble in the proper order.

Pro's Tip

When buying parts for faucets, try to buy the exact parts for that model and made by the faucet manufacturer. Sometimes these are the only parts that work. Substitute parts might work for a while but generally are not of so high quality.

Repairing a Single-Handle Cartridge Faucet

A cartridge faucet can leak from the spout or around the body. An expanded view of a cartridge faucet is shown in Figure 5.8. The repair work calls for taking apart the faucet in the proper order and examining the parts for wear. Even when parts do not appear worn, you might want to replace them when you have the faucet taken apart.

Follow these steps to repair the faucet:

1. Turn the shutoff valve off. Open the faucet to drain water; then close and cover the drain.
2. Pry off any trim cap to expose the handle screw below. Remove the handle screw. Lift up the handle and its handle body—this might take some tilting.
3. A retainer nut holds down the cartridge. Loosen and remove this nut, and then lift off the spout body.
4. Examine the O-rings around the faucet body, which is now exposed. Replace them if they appear worn. If the new O-rings are difficult to slide into place, lubricate them with soapy water. The new O-rings should fix any leak from around the spout body.

FIGURE 5.8

A cartridge faucet contains a cartridge with holes that move to allow for the flow of hot and cold water. Shop for the correct parts for your make and model.

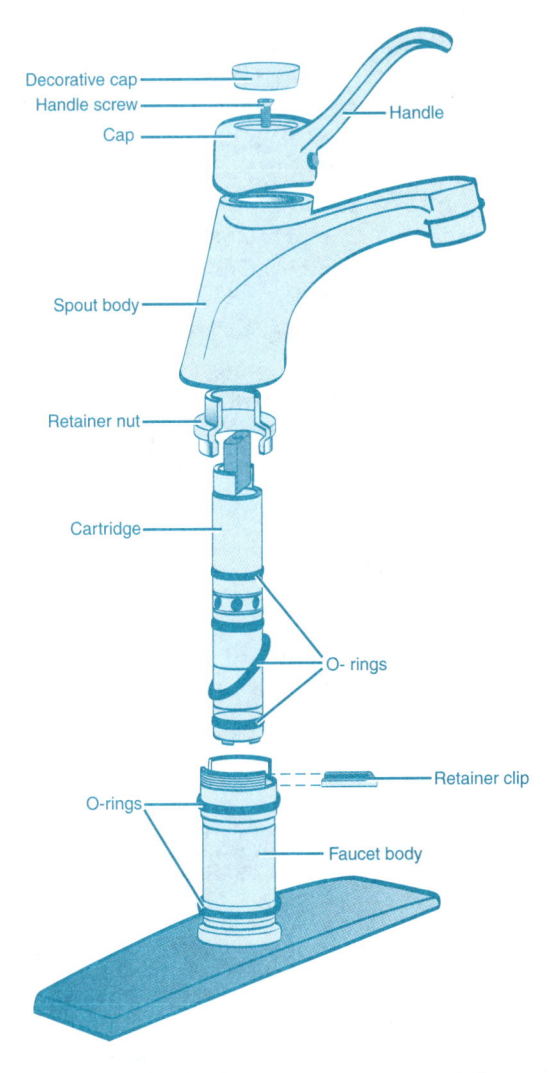

5. If the faucet body O-rings are in good shape, examine the cartridge. Take it out by using pliers or a screwdriver to pull back the retaining clip holding the cartridge in place. Then grip the top of the cartridge with pliers and pull straight up—this might require some strength. Note projections and slots; the cartridge or a replacement must go in the exact same way it came out.
6. If the O-rings around the cartridge look worn, replace them. If the cartridge itself appears worn, install an exact duplicate with its own new O-rings.
7. Reassemble the faucet in the reverse order. If, when you turn the water back on, the hot and cold are reversed, you have put the cartridge in reversed. Open the faucet again and turn the cartridge 180°.

CHAPTER 5   Plumbing   115

If you take a plumbing fixture apart to correct one fault but notice others—corrosion, stripped threads, deformed washers—correct them at the same time; they are likely to fail when you least want them to.

Repairing a Disk Faucet

A disk faucet is now common in bathrooms and rarely causes trouble (see Figure 5.9). In this type of faucet, a lower disk, usually fixed inside the faucet body, meets an upper disk mounted in a removable cartridge. Holes lined with seals align to let water flow. When trouble occurs, it is generally because of grit caught in the seals, worn seals, or a cracked cartridge.

FIGURE 5.9
Disk faucets have a top removable disk; the bottom one is stationary. Generally they require little maintenance.

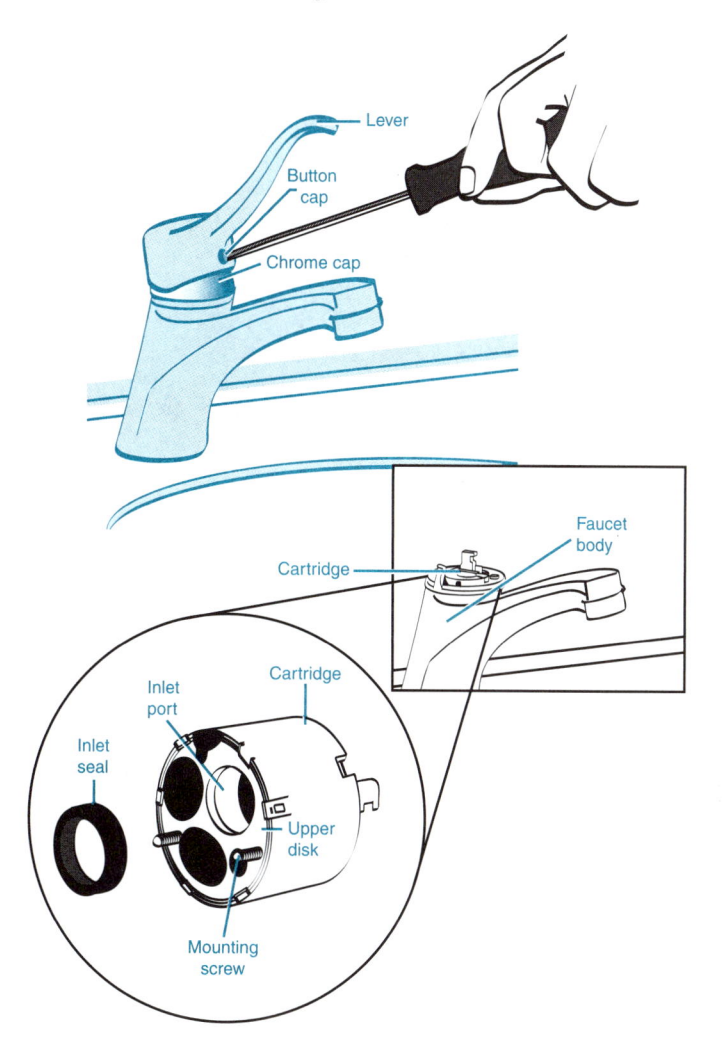

Disk faucet leaks might show up at the base, or even below the sink on the floor. Follow these steps to repair the leaks:

1. Turn off the shutoff valve. Lift the handle high to drain the faucet and expose the setscrew. Close and cover the drain.
2. Pry off any cap covering the setscrew. Loosen the setscrew and remove the handle.
3. There is a chrome cap below; pry it up or unscrew it. This pertains to newer models. Older models require that you remove the whole chrome body cover. You have to disconnect the pop-up stopper rod from below the sink (first mark the position of the thumbscrew on the clevis piece; refer to "Adjusting a Pop-Up Stopper") and unscrew two screws that project from beneath the sink up into the faucet body.
4. You should now be able to see what is often called the *cartridge* and which holds the upper disk. Loosen the two or three screws holding the cartridge down and lift it out, bringing with it the upper disk. Clean the ports and surfaces of grit or build-up on both the upper and lower disks. This might solve the problem.
5. If the rubber inlet seals appear worn, replace them; these are the sources of most leaks. If any portion of the disk mechanism appears worn or cracked, replace it.
6. Carefully align and replace the disk mechanism. Reassemble the faucet parts and test for leaks.

When repairing or installing faucets, remove any aerator, the mesh screen often screwed to the spout end that mixes air with the water flow, before you turn the water back on. You might have dislodged mineral build-up or grit in the pipes or faucet. This debris can get caught in the aerator and block the flow of water from the faucet when the water is turned back on. After you have reopened the water shutoff valve and checked connections for leaks, turn on both the hot and cold water forcefully for a few seconds to wash out any loose grit. Finally, turn off the water and reinstall the aerator. (Refer to "Cleaning a Faucet or Spray Hose Nozzle Aerator" for more on this process.)

Replacing a Faucet

Sometimes a faucet becomes so worn that it requires continual maintenance, is corroded, or simply shows too much age. When that's the case, you might want to replace the entire faucet.

If you have back trouble, it's probably best to avoid this job; you have to work on your back in an awkward space, and if the faucet is for a vanity's sink, you'll need to contort your body to replace the faucet. If you have any hesitation about this task, call in a professional plumber.

caution If you decide to replace an old faucet, wear eye protection while performing the job. You will be looking upward at threaded connections and could dislodge grit that will fall in your face.

Things You'll Need

- ❏ Eye protection
- ❏ Tape measure
- ❏ Vinegar, single-edged razor blade, and rags
- ❏ Pliers
- ❏ Adjustable wrench
- ❏ Basin wrench
- ❏ Screwdrivers
- ❏ Pipe joint compound or pipe-thread tape
- ❏ Plumber's putty

To replace a faucet, follow these steps:

1. Turn the shutoff valves beneath the sink to off. Turn on the faucet to let the residual water run out.
2. Loosen the setscrew holding the pop-up stopper to the clevis and pull the pop-up stopper lift rod up and out of the faucet (refer to "Adjusting a Pop-Up Stopper").
3. Use a basin wrench to loosen the coupling nuts holding the supply tubes to the underside of the faucet. Let the nuts slide down the supply tubes. Loosen the lock nuts holding the faucet in place. If the lock nuts are plastic, you might be able to loosen them by hand. If not, use the basin wrench. Lift the old faucet out of the sink.
4. Measure the distance between holes in the sink. Buy a new faucet that is going to fit these holes.
5. Clean mineral and soap deposits away from the faucet area.
   To clean soap and mineral deposits from the sink body, use a half-and-half combination of white vinegar and warm water. Carefully scrape with a single-edge razor blade. Dry the area.
6. If the new faucet has a gasket along the bottom surface, set it into place as is. If it does not, first prepare some plumber's putty. Do this by taking a wad of plumber's putty in your hands and rolling it into a string about 1/4" wide. Stick it along the underside perimeter of the faucet body. Repeat until the whole perimeter is laced with a thickness of plumber's putty. Set the faucet into place.
7. Follow the manufacturer's instructions for installation. They will call for threading the lock nuts onto either the mounting bolts or the inlet shanks. Gently tighten the nuts by hand or with a basin wrench. Before you make final tightening, stand in front of the sink and make sure the faucet is centered left to right and front to back; the holes in the sink are often large enough to allow for considerable movement.
8. Connect the supply tubes to the new faucet (see Figure 5.10).

FIGURE 5.10
Faucets require two fittings below the sink, for cold and hot water, and sometimes a pop-up stopper connection.

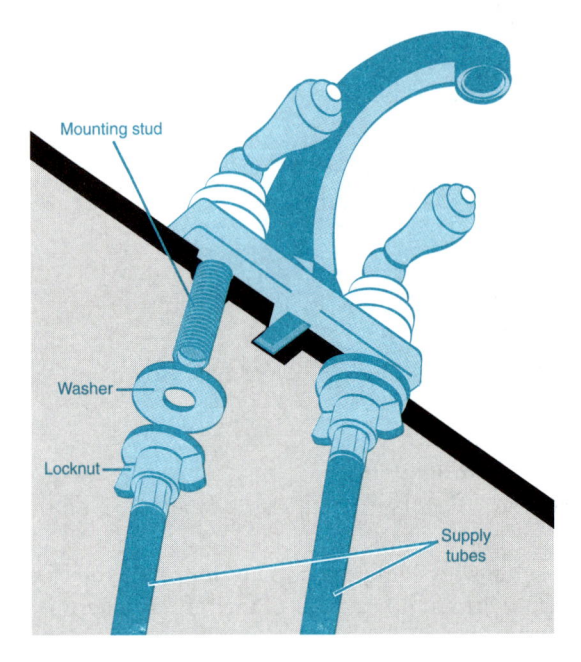

9. Use a putty knife or plastic knife to carefully scrape plumber's putty excess from around the faucet.
10. If the faucet has an aerator, remove it. Grit might have gotten into the pipes and you won't want it stuck on the aerator screen.
11. Connect the pop-up stopper lift rod to the clevis below the sink.
12. Turn on the shutoff valves and check for leaks. Run hot and cold water. Turn off the faucet and replace the aerator if you took one off.

Replacing Supply Tubes

When you peer up under the sink with the idea of replacing the faucet, you might decide you also want to replace the supply tubes leading to it. These can look corroded on the outside after long years of use and, although they might be serving their purpose well enough, new ones will look better.

These days there are four general types of supply tubing: woven stainless steel, woven vinyl, corrugated chrome-plated copper, and plain copper. The first three are the easiest for amateurs to work with. (Polybutylene supply tubes are sold in some places and are easy to work with but are not approved by plumbing codes in all localities; check before using this type.) Each type costs only a few dollars; some come in a kit of two; and replacement of a pair takes only about 30 minutes.

To replace the supply tubes, you need to use a basin wrench to loosen the coupling nut that connects the existing tube to the faucet, as shown in Figure 5.11.

CHAPTER 5 **Plumbing** 119

FIGURE 5.11
Cock the jaws of a basin wrench so that it can turn a supply tube coupling nut counterclockwise (as you look up at it). At the other end of the basin wrench, position the handle accordingly.

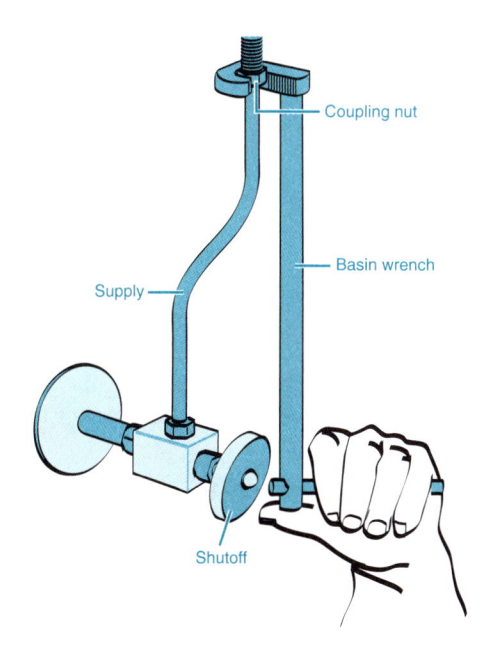

Things You'll Need

- ☐ Pliers
- ☐ Adjustable wrench
- ☐ Basin wrench
- ☐ Measuring tape
- ☐ Pipe joint compound or pipe-thread tape
- ☐ New supply tubes

Follow these steps to replace the water supply tubes:
1. Turn off the shutoff valve.
2. Unscrew the nut holding the old supply tube to the shutoff valve. Unscrew the coupling nut at the faucet inlet shank.
3. Take the old supply tube to a plumber's supply store or home improvement store for a replacement. Make sure that each end is going to be compatible with the shutoff valve and the faucet inlet shank (at the shutoff valve, the connection might not be threaded but rather something called a *compression fitting*, but these are no harder to deal with and still require a nut that is tightened by hand and wrench).
4. Bend a new supply tube in two gentle curves to run from the shutoff valve to the faucet inlet shank. You make the bends by hand.
5. Screw the fitting to the shutoff valve and to the faucet inlet shank. Turn on the shutoff valve and check for leaks.

Short Cut: Supply tubes come in varying lengths. If yours is too long, you don't have to cut it; just make more dramatic bends. Plumbers have even looped some entirely.

Replacing Shutoff Valves

If the supply tubes on your sink have become corroded and need to be replaced, chances are you might also want to replace the shutoff valves. These, too, can corrode and look bad, begin to drip over time, or become hard to turn. Replacing one is not particularly difficult, and a new one costs only about $4. Be sure to replace defective shutoff valves with ones that fit the *stub-out* (the pipe that protrudes from the wall or up from the floor) and the lower end of the supply tube running up to the faucet, as shown in Figure 5.12.

Call the Pro: Shutoff valves are usually screwed onto the stub-out. If it is soldered on, continue to live with it or call a professional. Otherwise, you will need copper soldering skills.

Things You'll Need

- [ ] Pliers
- [ ] Bucket and rags
- [ ] Basin wrench
- [ ] Pipe joint compound or pipe-thread tape
- [ ] Replacement shutoff valves

FIGURE 5.12
Shutoff valves are sometimes plainly visible in a bathroom. When they begin to drip or become unsightly, you can replace them.

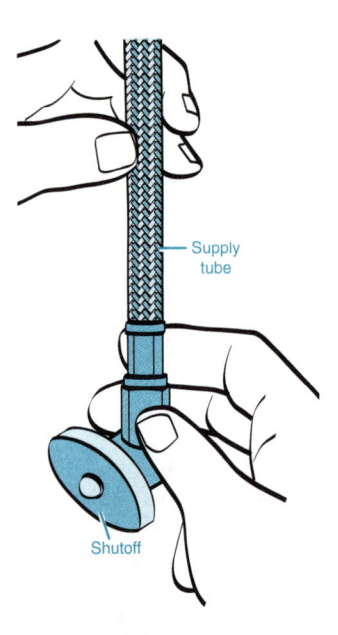

— Supply tube

Shutoff

To replace a shutoff valve, follow these steps:

1. Turn off the main shutoff valve to water for the whole house. Turn on the faucet above the shutoff valve to relieve pressure and then turn the faucet all the way off.
2. Unscrew the supply tube. Some water will come out. Wipe it up.
3. Unscrew the shutoff valve from the stub-out.
4. Take the old valve to the plumbing supply store and ask for the store's selection of replacements.
5. Clean the threads of the stub-out. Apply pipe compound or tape to the threads.
6. Start the replacement shutoff valve straight onto the stub-out threads and tighten it with an adjustable wrench.
7. Attach the supply tube.
8. Turn off the valve. Make sure the supply tube is well connected. Turn on water to the home, and then turn on the new shutoff valve. Check for leaks.

To do list

- ☐ Change a toilet tank flapper to stop a running toilet.
- ☐ Install a new toilet inlet valve.

Solving Toilet Tank Problems

When a toilet flushes, a flapper rises in the tank to let the water from the tank rush into the bowl. At the same time, a valve opens to let fresh water into the tank from the supply tube beneath the tank. In a few seconds, the flapper descends to seal the opening leading from the tank to the bowl and the valve continues to let fresh water into the tank.

Two things generally go wrong in tanks: The flapper distorts and no longer provides a good seal, or the valve gets old with age and does not function properly. A flapper can be replaced with little trouble, whereas a valve requires a half hour with tools. You'll be relieved to know that the water in a toilet tank is sanitary.

Changing a Toilet Tank Flapper

The toilet tank *flapper* is a piece of flexible rubber that normally seals water above an opening to the toilet bowl. It rises when the flush lever is raised, pauses as the water rushes out, and then lowers to seal off the water again (see Figure 5.13). If the toilet runs—that is, leaks water from the tank into the bowl—it's generally because of water leaking beneath the flapper at the bottom of the tank. Sometimes you can see water sliding down the bowl sides or, from time to time, you might hear the toilet tank valve open for a couple of seconds to allow in water to replace the amount that has leaked down into the bowl.

FIGURE 5.13
If the toilet runs, it's generally because of water leaking beneath the flapper.

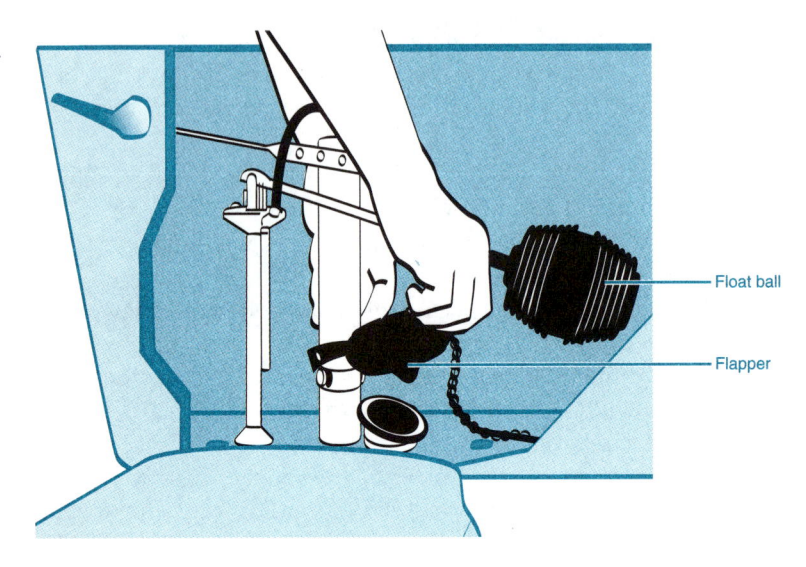

— Float ball

— Flapper

To remedy this problem, clean mineral build-up from the *seat*, which is the circular rim below the flapper, or replace the flapper with a new one.

Things You'll Need

- ❑ Utility knife
- ❑ Rag
- ❑ Replacement flapper

Follow these steps to change the flapper:

1. Turn off the shutoff valve beneath the toilet tank.
2. Flush the toilet to drain the tank. Raise the flapper and look at the seat against which the flapper rests. If you see mineral deposits or grit around the seat circumference, wipe them away with your finger or a rag. Wipe the underside of the flapper where it is meant to seal against the seat.
3. If this does not solve the problem, remove the old flapper, which is easily done by unhooking it from the chain that descends from the trip lever and from pegs on either side of the overflow tube. Look at the flapper edge-on. Over time the rims can become *scalloped*, meaning not perfectly flat, and it is under the raised scalloped portions that water is seeping. Throw such a flapper away and replace it with a new one.

   tip Replacement flappers often require trimming with scissors or a utility knife to fit a particular toilet tank model; instructions on the package show you where to do this.

4. Hook the chain to the new flapper, leaving no more than 1/2" of slack.

5. With the new flapper in place, turn the shutoff valve back on. Water should no longer be able to seep beneath the rim of the new flapper. With the lid off the toilet tank, flush the toilet a couple of times and watch how the flapper works. If it does not rise high enough to allow enough water to flow into the bowl, remove some slack from the trip level chain.

Installing a Toilet Inlet Valve

Toilet tanks have used a variety of inlet valves for refilling after a flush. Standard through most of the last century was a *ballcock valve*. This uses a float ball that rises with the rising level of water in the tank. When the float ball is high enough, the arm that connects it to the ballcock shuts off the valve. Today, most toilets use a *float cup valve*, which has a float cup attached to the valve itself (see Figure 5.14). As water fills the tank, the float cup rises and, when it rises high enough, turns off the valve.

FIGURE 5.14
Newer toilet inlet valves, called float cup valves, are not like old ballcock mechanisms that use float balls at the ends of steel rods.

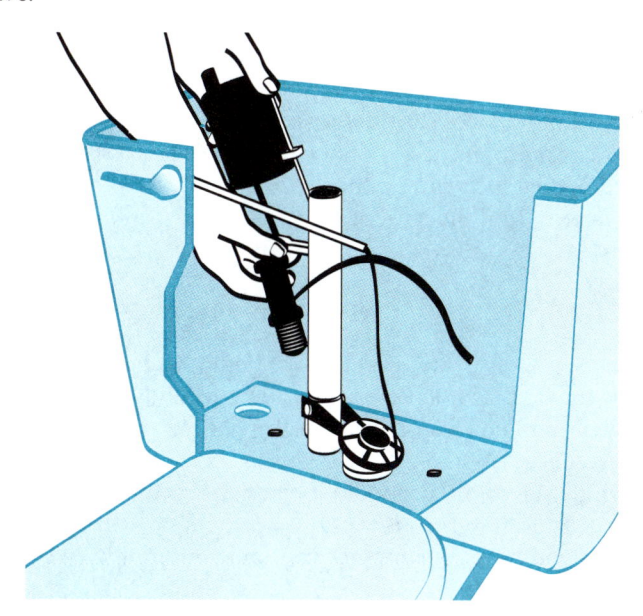

Things You'll Need

- Utility knife
- Channel-lock pliers
- Locking pliers
- Bucket and rags

If you have repeated difficulties with a ballcock valve, replace it with a float cup type, using these steps:

1. Turn off the shutoff valve beneath the toilet.
2. Flush the toilet to get most of the water out of the tank. Use a rag or old sponge to remove the remainder of the water from the tank.
3. Beneath the tank, loosen the nut that holds the supply tube to the inlet shank of the tank valve. Let this nut slip down the supply tube.
4. Still beneath the tank, loosen the lock nut holding the old valve mechanism in place. If the nut above it inside the tank turns as the outside one does, hold the inside one immobile with locking pliers.
5. Disconnect the old valve mechanism from the overflow pipe by pulling away the flexible tube. Lift out the old valve mechanism. Water remaining in the tank is likely to flow out of the hole to the floor below.
6. Manufacturers will have instructions for installing their valve mechanisms. Join threaded parts straight and avoid overtightening.
7. When the new valve is in, turn on the shutoff valve slowly. Look and feel for leaks. Connect the new mechanism to the overflow tube. A new flexible tube is typically supplied. Flush the toilet to test the new valve's operation.
8. If the new mechanism is a float cup type, adjust the level of the cup by pinching the pinch clip on the vertical rod. Lowering the cup turns the valve off sooner so that the level of the water in the tank is lower.

Summary

The plumbing system is a vital part of your home, and you should understand the basics of how it works. In addition, every home will have plumbing problems sometimes, if only a clog in a sink or toilet. In this chapter, you learned some remedies for these annoyances. You might also want to occasionally replace some plumbing parts; these might be small, out-of-sight components that cause leaks or such visible ones as faucets and showerheads that are worn out or look shabby. The more plumbing skills you have, the happier you and your family will be when those common problems arise.

Much the same can be said of the subject coming next: electricity. The principles of electrical wiring and connections are fairly simple; when small things go wrong, you'll be happy you have the skills to fix them.

6

Simple Electrical Repairs

For most people, the main problem with the electrical system in their home is that it sometimes stops working in a thunderstorm. There is nothing they can do about this, of course; the electric utility company has to remove tree branches that have fallen on power lines or repair a local transformer. But other minor ailments crop up from time to time that a homeowner can repair with relative ease. You might, for example, need to rewire a lamp because its cord has become frayed or the socket holding the light bulb has gone bad. Or the you might grow to dislike a chandelier or wall sconce inherited from the previous owner and decide to replace it with one of your own. Other upgrades homeowners frequently tackle include installing a dimmer switch, upgrading a bathroom fan, and installing a ground fault circuit interrupter (GFCI) receptacle. In this chapter, you learn how to do a number of minor electrical repairs, along with some sound tips for working safely with electricity. We begin, however, with a look at the tools you'll use to perform electrical repairs around your home.

In this chapter:

* Learn how to work with electricity safely.
* Rewire a lamp.
* Install a new light fixture.
* Install a dimmer switch.
* Install a GFCI receptacle.
* Extend a circuit to new places.

Putting Together Your Toolkit

Electrical work has the twin virtues of being simpler than other kinds of home repairs (for example, replacing a toilet tank valve or a floorboard) and being cleaner.

Electrical work also is entirely safe so long as you understand a few principles about electricity and follow some simple cautions. In addition, all electrical work that you do you can test with simple testing devices to ensure you have made the proper connections.

Before you begin your electrical repairs, however, you need to be sure you have a few simple tools, both for performing and testing your repairs. Here are my recommendations, all shown in Figure 6.1:

- **Voltage tester**—This simple and inexpensive device lights when its probes touch two parts of a live circuit. Buy one rated for 90–500 volts. Do not confuse it with one for checking low-voltage wiring.
- **Continuity tester**—Also simple and inexpensive, a continuity tester uses a battery and tests whether a continuous path for electricity exists between one of its probes (often an alligator clip) and the other (a thick blunt needle). A $15 volt-ohm meter combines the tasks of a voltage tester and continuity tester, plus other tasks as well, and can be purchased instead.
- **Multipurpose tool**—Vaguely resembling a pair of pliers, a multipurpose tool cuts wire, strips wire insulation, crimps various wire connectors, and cuts small bolts.
- **Cable ripper**—This is an inexpensive metal tool with a dulled tooth that slips over the end of nonmetallic (NM) electrical cable; when pulled, it cuts through the outer sheathing. A utility knife can do the same job but not as quickly and with more hazard of cutting into wires inside the cable.
- **Wire nuts**—These are plastic shells with copper lining that, when twisted over bared wires, hold them together and make electrical continuity between them. They are rated and colored for the size and numbers of wires to be gripped.

FIGURE 6.1
Here are some basic tools and supplies for electrical work, including a voltage tester, continuity tester, multipurpose tool, cable ripper, and wire nuts.

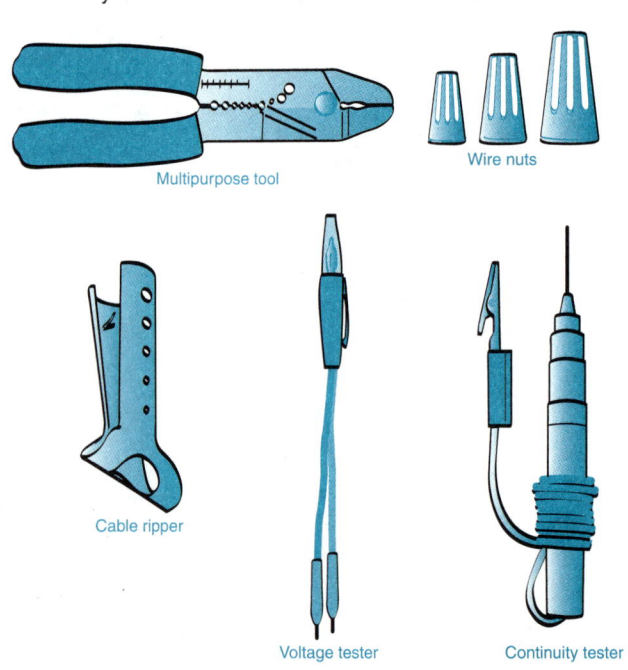

Multipurpose tool

Wire nuts

Cable ripper

Voltage tester

Continuity tester

CHAPTER 6   Simple Electrical Repairs   **127**

To do list

- ❑ Learn electricity principles.
- ❑ Understand safety precautions for working with electrical circuits.
- ❑ Learn how to test electrical circuits to determine whether voltage is flowing through them.

Pro's Tip

Most of the electrical supplies and tools discussed in this chapter are available in home improvement stores. But you might do well to go to the electrical supply store in your area where contractors buy their supplies and equipment. The salespeople are more knowledgeable there and, if you show them a part you need replaced or ask them an electrical question, they are more likely to have the right part and the correct answer.

Working Safely with Electricity

Working on your electrical system is generally safe and simple because you work on portions to which the power has been turned off, and you check your work with testers to ensure you have done the work correctly. For some work, however, you need momentarily to restore the power to the section you are working on to do the work properly. In this section, you learn basic principles, terms, and safety precautions for working with electricity. You also learn now to test circuits to be sure they're wired correctly.

Understanding Basic Principles of Electrical Wiring

To do electrical work, you need to understand a few electricity principles. Electricity needs to run in a loop. This is as true of the power grid in your neighborhood as it is the circuits of your home. The utility company power comes to your home in three intertwining cables. Two carry voltage of 120 volts each; the third is a neutral wire and has no voltage. In a standard 120-volt home circuit, power flows through a 120-volt live or *hot* wire (usually colored black or red) through a device (toaster, lamp, computer, and so on) in your home and out again through the neutral wire (usually colored white or gray). Some circuits, such as those used for an electric stove or water heater, require 240 volts. These have heavier duty cables and tap both 120-volt wires entering your home.

The utility power cables come to the outside of your house and first connect to an electric meter, which measures and records the amount of power that circuits inside are using. From the electric meter, the cables move inside the home to the service *entrance panel*, another name for the main circuit breaker panel or fuse box.

In the service entrance panel (for our purposes here we'll shorten this to *service panel*), the power is distributed among several circuits for your home. These can be few or many depending on the size of your home and the number of electrical appliances. If your home has an electric stove and water heater, they will have their own 240-volt circuits. Lights and receptacles to various parts of the house have lighter-duty circuits, some traveling to more than one room, or even more than one floor. But for all, the power flows into the circuits, through the water heater, light fixture, or other device that does the work (such as turning a motor, producing light, and so forth), back to the panel, into the power company neutral wire, and back to the power company.

It might do well here to review some basic terms. *Voltage* is a measure of electrical difference between one point and another. The wires leading from the service panel to devices on a regular home circuit are charged with 120 volts. *Ampere* (also called *amp*) is a measure of electrical flow, or current. *Watt* is a measure of work and is equal to voltage multiplied by amperes. When 120-volt electricity flows through a 60-watt light bulb it flows at a rate of 1/2 amp. Regular home circuits are designed to handle 15 amps at a time. Some are designed for 20 amps and some, as for an electric stove or clothes dryer, even higher. Any device you place on a circuit should be stamped to show that it meets the requirements of that circuit. For example, do not install a 15-amp-rated switch on a 20-amp circuit.

Working Safely with Electrical Circuits

All circuits have safety measures. Each is protected at the service panel by circuit breakers or fuses. If electrical current on a circuit rises to a level higher than it is designed for, say 20 amps on a 15-amp circuit, wires and elements on the circuit overheat, creating a fire hazard. But instead, the circuit breaker *trips*—that is, senses the surge in flow and flips itself off. If the service panel uses fuses rather than circuit breakers, the fuse *blows*—that is, interrupts electrical flow because a heat-sensitive strip inside melts apart—when the circuit overheats. Current could rise on a circuit if too many appliances on it were turned on simultaneously or if a wire in the circuit came loose and touched something that was grounded, producing a *short circuit*. In the latter case, current would rise very high very quickly, tripping the breaker or blowing the fuse.

In addition, each metal device and metal outlet box on the circuit is *grounded*, meaning it is connected all the way back to the service panel with a ground wire that attaches to a metal bar in the service panel called the ground/neutral bar, which is itself connected by a heavy wire to a cold water pipe (which connects ultimately to the main water supply pipe coming to the home from underground) or a metal stake outside the house hammered into the ground. If a *live wire*—these are normally insulated in black—loosens and touches something metal (the inside of a metal outlet box, for example), the danger is that someone would touch the metal cover plate of the box and conduct electricity through his body to the ground. With proper grounding, this does not happen because, when a short circuit occurs, electricity flows immediately through the ground wire to the ground. This flow, being greater than the circuit is designed for, also trips the breaker or blows the fuse, alerting the homeowner that there is a fault in the circuit that must be corrected.

The circuit breakers and fuses serve another purpose as well. They allow you to turn them off (or for a fuse, unscrew them) so that power cannot flow to a circuit you want to work on. You can perform your repair, check that it is done properly, and then turn the power back on again.

Follow these precautions when working with electrical circuits:

- **Never work on a live circuit, fixture, or appliance**—Turn off the circuit breaker, unscrew the fuse, or unplug the appliance. Touch parts of a live circuit, appliance, or fixture only with testing tools to check your work for safe wiring.
- **Before working on parts of a circuit, make sure it is really off**—Do this by testing it with a voltage tester (see the next section, "Checking Circuits with a Voltage Tester".
- **When working on circuits, do not touch metal plumbing or natural gas pipes, or work on damp or wet surfaces.**

Checking Circuits with a Voltage Tester

A voltage tester has no power of its own and lights only when its two probes touch a charged circuit, thus showing the presence of voltage. You use the voltage tester to ensure that no electrical current is flowing into a circuit, so you can safely work on outlets, fixtures, switches, and wiring connected to that circuit.

When you turn off a circuit breaker or remove a fuse, the circuit it serves should have no charge. To test the circuit, insert one probe deep into one slot of a receptacle on the circuit and the other into the other slot; the tester's light should not light (see Figure 6.2). Place one probe in one slot and the other in the rounded ground slot (if there is one); the tester should not light. Repeat with the other slot and ground slot; the tester should not light. Repeat for all the slots projecting through the cover plate (some dual receptacles gain power from more than one circuit).

Things You'll Need

- ☐ Screwdrivers
- ☐ Voltage tester

Before you make a test of a circuit you believe you have turned off, you should test the voltage tester on a circuit you know is live. It should light. Then if the tester does not light on the circuit you believe you have turned off, you know you have turned it off properly.

Now you can remove the cover plate. Test the receptacles again by touching the probes to opposite screws on the receptacle and by touching single screws and either the metal of the box (which should be connected to ground wires coming into the box) or, if the box is made of plastic, the ground slot.

FIGURE 6.2

Press one probe of the voltage tester into one slot and the other into the other slot or ground slot. Rub them up and down a bit to make sure you have a good connection. If the power is off, the tester should not light. If the tester lights, you need to go back to the service panel and turn off another circuit breaker or remove another fuse; penciled labels of circuits in a service panel are notorious for being incorrectly marked.

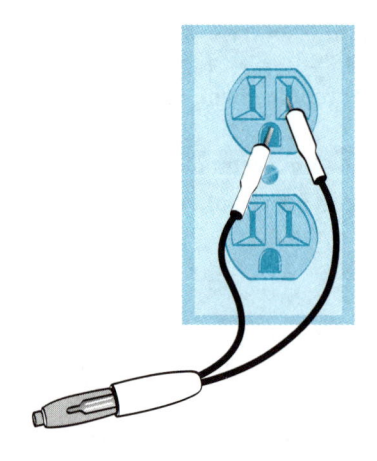

To test circuit power to a light fixture, first try to turn it on and off with its switch. If the light fails to come on, have a helper unfasten the fixture and hold it while you expose the insides of the outlet box. Untwist the wire nut that binds the black wires. Place one probe on the bare ends of the black wire coming from the cable entering the box and the other on the metal of the box or a bare ground wire (see Figure 6.3). If the tester does not light, remove the wire nut binding the white wires. Place one probe on the black wires and one on the white; the tester should not light. Check for power between the white wire and the ground wire. The tester should not light for any of these tests. In some instances, wires from another circuit might make connections in the box. If such wires are present, carefully remove their wire nuts and test them for voltage. If there is any, you need to turn off the circuit to these wires, too.

To check to see if power is going to a switch, remove the cover plate. Place one probe on the metal box or bare ground wire and the other on the screws (there might be more than two) of the switch (see Figure 6.4). If the switch has slots rather than screws, press the probe into each of the slots in turn. The tester should not light for any of these tests.

CHAPTER 6   Simple Electrical Repairs

FIGURE 6.3
Touch one probe of the voltage tester to the metal box and the other to the bare black wire coming from the cable that enters the box. If the power is off, the tester will not light.

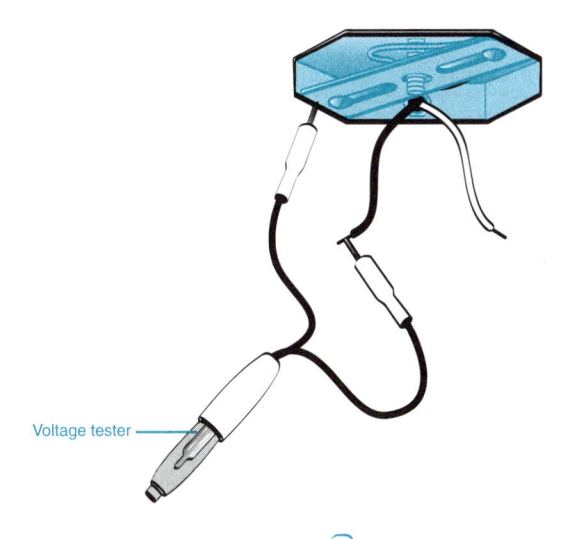

Voltage tester

FIGURE 6.4
Touch one probe of the tester to the metal box or ground wire and the other end to the terminals of the switch in turn. If the power is off, the tester should not light for any combination.

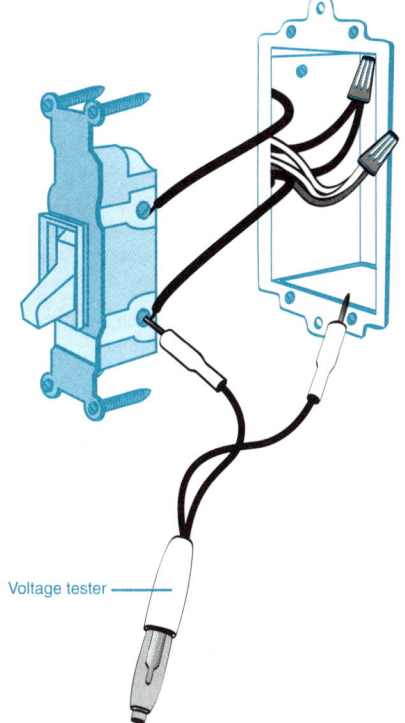

Voltage tester

Repair Your Home In No Time

To do list

- Rewire a lamp.
- Fix cords and plugs.
- Add a dimmer switch.
- Hang a new light fixture.
- Add a GFCI receptacle.

Minor Repairs and Improvements

You can perform many minor electrical repairs and improvements around the home without the need for an electrical permit or inspection by an electrical inspector. These include rewiring a lamp, replacing a light fixture, hanging a chandelier, replacing a light switch with a dimmer switch, and the like.

These kinds of tasks require disciplined sequential testing, proper wire connection techniques, and observation of safety principles. These repairs and improvements can make your home safer and more enjoyable, and the tasks themselves are clean and simple.

Things You'll Need

- Wire nut
- Electrical cable
- Utility knife or cable ripper
- Multipurpose tool
- Practice device, such as an old receptacle with screw connection and slot connection

Making Simple Wiring Connections

Wiring often begins with plastic-sheathed NM (nonmetallic) cable containing three or four wires, one being a noninsulated ground wire. A cable with two current carrying wires and a ground wire is called a *two-conductor cable*. To make connections, the outer insulation has to be stripped away and then the ends of the wires inside stripped an appropriate length for attaching to terminals.

DO YOU NEED A PERMIT?

You do not have to have a permit to perform many electrical replacements and repairs in your home. If you plan to extend or add a circuit, however, you should get a permit, and you need to call your local building department to learn the steps you need to follow. If building department officials are satisfied the extension of the circuit will be sound, they will issue the permit, but they will also require that they inspect the finished wiring. If you choose to do the work, they might require that you take a short written test on electricity principles before allowing you to proceed.

Many homes built before the mid-1950s were built with armored cable, sometimes also called *BX*. The conducting wires inside are insulated black and white just as with plastic-sheathed NM cable. Sometimes there is a bare ground wire, and sometimes not. When there is not, the metal sheathing of the cable itself serves as a grounding path for any short circuit. Accordingly, the sheathing has to be firmly clamped to metal boxes that hold the wire connections.

If you find wiring that is NM cable but without a ground wire or individual wires with no cables, you have especially old wiring and you should consider having the whole house rewired to modern standards.

To wire devices safely, the connections need to be done correctly. Sloppy connections can lead to short circuits. Most wire connections are made to a screw, into a slot, or with a wire nut.

Follow these steps to strip cables and wires in preparation for making a connection (you can practice these steps using a short section of scrap electrical cable):

1. To strip cable to be used in household circuits, insert about 8" through the end of a cable ripper, press down on the opposite sides of the cable ripper so that its tooth penetrates the outer sheathing, and pull the cable ripper down to the cable end to cut through the outer sheathing.
2. Alternatively, you can lay the cable end down on a flat surface and cut it with a utility knife. Penetrate the cable only as far as the thickness of the outer insulation.
3. After the outer sheathing has been cut, peel it down, along with paper insulation inside. Cut these away with the cutting surface of the multipurpose tool.
4. The ground wire is normally bare. To prepare the other wires for connections, open the handle of the multipurpose tool and place the wire end into the opening meant for that size of wire (the size is always written on the outer

sheathing of NM cable). Close the multipurpose tool around the wire, and then rotate the multipurpose tool several times to cut through the insulation, but without nicking the copper wire beneath.

5. Push away with the multipurpose tool to push off the cut insulation, revealing the copper wire below.

> **caution** Do not strip wire with a knife blade; it too often nicks the wire. Nicked wire can become overheated, creating a hazard. If you nick wire, cut it away and try again.

I recommend that you use a spare electrical device, such as a switch, to practice making these connections before you begin actual work on your home's wiring system. To make a connection with a screw terminal, follow these steps:

1. Strip 3/4" of insulation from a wire end.
2. With needle-nose pliers, shape the end into a *U*.
3. Slip this around the screw stem to make a clockwise loop. The end of the insulation should just touch the screw. The copper wire should extend almost all the way around the screw stem and end about at the end of the insulation.
4. When you tighten the screw, it tightens the copper wire around its stem. The final product should show insulation going up to the screw head and no or very little copper wire showing out from under the screw head.

Some switches and receptacles have push-in holes for making wire connections (if they have both slots and screws, either type of connection is all right). To make a push-in connection, follow these steps:

1. Hold the end of the wire to the strip gage on the back of the practice device to see how much insulation should be removed; then strip away this amount.
2. Insert the bare end of the wire into the push-in hole; a spring lock inside grips and holds the wire.
3. To remove a wire from a push-in hole, insert a small flat-head screwdriver into the slot near the wire. This releases the lock so you can pull the wire free.

To make a wire nut connection, follow these steps:

1. Strip about 3/4" of insulation from the two wires you'll be connecting.
2. Hold the stripped ends parallel and place the wire nut over them.
3. Twist the wire nut clockwise. This twists the wires around each other and up tightly against the copper inner shell of the wire nut. When you are done, no bare wire should be visible at the open end of the wire nut.

> **note** Use wire nuts that are the proper size for the wire you are using and the number of wires. The right size wire nut can accommodate up to four wires in a connection.

CHAPTER 6 Simple Electrical Repairs   135

ADDING A JUMPER WIRE

When wiring switches, receptacles, light fixtures, and the like that fit into outlet boxes, you are often called to connect the switch, receptacle, or fixture to ground wires in the box. To do so, you run a jumper wire from the device ground screw to the wire nut that has other ground wire ends in it. The jumper wire can be several inches long; it can be bare or have green insulation. Jumper wires are often cut from scrap pieces of wire, but they have to be the same gage as other wires in the circuit. Jumper wires ground the device by connecting it to other ground wires in cables coming into the box.

Things You'll Need

- ❏ Utility knife
- ❏ Multipurpose tool
- ❏ Needle-nose pliers
- ❏ Small flat-head screwdriver
- ❏ Replacement cord, plug, or both
- ❏ Continuity tester

Replacing Cords and Rewiring Plugs

Cords and plugs can go bad, often because users pull the plug from a receptacle by the cord rather than by the plug itself. The electrical connection in the plug becomes weakened or loose. If you see a plug with a bent prong or a damaged casing or faceplate, replace it. Cords that are frayed, brittle, or cracked also should be replaced.

Buy replacement cords and plugs that match the appliances and circuits they will be used on. Flat cords and small plastic plugs are for lamps and light appliances, whereas round cords and round plugs are for larger appliances that might be on larger ampere circuits. If the old plug had three prongs, buy a three-wire (the third being a ground wire) cord and plug. If the old plug was *polarized*, meaning it had one prong wider than the other, buy a polarized plug as a replacement.

To replace or rewire a plug, follow these steps:

1. If you are working with an appliance, unplug it. Cut away the old plug with the multipurpose tool.
2. If the cord is flat and has only two wires with no ground wire between them you can use what is called a *quick-connect* plug that does not require stripping the wires in the cord. There are different variations, but each has two metal prongs called *teeth*. Each tooth, when you press two parts of the plug

together or press a lever, penetrates one side of the cord to make contact with one of the wires. Then the job is done.

3. If the cord and new plug are round, remove the faceplate from the front of the plug (this might take prying with a screwdriver or removing screws). Push the end of the cable through the back of the plug until it penetrates about 5".
4. With a utility knife, carefully cut away 3" of outer cord insulation. Draw the wires inside apart. Use the correct hole of the multipurpose tool to strip off 3/4" of wire insulation from each wire.
5. If there is room, use the white and black wires to form an Underwriter's knot, as shown in Figure 6.5.
6. Curl the ends of the wires with the needle-nose pliers so that each makes a U. Pull the cord back until the stripped portion of the wires lie near the silver and copper screws of the plug.
7. Unscrew the brass and silver screws until they are raised higher than the wires are thick. Place the stripped portion of the white-insulated wire under the silver screw so that the open end of the U is on the right. Turn the screw down on the wire. Repeat this with the black-insulated wire and the brass screw. If there is a ground wire, screw it to the green screw.
8. Replace the faceplate. If there is a clamp at the base of the plug, use a screwdriver to clamp it down on the cord.

> **tip**
> If you are using flat cord, look for a white or gray stripe on one of the wires, ribbing, or a ridge that runs along one wire's length. This wire should be connected to the wide prong via the silver screw.

FIGURE 6.5
Some plugs have restraining clamps for securing cords. Where there is no clamp, tie an Underwriter's knot as shown and tug it back into the bottom of the plug.

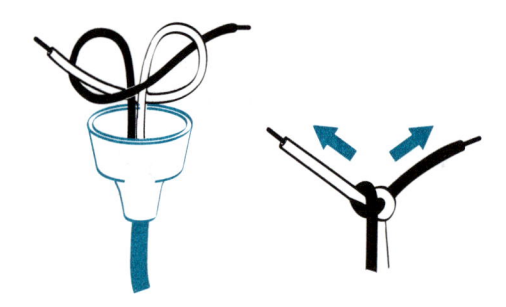

You can test your work with a continuity tester:

1. If you are working with an extension cord, bring the two ends of the cord close to one another, clamp the alligator clip to the wider of the plug prongs (for round cable), and press the probe into the wider slot of the plug at the other end. The tester should light. It should light for the narrow prong and the narrow slot and, if there is a ground prong, it should light for the ground prong and the ground slot.
2. If you are working with an appliance and have not opened the back to replace a cord, do not; merely plug the appliance in and see whether it works. But if the back is removed, test the new plug and cord with tests from

CHAPTER 6 Simple Electrical Repairs   137

the silver screw to the wide prong of the extension cord plug and the brass screw to the narrow prong. If there is a ground wire, test from the green ground screw to the rounded prong of the extension cord plug.

Things You'll Need

- ❑ Continuity tester
- ❑ Small flat-head screwdriver
- ❑ Multipurpose tool
- ❑ Replacement lamp cord

Repairing and Rewiring a Lamp

Normally, when a lamp fails, the problem is in the socket or the switch, which is often in the socket. The remedy is replacing the socket.

Follow these steps to determine whether the socket must be replaced:

1. Unplug the lamp and remove the light bulb.
2. Look for a place marked "press" on the socket shell, the name for the outer housing of the bulb's socket (see Figure 6.6). Press there and lift off the shell (you might have to twist it) and then the cardboard insulating sleeve underneath.
3. You can now test the socket with a continuity tester. Attach the clip end of the continuity tester to the metal screw shell and touch the probe to the silver screw. The continuity tester should light. If it does not, replace the socket.
4. Attach the clip to the brass screw and touch the probe to the rounded tab inside the bottom of the socket. If the tester does not light, turn the light switch knob (if there is one) and try again. If the tester still does not light, replace the socket.
5. If both tests show the socket is okay, the tab at the bottom of the socket might be too low for contact with the light bulb. Lift it slightly with a screwdriver end. Otherwise, the fault is with the plug or cord. Examine and replace them as necessary.

> **note** *Pro's Tip*
> If a lamp's cord becomes frayed or damaged, or if you simply don't like the cord's color, you can replace it using the steps listed in the preceding section for work on cords and plugs. If you replace the cord of a lamp (or the socket cap, the lowest part of the socket), however, be careful. When you remove the socket cap, the central shaft of the lamp might come loose. Make sure that the lamp is supported and will not roll. Take care to note where the cord has been knotted and knot the new cord in the same places.

FIGURE 6.6
The assembly of a socket goes as follows: socket cap, socket, insulating sleeve, and outer shell.

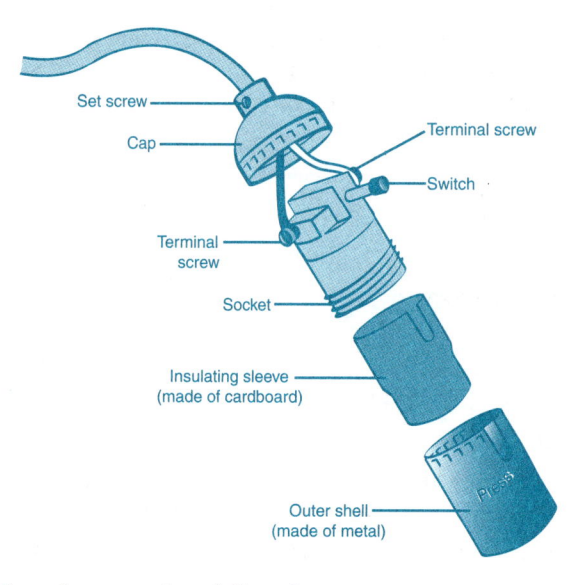

To replace a socket, follow these steps:

1. Unfasten the two wires attached to the socket and pull the socket away from the wires. You can reuse the existing socket cap if it is not damaged. If you want to replace it, unscrew the setscrew holding it to the lamp, untie the Underwriter's knot in it, and pull the cap away from the wires.
2. If you are replacing the socket cap, thread the wires up through the replacement and tighten the setscrew. Tie an Underwriter's knot with the wires.
3. Use a replacement socket marked with the same amp and volt rating as the old one. Connect the ridged or white-line wire to the silver screw of the socket and the smooth wire to the brass screw, as shown in Figure 6.6.
4. Slip the cardboard insulating sleeve over the socket and the outer shell over the cardboard. Press the whole assembly into the socket cap until it clicks into place.

Things You'll Need

- ❑ Screwdrivers
- ❑ New light fixture
- ❑ Wire nuts
- ❑ Ladder
- ❑ Voltage tester
- ❑ Helper, or heavy wire, to support fixture as you wire it

Installing a New Light Fixture

Installing a new light fixture is more a mechanical job than an electrical one. Fixtures have various kinds of mountings, but they come with black and white wires

CHAPTER 6 Simple Electrical Repairs   139

that are connected to the black and white wires in the junction box to which the fixture is attached.

When you're installing the new fixture, avoid letting the fixture hang by the wires alone; the connections might come apart, allowing the fixture to fall. Have a helper hold the fixture while you disconnect the wires or rig a temporary support with a bent coat hanger.

To install the fixture, follow these steps:

> **tip** Wear a tool belt for this job so you can reach the tools you need without descending from the ladder.

1. Turn off the circuit breaker or remove the fuse that controls the circuit the old light fixture is on.
2. Try to turn on the light fixture with its switch; it should not come on.
3. Remove the screws that attach the old fixture to the wall or ceiling. Lower the fixture into your hands. Have a helper hold the fixture while you work on the wires; if no helper is available, use a coat hanger or other heavy, bent wire to suspend the fixture below the junction box.
4. Disconnect the black wire connecting the old fixture. Generally this is a wire nut connection, but simple ceramic single-bulb fixtures of the type placed in garages and work rooms might have copper and silver screws rather than lead wires.
5. Test the black wire for power by touching it and the metal box or ground screw simultaneously with the two voltage tester probes. If there is no power, disconnect the white wire and, if there is one, the ground wire. If there are other wires in the box, remove the wire nuts and check the wires for voltage. If any are live, turn off the circuits to which they belong. Reattach the wire nuts of these wires.
6. Raise the new fixture close to the junction box. Connect the black lead wire of the new fixture to the old black wire protruding from the junction box and the white lead wire to the old white wire. Use the proper sized wire nut (see Figure 6.7). Check that the ground wire from the cable is connected to the box.
7. Attach the new fixture to the wall or ceiling with mounting bolts.

> **tip** A new fixture usually comes with directions on how the attachment is done. Some have holes that line up with holes in the junction box. Some require a *strap*, which is a piece of steel that mounts across the front of the junction box and has holes for the mounting screws.

Things You'll Need

- ❑ Screwdrivers
- ❑ New chandelier
- ❑ Volt tester
- ❑ Wire nuts
- ❑ Two ladders
- ❑ Helper

FIGURE 6.7
Connect the black cable wire to the black light fixture wire and the white cable wire to the white light fixture wire.

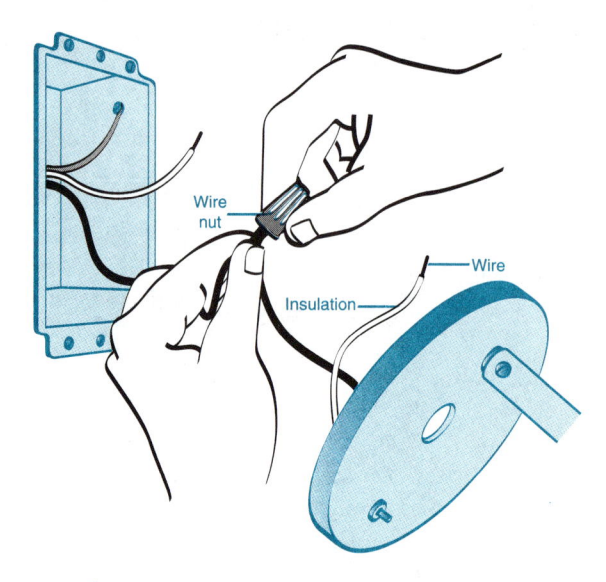

Installing a Chandelier

Installing a chandelier in the place of an old and smaller light fixture is a nice way to improve and brighten a room. Similar to installing a simple light fixture (refer to "Installing a New Light Fixture"), installing a chandelier is more a challenge mechanically than electrically. Fortunately, the procedure for hanging a new light fixture works for a chandelier weighing up to 10 lbs. Heavier chandeliers require a slightly different mechanical connection to the junction box as described here.

Follow the manufacturer's installation instructions for the chandelier, but they normally follow these steps:

1. Turn off the circuit breaker or remove the fuse that controls the circuit the old light fixture is on.
2. Try to turn on the light fixture with its switch; it should not come on.
3. Remove the screws that attach the old fixture to the ceiling. Lower the fixture into your hands and then look into the junction box. If the junction box has a bolt (called a *stud*) protruding from the middle, you can hang a chandelier of more than 10 lbs. Figure 6.8 illustrates the stud, along with the other chandelier assembly parts you'll use in installing a typical chandelier.

   If the junction box does not have a stud, you have to install a new junction box with a stud if you still want to hang the chandelier, and this is a job for a professional.
4. Have a helper (standing on a separate ladder) hold the fixture while you disconnect the wires, or rig a temporary support with a bent coat hanger.

> **caution** When you're installing a chandelier, you really need the assistance of a helper (with a second ladder) to hold the chandelier in place as you finish the wiring. Don't try to do this job on your own.

CHAPTER 6 Simple Electrical Repairs   141

5. Disconnect the wires connecting the old fixture and set it aside. Test all the wires in the junction box for voltage; if you find any that are live, turn off the circuit breakers or fuses to them.
6. Screw a piece of hardware called a *hickey* to the stud in the junction box.
7. Thread the chandelier wires through the fixture cover and then through a long hollow bolt called a *nipple*.
8. Have a helper hold the chandelier up while you thread the nipple into the hickey and secure it with a lock nut.
9. Use wire nuts to connect the black wire from the junction box to the chandelier black wire and the white wire from the junction box to the chandelier white wire, as shown in Figure 6.8. Make certain that the ceiling box ground wire is still attached to the screw attached to the box. Fold the wires gently into the box so the wire nuts are top up.
10. Raise the fixture cover of the chandelier to its position covering the ceiling box. The end of the nipple will come through the fixture cover's central hole.
11. Have the helper raise the chandelier. Screw the upper part of the chandelier chain, called the *collar*, to the end of the nipple. If the nipple projects too far through the fixture cover or too little, lower (or have the helper lower) the chandelier; then make adjustments to the height of the nipple by loosening its lock nut in the hickey and raising or lowering the nipple.

FIGURE 6.8
A typical chandelier assembly, from bottom to top: chain, collar, fixture cover, nipple, hickey, lock nut, and stud (which attaches to the ceiling box). The wiring is black to black and white to white.

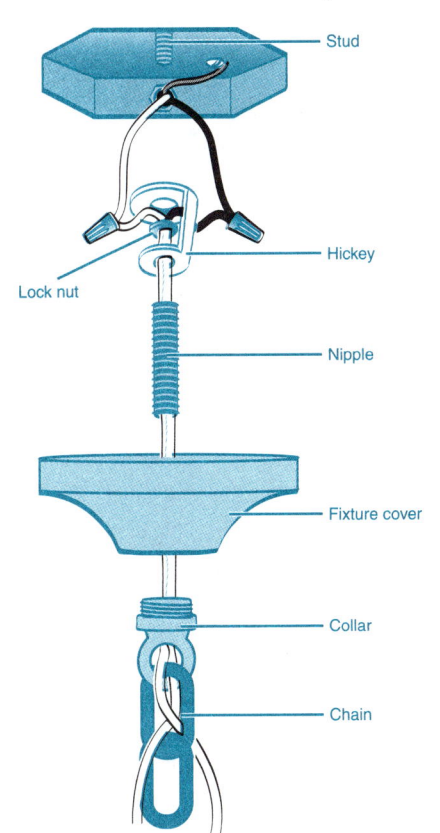

Repair Your Home In No Time

Things You'll Need

- ❑ Voltage tester
- ❑ Single-pole dimmer switch, properly rated
- ❑ Screwdrivers
- ❑ Multipurpose tool

Installing a Single-Pole Dimmer Switch

Dimmer switches are welcome additions in dining rooms, and sometimes in bedrooms and recreation rooms. They are not difficult to install, but as they work, they make small quantities of heat that must be dissipated. So, they can be installed only in junction boxes that are large enough for them and that are not crowded with wires and wire connections.

Several types of dimmer switches are available. The most common uses a dial that, when rotated, changes the intensity of the lights it controls. Another type resembles a toggle switch and dims according to the elevation of the toggle. Another has an electronic eye that senses natural light and makes adjustments accordingly, or the homeowner can adjust it by hand. Buy a dimmer switch that meets the voltage, amperage, and wiring type of the circuit into which it will be wired.

Single-pole switches are ones that alone control a light; no other switches turn that light on or off. Single-pole switches have only two wire connection screws (or slot connections) and are easy to wire. Three-way switches have three connection screws and work in pairs to control a light. A dimmer can replace one of these; to wire such a switch, see the next section of this chapter.

> **caution** In addition, a dimmer needs to be rated for the wattage that it will control. If a chandelier uses 10 40-watt bulbs, the dimmer has to be rated for at least 400 watts. Follow the manufacturer's instructions.

> **note** Fluorescent lights can be controlled by dimmer switches but require a different type of dimmer than those used for incandescent lights. Do not confuse the two types of dimmers. Installing a dimmer switch for fluorescent bulbs requires replacing the existing ballast (which is a part in a fluorescent fixture) with a dimming one as well as other complicated wiring tasks and therefore is not covered here.

To wire a single-pole dimmer switch, follow these steps:

1. Turn off the circuit breaker or remove the fuse controlling the circuit to the switch.
2. Remove the switch cover plate. Gently pull the switch out of the switch box. If the switch has only two wire connection terminals, it is a single-pole switch and you can proceed with step 3. If it has three terminals, it is a three-way switch and you need a three-way dimmer switch. Replace the switch in its

CHAPTER 6 Simple Electrical Repairs 143

box and remount the switch plate. Buy a three-way dimmer switch and follow the instructions in the next section.

3. Use the voltage tester to check for power. Touch one probe to the metal box and the other to each terminal screw in turn. The voltage tester light should not light. If there are no screws but slots instead, push the voltage tester probe into each slot in turn while holding the other to the metal box. If the box is plastic, carefully expose a ground wire and hold one probe to it rather than the box as you touch each of the terminals with the other probe. If the voltage tester light comes on during any of these tests, power is reaching the box. Return to the circuit breaker panel or fuse box and shut off power to the circuit.

4. One of two wiring patterns will be in the box. If the switch is in what is called *middle of the run*, two cables will enter the box (see Figure 6.9a). The neutral white wires are connected together, and the black wires attach to the two terminals of the switch. The ground wires all are connected to one another and to a screw mounted on the metal box (if you are dealing with a plastic box, the ground wires are just connected to one another).

   If the switch is in what is called a *switch loop*, only one cable enters the box (see Figure 6.9b). The black and the white wires attach to the switch terminals, and the white wire end should have a piece of black tape on it or be painted or otherwise coded black. The ground wire is connected to a screw mounted on the box.

5. Remove the old switch. If the dimmer switch has lead wires rather than screws or slots, connect the lead wires to the wires in the box with wire nuts. For a middle-of-the-run connection, connect the black wires to the dimmer switch—it does not matter which black wire connects to which terminal or lead wire. Leave the white wires alone.

   For a switch loop connection, connect the black and white (recoded black) wires to the dimmer terminals or lead wires.

6. Make the grounding connections. If the dimmer switch has lead wires, connect the green ground wire to the grounding screw in the junction box or to the wire nut containing the other ground wires. If the dimmer switch has a screw or slot grounding terminal, connect it to the cable's ground wire or wire nut holding multiple ground wires.

7. Gently press the wires into the box, keeping any wire nuts pointed up rather than down.

8. Mount the dimmer switch to the box with the mounting screws. Mount the cover plate over the dimmer switch. Attach the dimmer switch knob to the dimmer switch shaft that projects through the cover plate.

Things You'll Need

- ❑ Screwdrivers
- ❑ Three-way dimmer switch, properly rated
- ❑ Voltage tester

FIGURE 6.9A AND 6.9B

For a middle-of-the-run switch, as shown in frame A of this figure, connect the black wires to the dimmer switch and leave the whites alone. For a switch loop, shown in frame B, connect the black and white wires to the dimmer switch and code the white wire black. Make the ground wire connection.

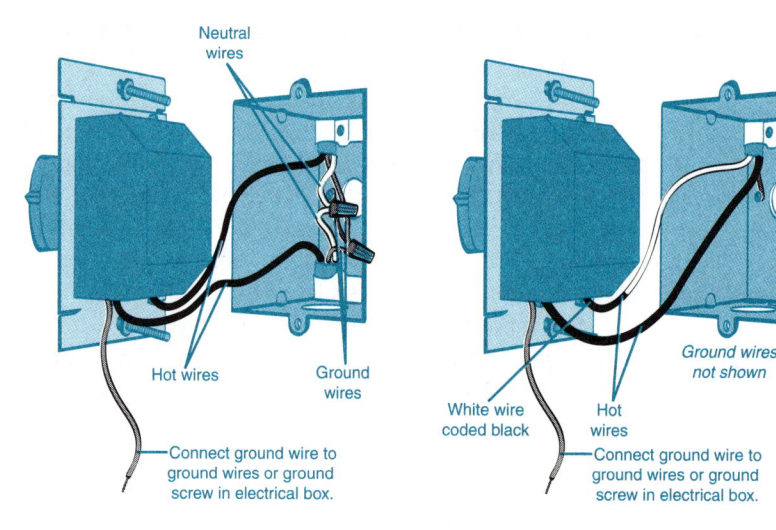

Frame A labels: Neutral wires; Hot wires; Ground wires; Connect ground wire to ground wires or ground screw in electrical box.

Frame B labels: White wire coded black; Hot wires; Ground wires not shown; Connect ground wire to ground wires or ground screw in electrical box.

Installing a Three-way Dimmer Switch

If you want to install a dimmer for a fixture controlled by two switches, buy a three-way dimmer switch and substitute it for one of the old switches; you do not need to replace both switches.

1. Turn off the circuit breaker or remove the fuse controlling the circuit.
2. Remove the cover plate of the switch you want to replace. Without disconnecting any wires, gently pull the switch from the outlet box.
3. Test for power. Hold one probe of a voltage tester to the metal junction box and each of the three switch terminals in turn—the voltage tester should not light. If it does, go back to the circuit breaker panel or fuse box and properly turn off the power to the circuit.
4. The three-way switch has three terminals, as shown in Figure 6.10. One is called common and, if it has a screw rather than a slot, the screw is black or copper colored. In addition, the common terminal is usually the one all by itself; the other two share a side on the switch or are together at the top or bottom. Place a piece of masking tape labeled "common" on the common wire.
5. Disconnect the three wires from the old switch and set it aside.
6. Connect the common wire to the black common wire of the dimmer switch. Connect the other two wires to the other two wires of the dimmer switch—it does not matter which connects to which.
7. Make the ground connections. If the dimmer has a green ground wire, connect it to the other ground wires. If it has a ground screw, use a jumper wire to connect the ground screw to the wire nut holding the other ground wires.

CHAPTER 6   Simple Electrical Repairs   145

8. Gently press the wire connections into the outlet box. Gently press the dimmer switch against the wires and into the box. Secure it in place with its mounting screws.
9. Screw the cover plate in place. If the dimmer switch uses a dial, press the dimmer switch knob onto the dimmer switch shaft protruding through the cover plate.

FIGURE 6.10
A three-way switch has a common wire. When you've identified it, connect it to the common terminal. Connect the other two wires to the other two terminals. Connect the dimmer switch ground terminal or ground lead wire to the other ground wires.

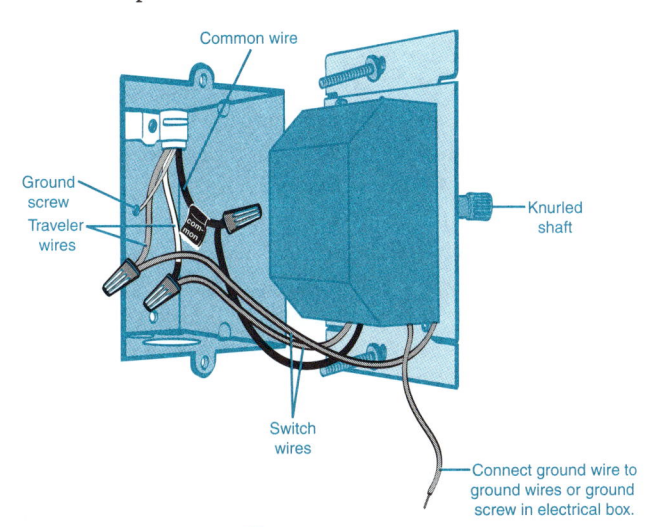

Things You'll Need

- A helper
- GFCI receptacle
- GFCI cover plate, if one did not come with the GFCI
- Voltage tester
- Screwdrivers
- Wire nuts
- Needle-nose pliers

Adding a GFCI Receptacle

A ground fault circuit interrupter (GFCI) is a device that can detect a very small amount of electrical leakage from a circuit (as little as .005 amp) and shut down power to those portions of the circuit it controls in as little as 1/40 of a second. As such, a GFCI provides better security against shock than a circuit breaker or fuse, which are not as sensitive or quick.

GFCIs are now required in locations where moisture or faulty appliances might cause a hazard, such as in kitchens, bathrooms, outdoor receptacles, garages, and the like. GFCI technology can be built in to circuit breakers. When one of these devices is installed in a service panel, it protects the entire circuit it controls. Where GFCI circuit breakers are not installed, GFCI receptacles are placed at appropriate locations. If the GFCI receptacles are at the end of a circuit, they protect at their own location; if they're in a middle-of-the-run, the receptacles protect their own location and all locations to the end of the circuit (away from the service panel).

> **tip**
> Both GFCI circuit breakers and receptacles have Test and Reset buttons. The Test button should be pressed once a month to ensure the GFCI is working properly. The Reset button reactivates the GFCI after the test.

1. Turn off power to the circuit. Remove the receptacle cover and gently pull the receptacle from the junction box. If two cables enter the box, skip step 2 and proceed to step 3.
2. If only one cable is entering the junction box, disconnect its wires. Attach the black wire to the GFCI terminal marked "hot" and "line." Connect the white wire to the terminal marked "white" and "line."

    If the GFCI has lead wires rather than screw or slot terminals, make the connections with wire nuts. Cap the load lead wires with separate wire nuts secured with a revolution of electrical tape. Run a short jumper ground wire from the green grounding screw of the GFCI to the grounding screw of the metal outlet box, or if a plastic box to the ground wire of the cable.
    Go to step 9.
3. If two cables enter the box, the receptacle is a middle-of-the-run receptacle and the sequence is more complicated. Gently pull the old receptacle from the outlet box. Now you need to discover which cable is coming from the service panel.
4. Disconnect the black wires from the old receptacle and bend them outside the box and away from one another. Expose one of the ground wire ends.
5. Now you need to restore power for a moment to the circuit. To do so, have a helper at the service panel turn on the power to the circuit. Hold one probe of the voltage tester to the ground wire and the other to one of the black wires, as shown in Figure 6.11. If the tester lights, this is the hot wire coming from the service panel.

    If the tester does not light, test the other black wire in the same way. When you have determined which black wire comes from the service panel, remember it and shout to your helper to turn off the power to the circuit again.
6. Disconnect the white wires and ground wire from the old receptacle.
7. Connect the black wire coming from the service panel to the terminal or black lead wire marked "line." Connect the white wire from this same cable to the terminal or white lead wire marked "line."
8. Connect the other black wire to the terminal or lead black wire labeled "load." Connect the white wire from this same cable to the terminal or white lead wire labeled "load." Connect the wire nut holding the ground wires to the GFCI ground terminal. (see Figure 6.12).
9. Gently press the wires and GFCI into the outlet box. Screw the GFCI to the outlet box and then screw the cover plate to the GFCI.

CHAPTER 6   Simple Electrical Repairs   147

FIGURE 6.11
Touch the end of one probe of the voltage tester to the ground wire in the box and the other to one of the black wires. One of the black wires will be charged with voltage; be very careful.

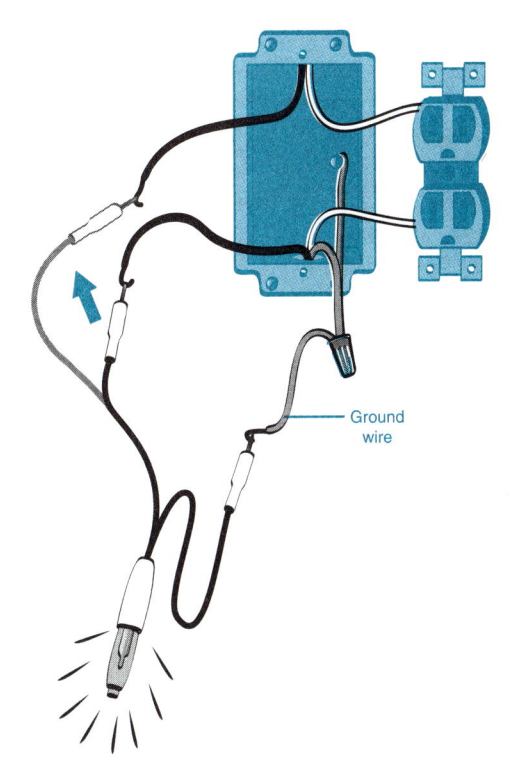

Ground wire

10. Restore power to the circuit. Press the GFCI Test button to check it and press the GFCI Reset button after the test.

FIGURE 6.12
Connect the wires coming from the service panel to the terminals marked "line" and the others to the terminals marked "load." Connect the ground wire of the GFCI to the other ground wires in the box.

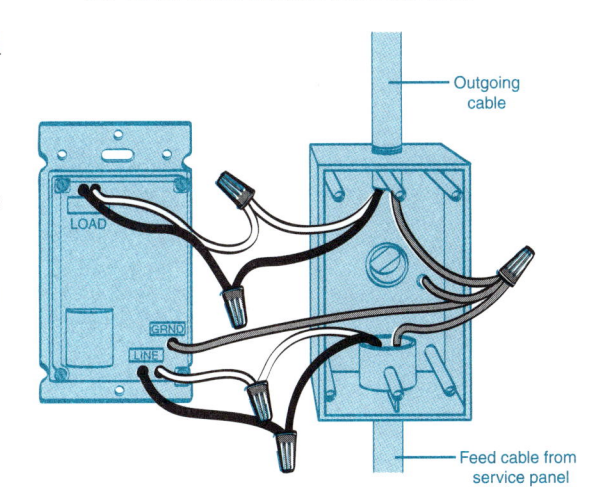

Outgoing cable

Feed cable from service panel

Summary

In this chapter we explored home electrical systems, how electricity works, how to work with it safely, and how to make some simple—but very useful—electrical repairs and improvements. These included rewiring a lamp, fixing a cord's plug, installing a dimmer switch, hanging a chandelier, and replacing a common receptacle with a protective GFCI receptacle. Each of these electrical wiring repairs or improvements saves you money that you would otherwise spend on professionals doing the job for you. Some of these tasks might seem small (replacing a plug), but they can have a measurable effect on how much you enjoy your home.

Now we move on to the really big and noticeable improvements, ones that give whole rooms brand new looks: painting and wallpapering. These are the home improvements that get everyone's attention.

Painting and Wallpapering

We live in rooms, and it's only natural from time to time to want to make them look better. A dramatic way of doing so is to paint or wallpaper them. Nothing so alters the aura of a room than a new paint color or new wallpaper. Even painting a room the same color as it has been makes it look fresh and newly decorated.

Anyone who has never painted a home might think, "Painting is simple; dip the brush in and spread the paint on the wall." But if this were all there were to it, there likely would be no professional painters. In this chapter, I explain the techniques used by professional painters to choose the right paint, prepare your interior walls for painting, apply the paint expertly, and clean up in a jiffy. (This chapter focuses on interior painting only; you learn about exterior painting in Chapter 8, "Outdoor Repairs and Maintenance.")

Wallpapering is trickier in many respects than painting, but a few simple procedures can make the task more manageable. In this chapter, you learn how to remove old wallpapering and get your room ready. You also learn how to hang that first tricky piece of paper and how to paper in and around corners, and around windows, doors, switchplates, and more.

But first, let's take a look at some of the tools you'll use for painting and wallpapering your home.

In this chapter:

* Learn how to choose the right paints and brushes; prepare and paint walls, doors, and windows; and clean up after oil-based and latex paints.

* Understand professional techniques for preparing and wallpapering around doors, windows, entryways, light switches, and more.

To do list

- Understand the tools and equipment you'll use.
- Choose and buy the right paint.
- Choose the proper brushes and rollers.
- Prepare walls, woodwork, paint, and equipment for painting.
- Paint walls and ceilings the right way.
- Paint windows efficiently.
- Paint doors, on or off hinges.
- Clean up with minimum mess.
- Learn tips for hiring a professional painting contractor.

Painting, from Setup to Cleanup

Professional painters have developed a number of techniques for preparing and applying paints, and you can use these methods to make your own painting projects go more smoothly and produce more professional results. The first task for any painter is to gather the necessary tools and equipment. One particularly important skill for getting a professional-looking paint job is choosing the right kind of paint for the job; another is choosing the right paint rollers and brushes. Painters also know how to prepare a room's surfaces and use a few professional techniques to ensure the paint they apply is going to look good and last a long time. And they know how to clean their equipment so it will be as good tomorrow as it is today. In the following sections of this chapter, you learn how simple these techniques really are. Finally, this chapter gives you some tips for hiring one of these professionals, just in case you'd rather *not* do it yourself.

Your Painting Tool Set

Figure 7.1 shows a variety of tools you'll use when painting. You might already have many of the tools you'll need for prepping your walls and applying paint. But here's a short description of the tools and equipment I recommend you have on hand for these jobs:

- **Scrapers**—A *regular scraper* resembles a putty knife but has a slightly wider and stiffer blade. *A hook-blade scraper* is a one- or two-handed tool for bearing down on loose paint to scrape it away. A *triangle scraper* is good for corners and grooves.
- **Paint brushes, rollers, roller frames, roller extension poles, and roller trays**—Have one set for latex paints, one for alkyd paints, and one for varnishes (see the section "Choosing Brushes and Rollers").
- **Beveled corner roller**—With this specialty roller, you can apply paint expertly to wall or wall-ceiling corners.

CHAPTER 7 Painting and Wallpapering   151

FIGURE 7.1
Good painting depends on good equipment. Shown here are three kinds of paintbrushes; a paint tray used with paint rollers; a putty knife, hook blade scraper, and broad knife; masking tape; a dropcloth; a beveled corner roller; and a brush spinner. If you keep painting tools clean, they can last for many years.

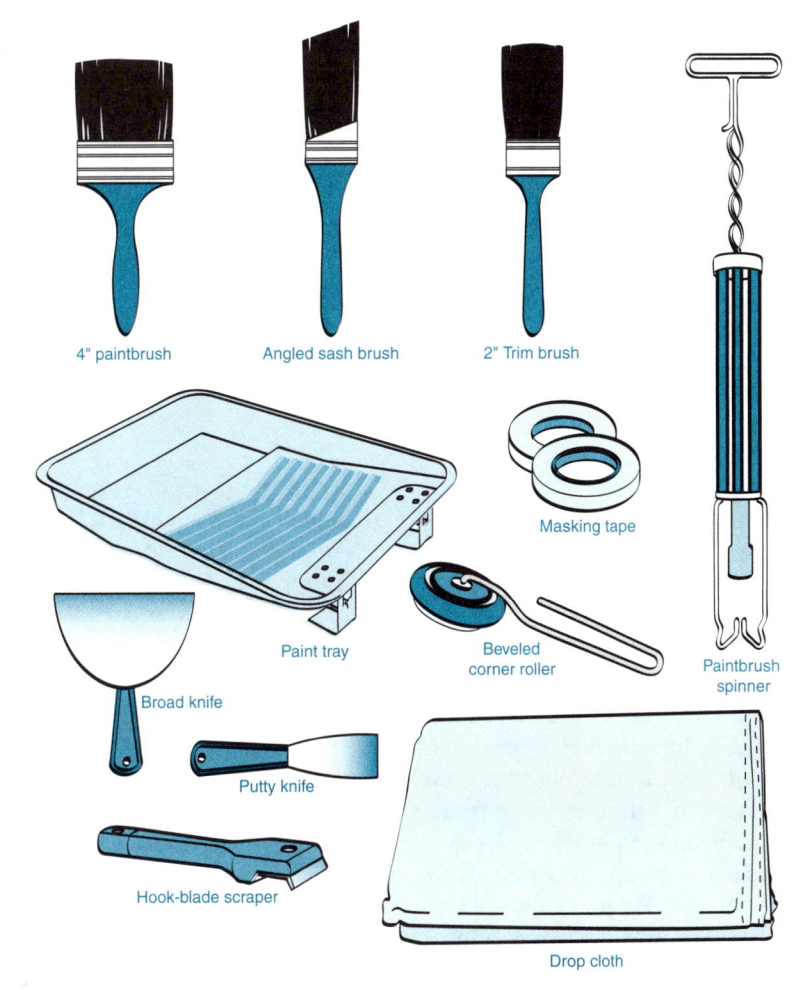

4" paintbrush   Angled sash brush   2" Trim brush

Paint tray

Masking tape

Beveled corner roller

Paintbrush spinner

Broad knife

Putty knife

Hook-blade scraper

Drop cloth

- **Edge guide**—This flexible guide allows you to paint on one surface without the paint lapping onto one alongside, for example, painting a baseboard alongside wall-to-wall carpeting. You move the edge guide along with the brush.
- **Paint mitt**—You put the mitt on one hand, dip the hand in paint (didn't you always want to!), and then paint such objects as balusters, radiators, pipes, and grills.
- **Canvas or paper dropcloths**—Canvas stays in place better than plastic. Both canvas and paper dropcloths absorb paint rather than pooling it in a slippery spot.
- **Step ladder**—A 5-foot aluminum ladder is good enough for most jobs and is light enough to pick up and carry.
- **Sawhorse braces and scaffolding boards**—Available in metal and common in tool rental stores, metal saw horse braces support several scaffolding boards a foot or so off the ground so you can reach high interior places.

- **Brush spinner**—This is a slender tool with a hand/plunger at the top and a paintbrush handle holder at the bottom. To finish brush cleanup, you clamp a paintbrush handle in the holder and then use the hand/plunger to spin the brush rapidly. Excess water or solvent is flung from the brush, which, of course, is held inside an empty bucket so the flying liquid is confined.
- **Bristle comb**—These metal-bristle combs are used on brushes to comb and separate the brushes' hairs during brush cleaning.
- **Tape**—For a crisp line, use higher-adhesion masking tape than general-purpose masking tape—the general-purpose variety can allow a bit of paint to seep under the edge. Where the surface is delicate, such as wallpaper, and where you do not want to leave any residue, use a kind of masking tape called painter's tape. This is blue and costs more than regular masking tape.

Choosing the Right Paints

Nine out of ten gallons of paint now sold are latex paints. These water-based paints use water as a solvent, making brushes, rollers, and hands easier to clean when the painting is finished. The other common type of paint is alkyd paint, which has a finish similar to the old oil-based paints but uses manmade alkyds rather than linseed oil as the binder. Both paints have their pros and cons, so you must consider each carefully before you decide which to buy.

You will run across the following terms for the types of paint finishes: *Gloss* (or *high-gloss*) has the most resins and is the most durable and smoothest, making it good for kitchens, bathrooms, and wood trim that might need frequent cleaning; *semi-gloss* has somewhat less resin than gloss, dries to a less shiny finish, and is applied where someone might use a gloss yet want less sheen; *satin* (or *eggshell*) is lower luster than semi-gloss and is popular on wood trim to set it off from a wall painted in a flat finish; and *flat* dries to the least luster but, because it is nonreflective, helps disguise imperfections on the surface. Flat paint is often applied to large surfaces such as walls and ceilings.

Although the following sections offer information to help you determine which type of paint is best for your paint job, remember that employees in a good paint store can also give you advice on which kind of paint to choose. Describe the surface you intend to paint, the level of preparation you can afford, and the kind of finish you want to achieve—matte, eggshell, or high gloss—and they can offer valuable suggestions.

Latex Paints

Latex paints are easier to clean up, are more tolerant of humidity, and dry more quickly than alkyd paints. Because they release fewer volatile organic compounds (VOCs) to the atmosphere, latex paints also are more environmentally friendly than are alkyds. They are almost odorless and do not yellow with age. Latex paints can be applied to slightly damp surfaces (after all, they are partly water themselves), but the surfaces have to be clean and primed for durable adhesion. The highest-quality latex paints, that is, the most durable, use 100% acrylic resin for the binder. The lowest-quality uses only vinyl for the resin, and the middle-quality uses vinyl acrylic resin.

Latex paints are used in many applications, but there are some situations in which they probably shouldn't be used. Latex does not stick well to some alkyd paint surfaces or high-gloss finishes. The water in latex paint causes rusting if applied to bare metal, and it raises the grain of uncoated wood. Latex paint can be applied over wallpaper, but the water in it can weaken the glue that holds the wallpaper to the wall. Finally, latex paint—especially in the flat finish form—does not stand up as well as alkyds to abrasion and cleaning, so you might prefer to use a more durable alkyd paint for any area that's bound to need frequent cleaning (such as kitchen cabinets).

Alkyd Paints

Alkyd paints can make a harder, smoother finish, leveling out better than latex paints and drying without showing brush marks. But they are more difficult to work with; take longer to dry; have strong odors (requiring ventilation and even respirators); and require solvent (also called *paint thinner*) for cleaning up brushes, rollers, and skin. Some alkyds are made to have low odors but still release vapors and so still require ventilation and possibly respirators. Alkyd paints adhere better to poorly prepared surfaces (making them useful when you cannot spare the time for adequate surface prep) and to cold surfaces or ones that might soon be rained on. Because their semi-gloss and high-gloss finishes are so durable and cleanable, alkyds are a favorite for wood trim work. This is especially true of door trim and window trim, which tend to get bumped and marred, but alkyds are also a favorite for chair rail, crown molding, and baseboard molding.

> **note** You also might choose to apply varnish over painted surfaces for added protection. Varnishes, including polyurethanes and shellac, are tough, transparent, and translucent finishes normally used over unpainted wood. Varnishes are used to protect painted surfaces or where wood grain is meant to be visible. Polyurethanes come in gloss, semi-gloss, and satin finishes—with gloss being the shiniest and most transparent.

Things You'll Need

- ❏ Calculator
- ❏ Pencil and paper
- ❏ Measuring tape

Estimating Paint and Work Time

To estimate the number of gallons of paint you'll need, you must consider the room's size and shape. If a room is fairly rectangular, add the width to the length and multiply by the height. Double this number to get a figure for the square footage of the walls. Subtract 21 square feet per door and 15 square feet per average-size window. If you are painting the ceiling, multiply its length by its width.

A gallon of paint covers an average of 400 square feet, although you should check with the paint you are considering buying. (Surfaces that have never been painted will absorb more paint; well-covered surfaces absorb less paint.) Divide 400 into the square footage you intend to cover to get the number of gallons you will need.

For trim paint, figure 21 square feet for a door (both sides) and 7 square feet for a window (inside only). For a baseboard, multiply the height by the length.

You can paint a small room in an hour if you are applying only one coat. If you are applying more than one coat, remember to consider drying time, which can be as little as 2 hours or as many as 36 depending on the paint. Adding another color for trim or ceiling adds time. And remember that most of the time a person spends on a paint project is in the preparation, not the painting.

Choosing Brushes and Rollers

Use one set of brushes for latex paints and one set for alkyd paints, never mixing them. Buy one set for varnishes, too, if you are going to use these tough, clear finishes. Buy quality paint brushes and then build enough time into your project to clean the brushes well—a paint brush is only as good as its last cleaning. A good paint brush properly cleaned can last a lifetime.

For latex paint, use brushes with synthetic bristles, normally nylon or nylon polyester. For alkyd paints, use natural bristle brushes. If you use a natural bristle brush with latex paints, the water in the latex paint will eventually ruin the bristles. Mark each brush as latex or alkyd.

> **note** A good nylon-polyester brush is acceptable for working with alkyd paints, but don't use a 100% nylon brush for this purpose.

Buy high-quality brushes and treat them well. High-quality brushes are expensive but have better balance (reducing fatigue), are constructed for long service, and have bristles that hold more paint and stay where they should rather than loosening or splaying. Good brushes have bristles with *flagged*, or split, ends—the better to hold more paint. A brush should feel comfortable in your hand and the bristles should be thick—though thicker near the handle than the tip—and flexible.

A standard collection includes a 3" or 4" straight-edge brush, a 2" chisel-edge trim brush, a 1 1/2" angled (*sash*) brush, and a 1" trim brush for hard-to-reach places.

When buying rollers, get a nylon nap for latex paints and get nylon and wool blend, mohair, or lambskin for alkyd paints. Three thicknesses are commonplace: 1/4", 1/2"–3/4", and 1"–1 1/4". Use the shorter naps for smoother and glossier surfaces, and use the longer naps for rougher and duller surfaces. For general work, chose the medium nap; it holds more paint than the shorter nap rollers do and leaves a pleasant-looking finish.

Buy a roller handle that has threads at the end to accommodate an extension pole, which is good for painting walls and ceilings. A 9" long frame is the most common, but it holds more paint than the 7" ones and will tire you more quickly. Chose a frame with five wires rather than four; five wires help hold the shape of the roller tube better than four do.

Various kinds of paint pads are also available and can be useful in some situations, but only if you are careful not to overload the pad with paint. I have never found them to be real time-savers, except when using small ones for painting along a straight line. Paint pads with wheels can be useful on walls along the edges of window and door trim, but a steady hand with a paintbrush can be just as fast.

PRACTICE SAFE PAINTING!

Painting seems safe enough, but there are dangers so you need to use these precautions:

* **Make provisions to keep children and pets out of painting areas**—Keep them away from paint cans, solvents, and drop cloths with paint on them as well as rooms where you have removed electrical outlet covers and switchplates. Pets are particularly susceptible to fumes, particularly pet birds. If a pet gets paint or solvent on its fur, there is a double danger: It can burn its skin, and it wants to lick the substance off. If the paint is latex, rinse it off with water. If the paint is alkyd, do not try to remove it with solvent, which can harm a pet's skin. Instead, use a cloth soaked in cooking oil and wipe off the offending substance.

* **Read all instructions on paint cans**—Try to keep these labels free of paint because they also contain information on antidotes in case paint is swallowed.

* **Ventilate rooms**—If you are using alkyd paints, open windows and doors and even place exhaust fans in windows or doorways if you can. Check paint and solvent labels to see if you should extinguish pilot lights in rooms where you are painting. If you cannot ventilate a room, wear a respirator (not a mere dust mask).

* **When sanding, wear a dust mask and eye protection**—Before working with liquid or paste paint strippers, read the sidebar "Using Heat Guns and Chemical Strippers," later in this chapter. When painting a ceiling, wear eye protection.

* **When working with solvents, wear rubber gloves.**

* **For safety when climbing ladders or using scaffolding, read the section "Positioning a Ladder," later in this chapter.**

Proper Painting Preparation and Techniques

Alas, as with many other things in life, with painting there is a hurdle of preparation before the real fun begins. One report shows 60% of a painting job goes to preparation and 15% to cleanup, leaving 25% of the time devoted to actual painting. But without proper preparation, the paint may all too soon pucker or peal and confront you with yet another painting project.

As everyone knows, paint needs to be applied to a clean, dry surface. How little this sentence looks…and how huge the surfaces are in the rooms you want to paint! But with a good radio and perhaps some hearty companionship, you can make those surfaces just the way they should be to receive the paint you have in mind. And your prep work will pay off: The better the prep is, the longer the paint will last in a good and true condition.

Things You'll Need

- ❑ Screwdrivers
- ❑ Dropcloths
- ❑ Garbage bags
- ❑ Masking tape
- ❑ Newspapers
- ❑ Cleaning solutions, as appropriate (bleach, soap, water, and so on)
- ❑ Sponges and rags
- ❑ Paint scrapers
- ❑ Sandpaper
- ❑ Spackling compound/plaster, as necessary
- ❑ Liquid deglosser, as necessary
- ❑ Vacuum and sponge mop

Preparing the Room

Yes, you should even prepare for the preparation. This means organizing the room so the preparation and the painting go smoothly, without mess or accident. Here are some things to do to get your room ready for painting:

1. Remove light furniture, curtains, and blinds from the room.
2. If you can, move heavy furniture to the middle of the room. Cover the furniture with dropcloths.
3. Unscrew and remove heating and cooling grills. Place newspapers over radiators and cover thermostats. For receptacles and switchplates, either carefully paint them in place or turn off power to the room, remove the plates, and paint them separately before reinstalling them. You can restore power when they are removed, but keep children and pets out of the room.

CHAPTER 7 Painting and Wallpapering

4. If you are painting the ceiling, cover a chandelier with a garbage bag drawn up from the bottom and closed with a twist-tie at the top. Run the bag up the chain as high as you can. Cover the rest of the chain with a cut garbage bag and masking tape. Cover windows with plastic or sheets.
5. Lay dropcloths on the floor.
6. Tape over exposed portions of door hinges.
7. If you are painting windows, remove the hardware.
8. If you are not painting window and door trim, you can use painter's tape to protect them from accidental paint smudges. This adds to both preparation time and expense, and you can skip it if you like, though you will move more slowly with a brush than you would otherwise.

Preparing the Surfaces

Walk around the room and see where the problems are. New paint has to be applied to clean, dry areas on new materials or on old paint or wallpaper that is sound and solidly attached to the surface below. If any of these conditions is not met, there is going to be trouble.

Look for mildew; grime; or puckered, cracked, or peeling paint. Check for bleeding wood knots. These release resins that stain the wood and even paint that has been coated over them. Here are remedies for problem areas you can encounter during preparation for painting:

- **Mildew**—Wash away mildew with a solution of equal parts laundry bleach and water. That's the easy part. More difficult is discovering and removing the cause of the mildew buildup. If you don't, the mildew is likely to come back when the weather gets warm and humid. Mildew can arise because of a leaky pipe within the wall or rain water seeping in from a roof or around a window or door. Mildew can also merely be the result of warm humid days, especially in basements. Here the long-term solution might be the installation of dehumidifiers. They consume electricity and create warm air, but they keep the humidity in a room below 60%, thus preventing mildew from settling.
- **Puckered, cracked, or peeling paint**—Scrape away any paint that is not firmly adhering to the surface below. Use regular, hook-blade, and triangular scrapers. If the old paint is thick, you might end up with visible depressions. Sand the depression edges or, if the depressions are deep, fill them with spackling or drywall joint compound and sand them smooth when the compound is dry. If you want to use chemical paint strippers, see the sidebar "Using Heat Guns and Chemical Paint Strippers," later in this chapter.
- **Gouges, cracks, and holes**—To learn how to fill or smooth gouges, cracks, and holes in plaster and drywall, see "Repairing Walls," in Chapter 3, "Walls and Floors."
- **Hard, slick surfaces**—New paint adheres better when the surface on which it is spread is slightly roughened, even microscopically. Sand walls lightly; you can use sanding pads attached to poles—a technique used by drywall finishers. You can sand either alkyd or latex paint. Alkyds also respond well

to liquid deglossers as well as to solutions of trisodium phosphate (TSP), if TSP is allowed in your community (they introduce phosphates into the water supply). Liquid deglossers are good in places that are difficult to sand. They also remove old floor wax that has splashed on baseboards. If you are going to paint metal, such as radiators, sand off any rust.

> **caution** Wear rubber gloves when you use a liquid deglosser, TSP solution, or laundry bleach. Also wear light gloves if your fingers are going to be in contact with sandpaper.

- **Dust and dirt**—Use a vacuum or damp rag to remove dust from the tops of doors, the tops of door and window trim, and the tops of baseboards. Use a mild diluted household cleaner and a long-handled mop to wash walls and wood trim. This can be a two-person job: One person sponges on the cleaner, and the other waits for 2 minutes to let the cleaner lift off dirt and then rinses with another sponge mop (rinsing with a second bucket of clear water).

USING HEAT GUNS AND CHEMICAL STRIPPERS

Heat guns are sold in home improvement stores to remove paint. They operate at very high temperatures and can ignite sawdust or paper. If you use one, wear protective gloves. Hold it in one hand several inches away from the painted surface. When the paint bubbles, scrape it with a scraper held in the other hand.

If you use chemical strippers, read the cautions and instructions carefully. Wear goggles, thick rubber gloves, and old clothes that cover your arms to the gloves. Ventilate the room well, and wear a respirator if the instructions call for one. Apply chemical paint strippers with a cheap, disposable paintbrush to areas about 2 feet square at a time. When the paint begins to blister, scrape it up and wipe it into newspapers. Dispose of these in a manner prescribed by your community's hazardous waste department. Clean the stripped area as called for by the stripper's instructions. Finish by lightly sanding the area and then cleaning away the dust.

CHAPTER 7   Painting and Wallpapering   159

Things You'll Need

- ❑ Paint can opener
- ❑ Paint can stirrer
- ❑ Paper plate, tape, hammer, and small nail (optional)

Stirring the Paint and Getting It Ready

Preparing the paint and the paint can to help ease your work makes the whole job faster and better. Here are some tips on making the paint debris-free and the can dribble-free:

1. Remove dust or debris from the top of the paint can before you open it so nothing falls into the paint.
2. Use a paint can opener to pry off the lid; then set the lid aside. The best way to ensure your paint is well-mixed is to have the paint store do it on its oscillating machine and then use the paint shortly thereafter. If you can't use the paint soon after the paint store has mixed it, you can use a variable speed drill attachment for mixing or, failing that, use a wooden stirrer given out free at paint stores. Stir with a wooden stirrer, taking care to lift up pigment that has settled. The paint is well-stirred when you see no streaks of base and pigment, even when stirring from the bottom and sides of the can.
3. If the paint is an alkyd and has been used before, it might have a skin on top. Cut around its circumference and lift it out with a stirrer; dispose of it in newspaper.
4. If there is debris in the paint, you can pour the paint through cheesecloth bound to the top of an empty can or paint bucket.
5. If you are working with several gallon cans, mix portions together in a paint bucket so you do not run the risk of different tints in each can.

Pro's Tip

If you will be carrying around a gallon can of paint, you need to minimize the problem of leaving paint rings wherever you set the can. Take a paper plate (plastic-coated is better) and, with double-sided tape or tape made into a couple of loops sticky-side out, tape it to the bottom of the can as shown in Figure 7.2. Drips will be caught on the paper plate and not end up on any surface you put the can on.

Pro's Tip

You can minimize drips down the side of a paint can by making half a dozen nail holes in the depression or channel of the rim at the top of the can. Use a finishing nail or other small nail and, with a hammer, punch holes at equal distance around the circumference as shown in Figure 7.3. Any paint that then gets in the rim will drip back into the paint below. With thick latex paint, you might have to clear the holes from time to time.

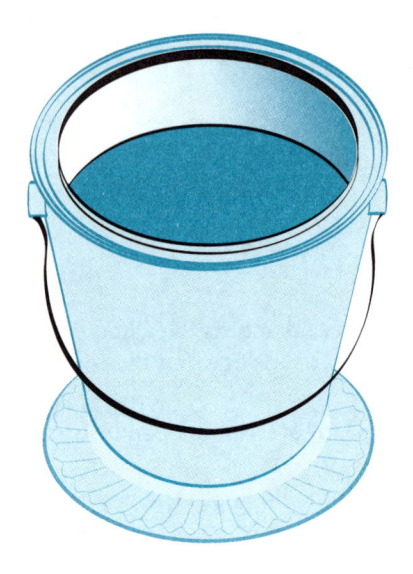

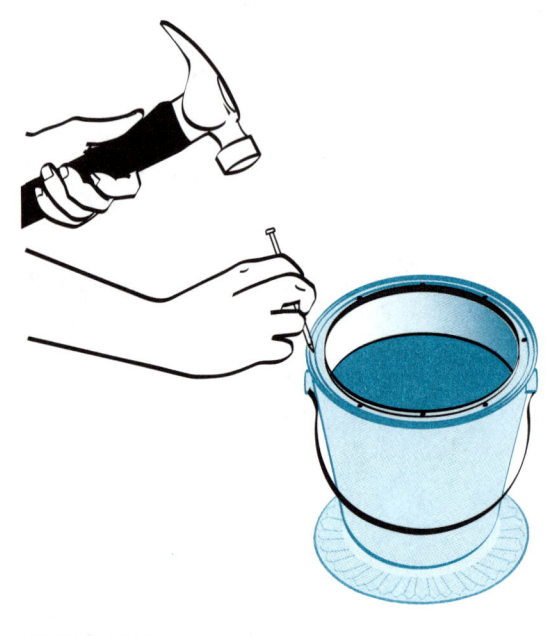

FIGURE 7.2
To keep paint dribbles off surfaces where you place a paint can, tape a paper plate to the bottom of the can.

FIGURE 7.3
Poke several holes in the depression of the rim at the top of a paint can. Paint in the groove will drip through the holes back into the paint can.

Things You'll Need

- ❏ Brushes
- ❏ Water and paint solvent
- ❏ Roller tray, roller, and extension pole
- ❏ Aluminum foil
- ❏ Five-gallon bucket and a roller screen (optional)

Positioning a Ladder

Step ladders are generally all that are needed for interior painting. Make sure your step ladder is sturdy and free of defects; then follow these guidelines for its safe use:

- Do not set up a ladder in front of a closed door unless you lock the door to prevent a person coming through.
- Set tools, brushes, and paint cans on the bucket shelf before you begin to climb the ladder so you can use both hands as you climb.
- Do not stand on the top of the ladder, the bucket shelf, or the step below the top.
- Do not lean any farther out left or right than making your belt buckle move to the left or right rail.

CHAPTER 7 Painting and Wallpapering

- If you have to paint a stairwell, erect a step ladder on the top landing and a straight ladder on the stairs (see Figure 7.4). Run a scaffolding-strength 2-by-10 between them.

FIGURE 7.4
To reach high areas in a stairwell, place a step ladder on the landing and a straight ladder on the stairs. Pad the tops of the straight ladder. Run scaffolding-grade 2-by-10s between ladders so the boards are level.

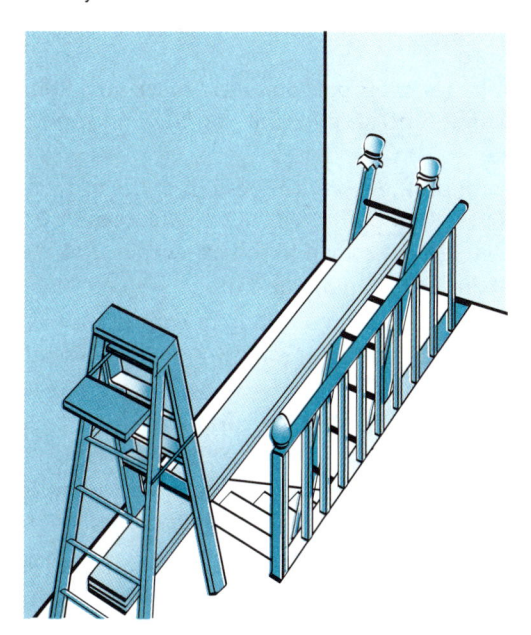

Painting with Brushes and Rollers

Everyone has probably painted before, but professionals have learned ways to reduce the mess, make the job faster, and minimize fatigue. Use these tips when painting with a brush:

1. Condition the brush. If it is new, rub it between your palms to dislodge loose bristles. It's also a good idea to break in a new brush on a primer or undercoat—that way, any remaining loose bristles won't be dislodged onto a top finish coat. If the brush is for latex, dip it in water. If it is for alkyd, dip it in paint solvent. Wipe away excess moisture.
2. Hold the brush with the thumb on one side of the metal portion (called the *ferrule*) and the other four fingers on the other side.
3. Dip the brush one third to one half the way down the bristles.
4. Draw the brush up and tap it against the insides of the paint can. Do not wipe it along the rim. Doing so removes too much paint and increases the risk of dribbling paint down the outside of the can.
5. Paint about 3 square feet at a time. Paint from a dry area to a wet edge. For smooth surfaces and wood, finish your strokes all in one direction.

When painting with a roller, use these techniques:

1. Fit the roller tray to the size of job. Use a regular roller tray for a regular job and use a deeper roller tray for larger jobs. If you are going to paint a whole

Short Cut

room, consider using a 5-gallon bucket with a course screen that hooks to the edge and descends into the paint.

To make the cleanup quicker, line a roller tray with aluminum foil before pouring in the paint. When the paint is used up at the end of the job, toss the aluminum foil away.

2. Pour paint into the reservoir portion of the roller tray. Roll the roller in and then run it back and forth several times on the ribbed portion of the tray to squeeze off excess.
3. Avoid getting paint on the steel arm portion of the roller that supports the roller frame; paint will drip off it where you don't want. If you are using a bucket and screen, use the screen to roll excess paint off the roller.
4. Paint sections about 3 feet square at a time.
5. Make the first roll—whether on a ceiling or wall—away from you.
6. Return on the diagonal, and then roll away from you again, making an *M* or *W* shape as shown in Figure 7.5.
7. Without removing the roller from the surface, go back over the same area filling in unpainted portions, again in an M or W fashion.
8. If paint splatters from the roller, you might have too much paint on it—remove more next time on the ribbed portion of the tray. More likely, you are simply moving the roller too quickly.

FIGURE 7.5
Make the first roll away from you and then come back on a diagonal. Roll away on another diagonal, creating an *M* or *W* shape.

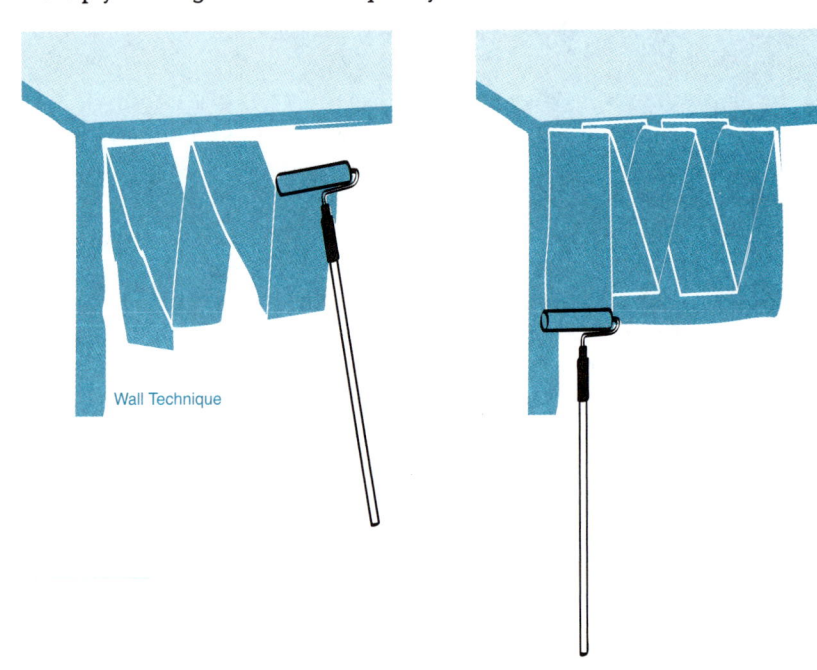

Wall Technique

CHAPTER 7 Painting and Wallpapering

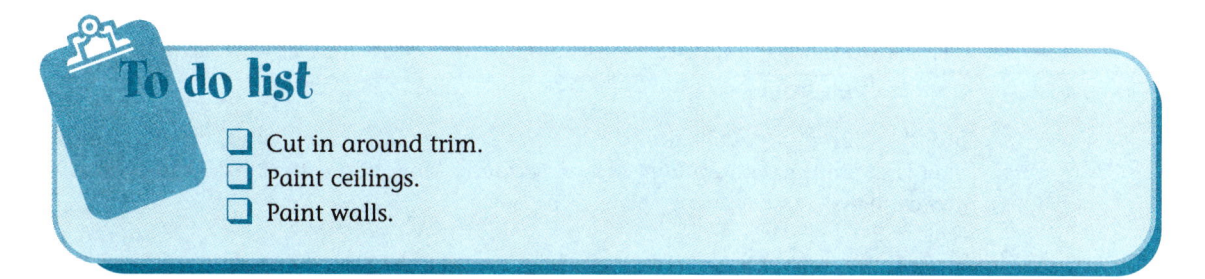

To do list

- ❏ Cut in around trim.
- ❏ Paint ceilings.
- ❏ Paint walls.

Painting Walls and Ceilings

If you are painting a room, most likely you are using a roller. Even so, you need to begin by cutting in around door, window, and baseboard trim with a brush. By painting around trim with a brush, you get a cleaner edge and avoid having to paint near trim with the roller. After cutting in comes the rolling and then painting trim and cleaning up—all techniques you learn in this section of the chapter.

> **caution** If you are using latex paint, do all the cutting in before you fill in with rollers. If you are using alkyd paint, cut in only where you can fill in within 20 minutes; otherwise, the cut-in portion will have dried so much that it might look different from the rolled portion when the whole job is done.

Things You'll Need

- ❏ 2" trim brush
- ❏ Corner roller
- ❏ Paint (prepped as described earlier)
- ❏ Prepped room (as described earlier)
- ❏ Roller and roller tray

1. Use a 2" trim brush to create a 2" border of paint on the wall next to wooden trim and other objects. At the line where the two colors are going to meet, you can—with practice—make a fairly sharp line by pushing a bead of paint just ahead of the brush's bristles.

> **tip** At corners where both areas are to be the same color, you can use a special roller called a *corner roller*. It applies an inch or so of paint to both sides of the corner.

2. Roll the ceilings in the narrowest direction, covering about 9 square feet at a time. Wear eye protection and a painter's hat.
3. Roll the walls beginning at a top corner, as shown in Figure 7.6. Most people like to work to another corner, covering about 9 square feet at a time and moving horizontally rather than vertically. This allows them to do all their

work with the extension pole attached before they remove it to paint at their waist height and below. Most right-handed people prefer to work left to right, left-handed people the opposite.

After the ceiling and walls are painted, the general plan of attack for completing the room is to paint crown moldings, then windows, then doors, then baseboards, and then cabinets.

FIGURE 7.6
Begin rolling at a top corner, using the *W* or *M* pattern. Continue at this height to the far corner.

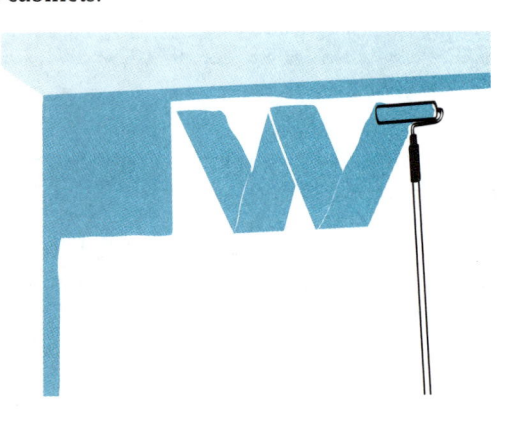

Painting Windows

Double-hung windows are always a challenge to paint. A well-considered sequence helps.

Things You'll Need

- ❏ Proper paint
- ❏ 1 1/2" sash brush
- ❏ Single-edge razor

1. Lower the exterior sash and raise the interior sash each about two thirds of the way, as shown in Figure 7.7.
   If the upper sash is painted shut and you do not want to free it, paint as best as you can without moving it. Its lower horizontal rail will appear with its old paint when the interior sash is raised, but that is the only price you pay for not going to the trouble of freeing the sash.
2. With the sash brush, paint the interior-facing portions of the interior sash and the portions of the exterior sash you can reach. Do not paint the top edge of the interior sash or the lower edge of the exterior sash; you will need to put your fingers there to move the sashes.

CHAPTER 7 Painting and Wallpapering   165

When you are painting near panes, allow 1/16" of paint to flow onto the glass, weatherproofing the seal between wood and glass.

3. Move the exterior sash up and the interior sash down. Paint the portions of the exterior sash you could not reach before. Paint the upper edge of the interior sash. Leave the lower edge of the exterior sash for when you paint the outside of the window.
4. Paint the window trim from top to bottom. Where the trim meets the wall, work a brush carefully to make a straight line. If you prefer, use painter's tape on the wall, although this adds to the expense and you must be certain the wall paint is thoroughly dry. Use a small paint pad on the wood trim if you prefer these tools.
5. When the paint is dry, move both the top and bottom sashes up and down a couple of times. Then push both sashes down all the way. Paint the channels in which the sashes move. Paint as lightly as possible here because paint buildup can make sash movement difficult. If there are sash cords, keep paint off them. Raise the sashes and paint the lower portion of the channels.
6. When the paint is dry, trim away excess paint on glass with a single-edge razor blade. You can hold the razor in your hand or use a holder for it sold in home improvement stores. You can also do this freehand or use a ruler as a guide. Hold the ruler edge along the edge of the glass and run the razor point down the ruler edge, cutting the dried paint. Remove the ruler and scrape paint toward the scored line; paint the thickness of the ruler will remain on the window glass.

FIGURE 7.7
To begin painting a double-hung window, lower the exterior sash and raise the interior sash each about two thirds of the way. Paint the exposed parts of the sashes.

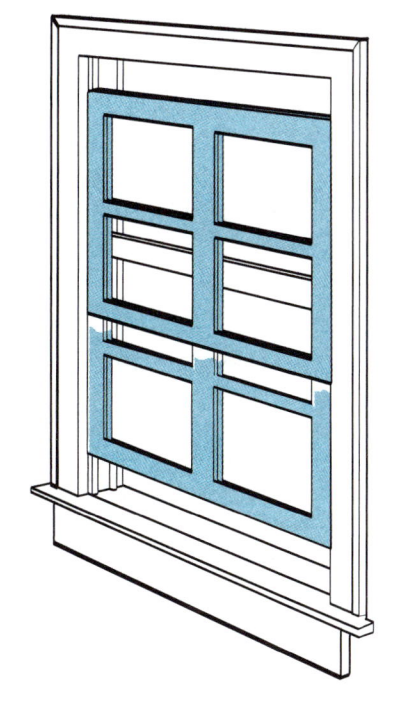

Painting a Door

You can paint a door in place or take it off its hinges. To take it off its hinges, leave the hinge plates in place. Tap a nail up into a hinge barrel to raise the hinge pin. When the pin is high enough, remove it with your fingers or grip the shaft with a pair of pliers and tap the pliers up with a hammer. Do the lower hinge first. Note that some pins are not removable, in which case you have to remove the hinge plates by removing the screws.

You can remove the lock and strike plate (see "Replacing a Lock" in Chapter 4, "Doors and Windows"), or you can leave them in place and cut in around them with a sash or trim brush.

If the door has never been painted, you need to paint the bottom edge. If it has been painted once, there is no need to paint it again.

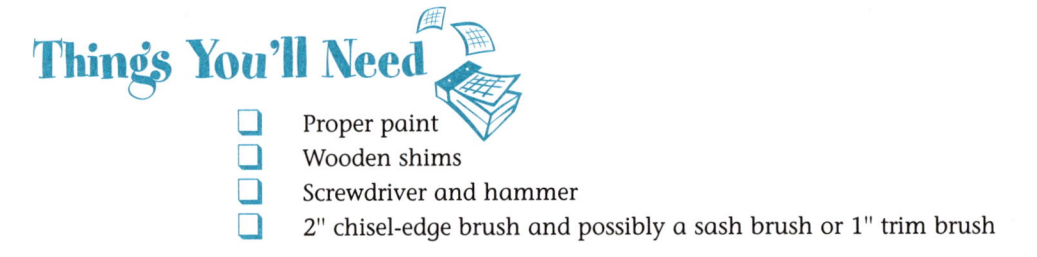

Things You'll Need

- ❑ Proper paint
- ❑ Wooden shims
- ❑ Screwdriver and hammer
- ❑ 2" chisel-edge brush and possibly a sash brush or 1" trim brush

Painting a door also follows a sequence:

1. Paint any panels first, the horizontal portions, and then the vertical portions.
2. If you're painting the door in place, wedge the door open with shims beneath the bottom edge. Paint the latch edge the same color as the door color on the side toward which the door swings.
3. Paint the door trim, top to bottom. Paint the jamb the same color as the trim up to and including the narrow face of the doorstop against which the door comes to rest; the other portion of the stop should be the color of the trim in the other room, as shown in Figure 7.8.

Taking a Break and Cleaning Up

When you want to stop painting for just a bit or overnight, there are several things you can do to keep the brushes and rollers in good condition.

If you are going to stop painting for less than 20 minutes, you don't need to clean or protect your brush or roller. Rest your brush on the paint can rim. You can set a coat hanger across the top of the can as a partial support if you like. Perch rollers on the grid portion of a roller tray.

If you are going to resume painting the next day, you can avoid cleaning brushes and rollers with a couple of simple tasks:

CHAPTER 7　Painting and Wallpapering　　167

FIGURE 7.8
Paint the narrow face of the doorstop against which the door comes to rest the same color as the trim in the room into which the door swings. Paint the jamb between here and the door the same color.

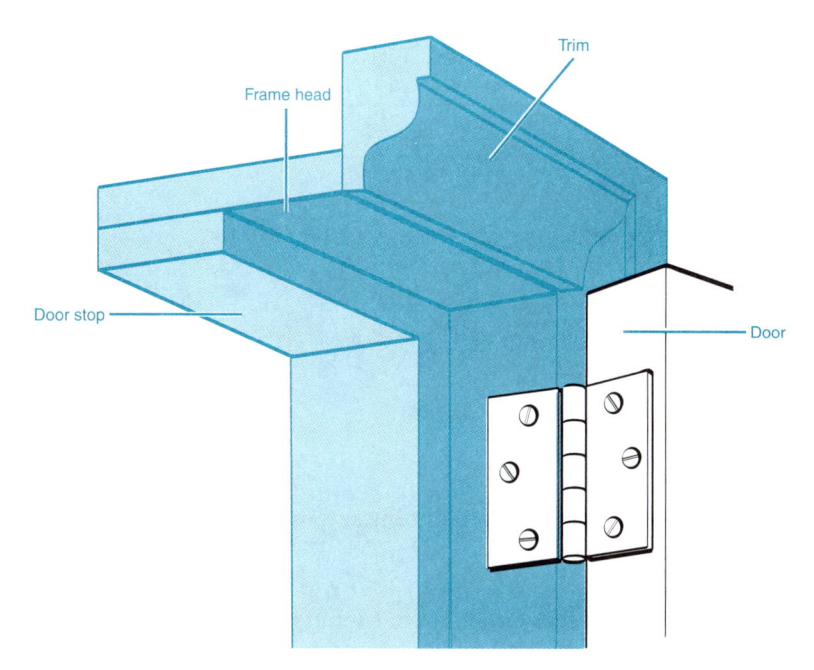

Labels: Trim, Frame head, Door stop, Door

Things You'll Need

- ☐ Rag
- ☐ Aluminum foil
- ☐ Hammer or rubber mallet
- ☐ Coat hanger

1. If there is paint left in a roller tray, pour it back into a paint can.
2. Tap the lid back on the paint can with a hammer or rubber mallet for a good seal. If there is paint in the rim's channel, cover the top of the paint can with a rag or newspaper before you hammer it down; otherwise you might be splattered.
3. Stroke a paintbrush on newspaper until no more paint comes out. Wrap the bristles up to the ferrule in aluminum foil. Fold the aluminum foil back at the bottom to make a good seal, but without crimping the bristles. Make a fairly good seal at the ferrule. Place the brush in a freezer.
4. Leave a roller on its frame. Wrap it in aluminum foil and place the roller and frame in the freezer.
5. The next day, remove the brush and roller from the freezer and allow them several minutes to thaw. You can leave a wrapped brush or roller in a freezer for several days.

Cleaning Up After Latex Painting

Remember that your brushes and rollers are only as good as their last cleaning. With proper care, these tools can last a lifetime; if they're abused, they can be ruined in a day.

Things You'll Need

- ❑ Paper towels
- ❑ Bristle comb
- ❑ Brush spinner
- ❑ Dishwasher detergent
- ❑ Stiff paper

1. Wipe out reusable paint buckets with dry paper towels. Finish with damp paper towels.
2. Wipe brushes and rollers as dry as you can make them.
3. Hold brushes under warm running water, working your fingers gently through the bristles.
4. Work a bristle comb through the bristles.
5. If you have a brush spinner, use it to spin brushes inside a bucket or empty paint can to help expel water. Comb the brush again and let it dry.
6. When the paintbrush is dry, place it in its original stiff paper holder—or wrap it gently in kraft paper—and hang it on a nail.
7. Hold the roller under warm running water and massage it with your hand until the water runs clear. Use a bit of dishwasher detergent if you like.
8. Dry the roller by rolling it on newspaper. Set it on end to dry thoroughly.
9. When it is dry, wrap it in heavy paper or in a perforated plastic bag. Store it on end. Alternatively, when your painting job is done, throw the roller away and use a new one for your next large paint roller job.
10. Wash your skin with soap and water.

Cleaning Up After Alkyd Painting

Cleaning up after work with alkyd paints is more troublesome, but the result needs to be the same: brushes and rollers that are ready for the next job.

> **caution** Observe all safety requirements with solvents:
> - Work in a ventilated area or wear a respirator.
> - Protect skin with rubber gloves and a long-sleeved shirt.
> - Keep solvents away from open flames and pilot lights.
> - Read the can label for instructions on disposal. Do not pour solvents out on the ground or down a drain. Call your community's hazardous waste office to learn how it prefers proper disposal.
> - Do not leave solvent-soaked rags in a heap. Wash them or let them air outdoors, then dispose of them in the trash.

CHAPTER 7   Painting and Wallpapering

Use the solvent (paint thinner) recommended on the paint's label; they can vary owing to the different solvents used in individual paints.

Pro's Tip You can use solvent several times. When solvent gets cloudy, pour it into a large coffee can and continue to do so as you clean your brushes and rollers with fresh solvent, as many times as needed until the brush and roller are clean. Cap the coffee container tightly. After a few days, the paint pigment within the solvent settles to the bottom of the can. Without disturbing the sediment, pour the top four fifths of solvent into a fresh can and cap it tightly for use after the next job. Dispose of the first can with the sediment in it.

Things You'll Need

- ❑ Paper towels
- ❑ Rubber gloves
- ❑ Coffee cans and tennis ball cans
- ❑ Paint solvent recommended by paint manufacturer
- ❑ Bristle comb
- ❑ Brush spinner
- ❑ Dishwasher detergent
- ❑ Stiff paper

Put on your rubber gloves; then follow these steps:

1. Use dry paper towels to wipe out paint pails and roller trays of as much paint as possible. Use paper towels dampened with solvent to wipe them clean.
2. Swirl brushes in a coffee can half filled with solvent. Knead the bristles with your gloved fingers. Pour cloudy solvent into another coffee can, and pour clean solvent into the original can; continue this until the solvent is tinted only slightly by the paint in the brush.
3. Remove solvent from the brush with a brush spinner if you have one.
4. Wash the brush with warm, soapy water and hang it on a nail to dry. When it is dry, place it in its original stiff paper container or wrap it in kraft paper.
5. Dip rollers in solvent in a paint tray or tennis ball can. Knead the nap with your gloved fingers. Replace the solvent periodically until the roller barely tints it.
6. Dry the roller on newspaper and then set it on end to dry thoroughly. When it is dry, store it in heavy paper or a perforated plastic bag.
7. Remove your gloves; then clean your skin with solvent, followed by a good washing with warm, soapy water.

tip Do not let brushes sit in cans of solvent; it bends the bristles. If paint has partly dried in the bristles and you want to let a paintbrush soak, rig a coathanger wire holder suspended on either side of the can so the bristles enter the solvent but the ends are suspended above the container's bottom.

Hiring a Professional Painter

Call a professional painter when you don't have the time to do it yourself. Painting takes lots of time, and proper preparation takes two or three times the hours put into actual painting. Likely, you can do the work as well or better than a professional; you are much more interested in seeing straight lines along windows and the general appearance of your home than any contractor. But after all, a contractor can bring in a crew and get the job done in several days.

If you consider hiring a contractor, follow these guidelines:

- Get recommendations from neighbors and paint stores.
- Walk through the rooms with an estimator.
- Ask for a separate quote for the preparation work, and demand the estimates in writing.
- Require that the painter use the best paints, find out if the finish coat will be scrubbable, and ask that the paint type be written into the contract (about 85% of a painting contract is for labor and only 15% for paint, so you should get the best paint for the job).

To do list

- ☐ Gather essential tools and supplies.
- ☐ Choose the kind of wallpaper to use.
- ☐ Prepare a room for wallpapering.
- ☐ Lay out where the strips will go.
- ☐ Paste strips to the walls.
- ☐ Move around corners, windows, and other objects.

Working with Wallpaper

You might think that wallpapering is too difficult to tackle, but homeowners do it all the time, and to very good effect. Wallpapers are easier than ever to apply—and even take down, such as when a nursery is upgraded to a child's room. It's probably best to begin on a simple space like a hall or rectangular room. Then with that kind of experience behind you, the rest of the home beckons. In the following sections, you learn about the tools and equipment you'll use when wallpapering and how to get the walls and room ready for the job. You'll also learn how to hang wallpaper on flat surfaces and around corners, windows, and other wall openings.

Gathering Your Wallpapering Tools and Equipment

Figure 7.9 shows some of the tools and equipment you'll use when wallpapering. You might already have some of these items on hand; others you might choose to rent, rather than buy:

- **Pasting table**—You can rent one from a wallpaper store or make one with two saw horses and smooth wood. An adequate one is 6 feet long and 30 inches wide.
- **Wallpaper scissors**—These should be large, sharp, and comfortable to grip.
- **Spare razors for your razor or utility knife**—Dull razors can tear wallpaper, so change the blades often.
- **Water tray**—A water tray is a narrow container used for soaking rolls of prepasted wallpaper.
- **Paste, paste bucket, and brush**—Paste comes premixed or as a powder you mix with water; use one recommended by the manufacturer of the wallpaper you are using. If you're using paste, you'll also need a paste bucket and brush for mixing the paste and applying it to the backs of wallpaper strips.
- **Smoothing brush**—A long brush with short bristles, it smoothes the paper after the paper is on the wall.
- **Seam roller**—This small, handheld roller smoothes and presses the wallpaper at seams.
- **Large sponge**—Use a large sponge to smooth the wallpaper and wipe away paste that has gotten onto the pattern side.
- **Bubble stick, a level, or a plumb line**—A *bubble stick* is a lightweight level. Any level you use should be 4 feet long. A *plumb line* or *bob* is essentially a weight and a string by which you can draw vertical lines on walls that are straight up and down (plumb).
- **Tools for removing wallpaper**—These include scrapers (a 4" blade also helps in the trimming process for new wallpaper), any of several types of scoring or perforation tools that pierce old wallpaper for water or steam removal treatment, and possibly a rentable steamer. Scoring tools have teeth that are pulled across the old wallpaper, whereas perforation tools have disks with points that are rolled across and make holes in the old wallpaper.

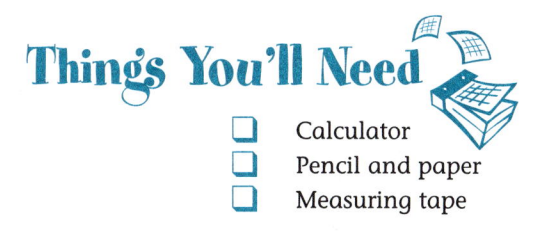

Things You'll Need

- [ ] Calculator
- [ ] Pencil and paper
- [ ] Measuring tape

Choosing and Buying Wallpaper

Most wallpaper is sold in lots of two rolls, called *bolts*. Make sure the rolls you buy are from the same printing run so the colors match.

When you wallpaper a room, you generally must cut and hang the pieces so the pattern matches along all the seams. Your first wallpapering jobs should probably be ones called *random texture* and *random match*. With these choices, you actually won't have to match designs along the seams, and you use the least amount of paper. Next in simplicity is called *small pattern*, although these require some matching. The pattern is relatively easy to line up and requires minimal excess paper. The most difficult to deal with is called *large pattern*; you might have to cut away large amounts of paper to match one strip's pattern with the next, so papering with a large pattern can require more rolls. If you want to use a large pattern, ask your wallpaper dealer about the need for extra wallpaper.

Wallpaper comes in a variety of types. *Vinyls*, including fabric-backed vinyl and paper-backed vinyl, are very popular because they are fairly easy to work with. Heavy-duty vinyls are used in damp locations such as kitchens and baths or where cleaning is frequent. Foils are reflective and brighten a room, but they show wall imperfections more than do vinyls so wall preparation needs to be more careful. In addition, they can be difficult to handle. *Organic* types are made from grass cloth and burlap. *Flocked*, *embossed*, and *hand-printed paper* can be exacting and unsuitable for a beginning wallpaper project.

FIGURE 7.9

Wallpapering tools are small and large. You need sharp blades for trimming wallpaper, a level or plumb bob for indicating true vertical, sturdy scissors, a large sponge, a smoothing brush, and a seam roller to press down seams. If you are removing wallpaper, you need at least one kind of scraper. If you are using paste, you need a paste bucket, and if you are using prepasted wallpaper, you need a water tray. Largest of the equipment is a pasting table, which is often available at wallpaper stores

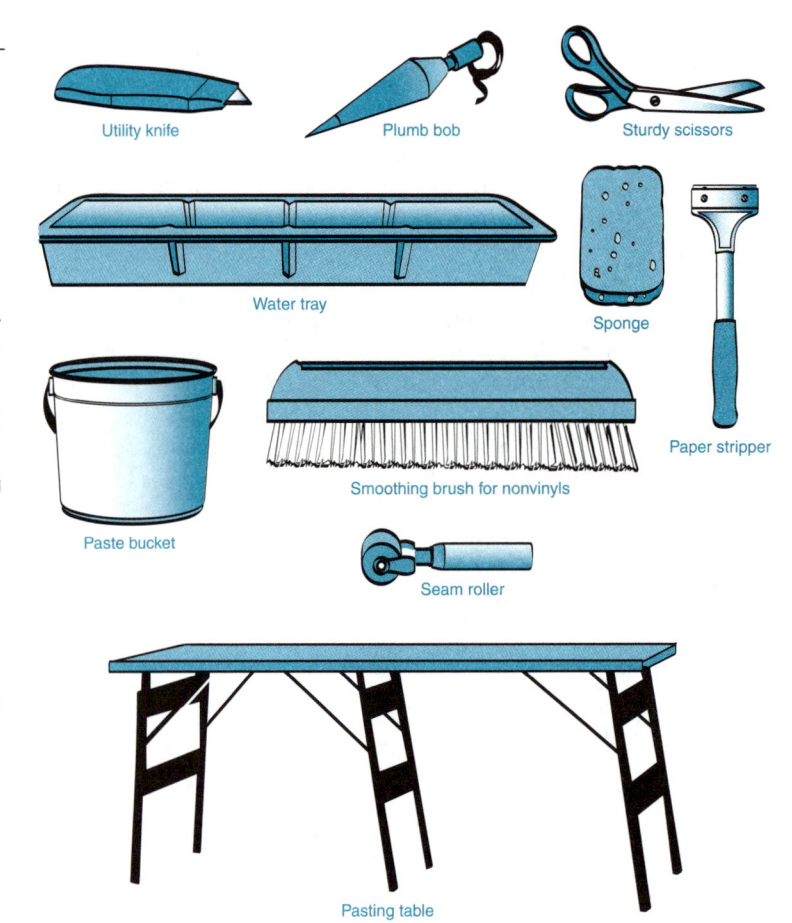

CHAPTER 7 **Painting and Wallpapering**   173

To determine the number of rolls you will need, measure the width and length of the room. Multiply by two and multiply again by the height of the room from the baseboard top to the ceiling. Subtract square footage for doors and windows: 21 square feet for a door and 15 for a window if you want a rough estimate. Divide the square footage by 30 to get a figure for the number of single rolls you will need. Always round up—for example, if the number you get from the division is 7.4, buy eight rolls. Always buy more than you think you will need. Some stores refund money on unopened rolls and, if you have to buy more later, you can end up with rolls slightly mismatched in color.

Things You'll Need

- ❏ Scrapers
- ❏ Sandpaper
- ❏ Cleaning solutions, as appropriate (bleach, soap, water, and so on)
- ❏ Sponges and rags
- ❏ Spackling compound/plaster, as necessary
- ❏ Liquid deglosser, as necessary
- ❏ Vacuum and sponge mop
- ❏ Paint, brushes, and rollers, as necessary

Getting Your Room and Walls Ready for Wallpapering

Like paint, wallpaper should be applied to smooth, clean surfaces. Consult Chapter 3 for how to repair plaster and drywall gouges. Also, read "Preparing the Surfaces," earlier in this chapter, to learn how to handle smaller repairs. Figure on two days to strip wallpaper from a 12' × 15' room, prep the walls, and apply new wallpaper. After the walls are prepped, you also need to organize the room for the most efficient work.

General Wall Preparation

Different wallpapers require different surface preparations. Consult with your wallpaper supplier about the requirements for the paper you are considering buying. Some papers can be pasted to existing papers so long as the existing paper is well bonded and not more than three layers thick. Some papers require a lining paper applied to the walls first. Following are general wall conditions and the preparations needed for each:

- **Unpainted drywall or unpainted plaster**—Paint first with a latex or alkyd primer.
- **Latex paint**—Sand the surface with fine sandpaper.
- **Flat oil-based paint**—Wash the paint with a mild detergent and then rinse. See cleaning advice in "Preparing the Surfaces," earlier in this chapter.
- **Glossed oil-based paint**—Sand the paint or use a liquid deglosser (also described in "Preparing the Surfaces") to roughen its surface.

Leave wallpapers that are well adhered or that would lead to your damaging the walls in a removal attempt. Follow these steps to prepare the surface for a new layer of wallpaper:

1. Glue down curling corners.
2. If the old wallpaper is a shiny vinyl or foil, sand it.
3. Seal the old wallpaper with a glue called wallpaper size, which comes as a liquid or a powder you mix with water. Apply it like paint with a brush or roller.

Things You'll Need

- ❑ Knife
- ❑ 4" flexible wall scraper
- ❑ Large garbage pail
- ❑ Bucket for water, as necessary
- ❑ Large sponge
- ❑ Perforating tool, liquid paper remover, or a rentable steam stripper, as necessary
- ❑ Wallpaper size and brush or roller if papering over old wallpaper.

Removing Wallpaper

If your walls have wallpaper that should be removed (three layers thick or poorly bonded), there are various methods you can use. Some wallpapers are meant to peel off; these include some Mylars, vinyls, and vinyl-coated papers, typically called *strippable* wallpapers. So, try peeling first. Use a knife point to work under a top corner of a piece. Pull down and close to the wall, not out. Strippable wallpaper should come off in whole sheets. Some might leave behind a fuzzy residue on the walls. Leave it because it helps the next wallpaper bond better.

Some papers can be stripped dry with a scraping tool—you cut through the wallpaper with a utility knife, work the blade of a flexible wall scraper underneath it, and start scraping up under the paper. This is the preferred method for a wall of drywall, which can be damaged by using wet methods such as water or steam.

If handstripping or dry stripping does not work, proceed as follows:

1. Perforate the wallpaper with a wallpaper scoring or perforation tool.
2. Use a large sponge to apply warm water to a section of wallpaper and allow it to soak in for 10 minutes.
3. Use a 4" flexible blade scraper to scrape away paper. If water alone is not doing the job, adding detergent might help.

    If stronger means are necessary, wallpaper stores sell liquid paper remover that can be applied to the wallpaper. Wear rubber gloves and ventilate the room if you use one of these.

CHAPTER 7 Painting and Wallpapering   175

If all else fails, rent a steamer. These heat water to steam and conduct it through a hose to a flat, perforated plate. Fill the steamer with water and allow it to heat up (the steamer will have an indicator). Hold the plate to the old wallpaper to soak the old paper and adhesive with steam. Use the scraper to strip off the section of steamed wallpaper.

> **note** The preceding instructions are general guidelines only. Consult with your paper supplier about what other preparation should be made before applying the paper you have in mind to the wall surface you have.

4. After the paper has been removed, allow the wall to dry thoroughly. Patch gouges with drywall joint compound and sand smooth.

Marking and Setting Up the Room

Wallpapering calls for planning. Large patterns especially need to be started with care. So must the position of the last strip as well as planning for large obstructions such as doors and bookcases.

Preparing a room is like preparing for painting but not as intensive. You need to remove the curtains and move furniture out of the room or away from the walls. Place a pasting table in the middle of the room, and then lay down dropcloths where you will have water trays or water buckets. Turn off electrical power and remove the switch plates and outlet covers. Cover outlet faces with masking tape. You might have to bring in lighting from another room by using electrical extension cords.

Things You'll Need

- ❑ 4-foot level
- ❑ Tape measure
- ❑ Plumb bob
- ❑ Roll of chosen wallpaper
- ❑ Pencil or other erasable marking instrument
- ❑ Pasting table
- ❑ Dropcloths

1. Choose a position for the first piece. Large patterns require the most consideration. Center them over a fireplace if there is one in the room. If not, center the pattern between two windows opposite the main entry door to the room.
2. Mark the tentative location of the first strip and then mark the locations of each subsequent strip. Strips should not end exactly at an interior corner but have at least a 1/4" wraparound; outside corners should have 1 1/2" wraparounds. The last strip will not exactly meet the pattern of the first, so it should be in an inconspicuous place; over a door is a good option. Avoid a strip's edge coming within 6" of a window or door.

3. If the first sequence does not work out, erase your marks and begin in another location, testing this one.
4. When you are satisfied with the planned sequence of strips, mark the location of the first roll. With a level or a plumb bob, mark a plumb line 1/4" to the right of the location of the right side of the first roll.
5. Unroll one roll of wallpaper and hold it in place against the wall. If the pattern is large, adjust the roll up and down until you like where the pattern is located vertically. Mark the roll at the baseboard or ceiling to record this height.

FIGURE 7.10
If there is a fireplace breast, center a roll or a seam there and work around to the interior corners. Then move around the room in one direction. If centering is not so important, begin near an inside corner.

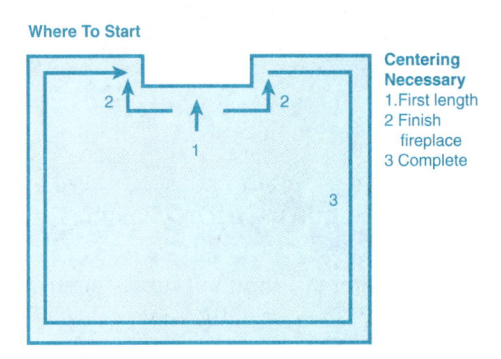

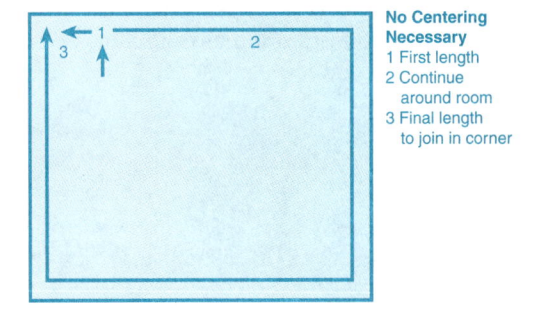

Where To Start

Centering Necessary
1. First length
2. Finish fireplace
3. Complete

No Centering Necessary
1 First length
2 Continue around room
3 Final length to join in corner

Pasting the First Piece

Try to do wallpapering in daylight because you will be able to see adjoining edges better. Lamps create too many shadows.

If you are using paste, buy a type recommended by the wallpaper manufacturer. Mix it with water in a 5-gallon bucket according to the paste maker's instructions. You can apply it with a wide paint brush or a short-nap or sponge roller, for which you will need a roller tray.

CHAPTER 7   Painting and Wallpapering   177

Things You'll Need

- Wallpaper
- Straight edge
- Cutting tool (razors and/or scissors)
- Plumb bob with chalked plumb line
- Smoothing brush and large sponge
- Water tray or paste, paste bucket, roller trap and short-nap or sponge roller

1. Unroll a strip of wallpaper, pattern side up, onto your table. Cut the strip 4" longer than the distance between the ceiling and the top of the baseboard.
2. Unroll the next strip of paper alongside the first. Align the patterns and then cut the second strip so that it is the same length as the first.
3. If your wallpaper is prepasted, roll the first strip pattern side in and place it in a water tray half filled with lukewarm water. Allow the strip to soak for a duration specified by the manufacturer (usually less than a minute). After this time, lift the strip from the water tray and unroll it pattern side down on the table.

   If your wallpaper is not pasted, unroll it on the table pattern side down and apply paste with a clean short-nap paint roller.
4. For either prepasted or hand-pasted wallpaper, gently fold the top half of the strip back on itself and the bottom half back on itself so the pasted side is now on the interior of a large flat loop. This is called *booking* the strip, and it allows the paste to spread, smooth, and cure. Leave the strip in this position for a duration specified by the manufacturer (generally several minutes).
5. Carry the booked strip to the wall. Carry it up the step ladder and unfold the upper section. Position this to the wall 1/4" away from your plumb line and vertically so that about 2" overlaps the ceiling or crown molding. Use the smoothing brush to press and smooth this portion of the strip to the wall (see Figure 7.11).
6. Unfold the lower portion of the strip and align it. The whole edge should be 1/4" away from the plumb line. Smooth the strip with the smoothing brush, working out from the middle. You can make small adjustments by sliding the paper along the wall's surface. If you are far off, remove the strip and try again. Wipe and smooth the strip with a large damp sponge, removing any paste that has reached the pattern side.

Hanging the Second and Subsequent Strips

After you've hung the first strip, you're ready to continue hanging wallpaper around the room. Follow these steps:

FIGURE 7.11

With the lower half still folded, position the upper half alongside the plumb line and with 2" overlap at the ceiling. Smooth the top half with a smoothing brush.

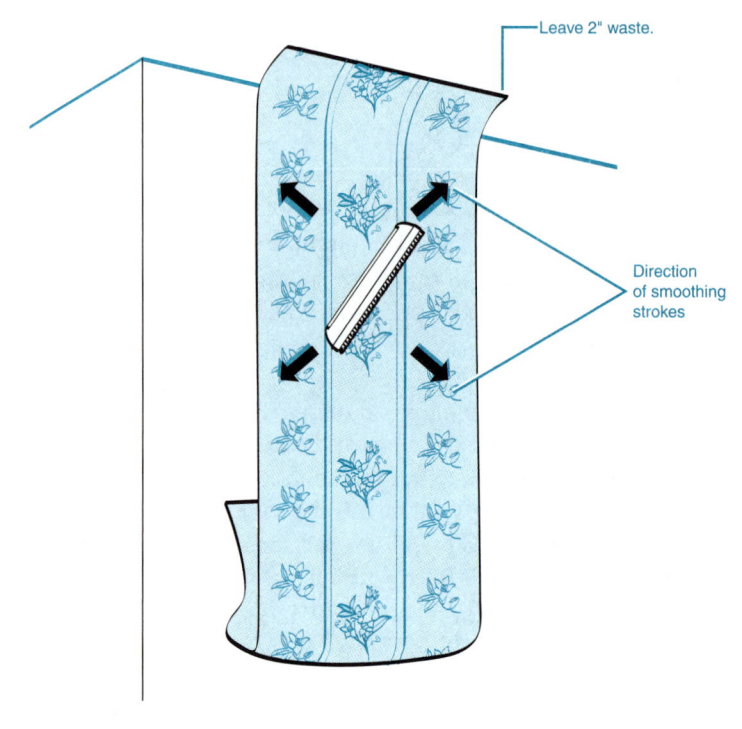

Leave 2" waste.

Direction of smoothing strokes

1. Clean the pasting table of paste and dry it. Shift the second strip to the former location of the first and bring a third into the former place of the second. Shift the third to match the pattern of the second and cut it to length.
2. Paste the second sheet as you did the first and let it cure for the appropriate time.
3. Position the second sheet alongside the first. Shift it until the edges meet; try to move the whole sheet instead of merely stretching the paper near the edge. Smooth the second sheet with the smoothing brush and sponge. Smooth the seam with a sponge or seam roller.
4. Trim the top and bottom of the first strip. A metal straight edge and a very sharp razor suffice for this, as shown in Figure 7.12. Alternatively, you can crease the strip at the ceiling and baseboard and then pull it back enough to cut it along the crease with scissors. Repress the areas you have pulled away from the wall.
5. Continue working with strip after strip in this fashion.

Wallpapering an Inside Corner

You might be tempted to end with a strip of wallpaper that aligns exactly along an inside corner, but don't do it. The strip has to go around the corner at least 1/4" for the paste to hold. In addition, corners are rarely so true and plumb that two strips can meet perfectly there. Follow these steps:

CHAPTER 7   Painting and Wallpapering   179

FIGURE 7.12
Hold a wide bladed scraper or a straight edge to the top edge of the strip and cut away the excess with a sharp razor.

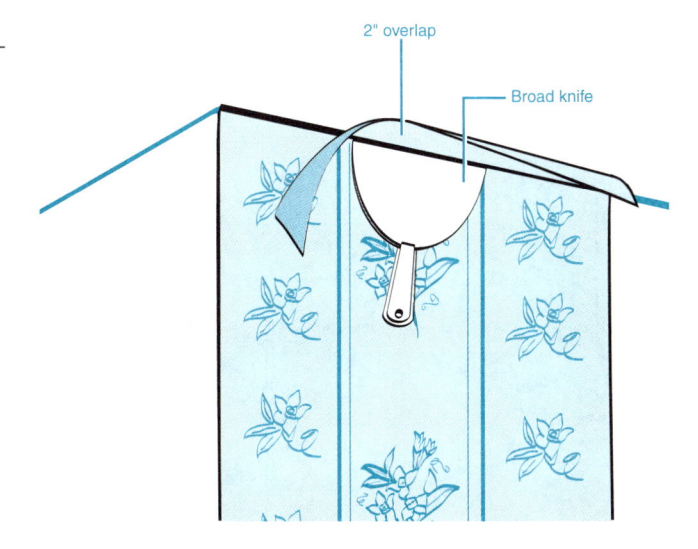

2" overlap

Broad knife

1. When you are less than a strip's width from an inside corner, measure from the last strip edge to the corner at the ceiling, the baseboard, and halfway in between. Add 1/4" to each of these measurements.
2. Cut an unwatered or unpasted strip lengthwise to match these dimensions, and save both halves.
3. Water or paste the first strip and place it in position. Snip the wallpaper at the top and bottom so it turns the corner without buckling. The long cut edge will extend beyond the corner by 1/4".
4. Measure the width of the strip that has been cut away. Mentally add 1/4" to its width at the top, middle, and bottom. Measure these distances on the uncovered wall from the corner, and then mark a plumb line through these marks, as shown in Figure 7.13.
5. Water or paste this strip. Locate it so that its close edge overlaps the previous strip and its other edge runs 1/4" shy of the plumb line. Note: If you are using vinyl wallpaper, use a vinyl-on-vinyl glue available in wallpaper stores for the lap seam.

Papering Around an Outside Corner

Outside corners can be easier than inside ones. But they still require care, and the technique for dealing with them is often the same as for inside corners:

1. Wrap around an outside corner by 1 1/2"–6". You might be able to do this and still have the leading edge of the wrapping strip be plumb.
2. If the leading side of the strip is going to be out of plumb, proceed with the method for an inside corner, as shown in Figure 7.14.
3. When the strip goes up, cut 2" into the top and bottom at the corner's location so the strip can fit around the corner. After hanging the adjoining strip, trim away the excess at the top and baseboard.

FIGURE 7.13

Cut a strip so that all along its length it overlaps around the corner by 1/4". Measure from the corner on the unpapered wall the width of the remaining piece plus 1/4", and draw a plumb line. Paste the remaining piece 1/4" back from the plumb line. Its left edge will overlap the first piece slightly, but this will not be noticeable.

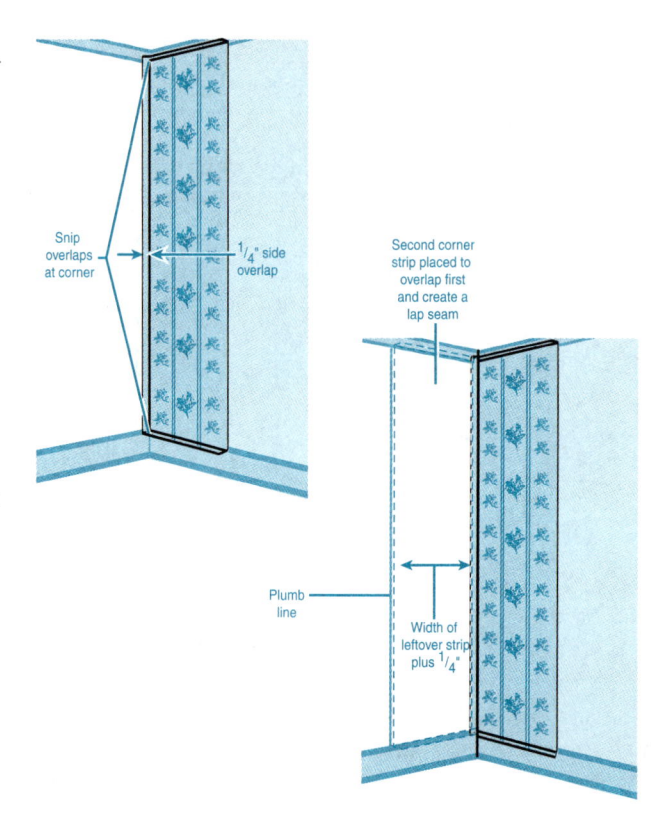

Papering Around Windows, Doors, and Entryways

You will meet windows, doors, and more as you proceed around a room. These are dealt with by careful trimming. Though these steps describe papering around a window, you can use the same process to paper around doors or other openings:

1. When a strip overlaps a window, set it into place as you would a regular strip, aligning its edge with the edge of the last strip hung. With the smoother or sponge, smooth the piece on the wall as close to the window trim as you can without tearing the paper.
2. Cut the strip's portion that covers the window, leaving 2" of overlap along the window trim. Make a 45° slit at the window trim corners to the point where the window trim corner meets the wall, as shown in Figure 7.15.
3. Trim the strip tight against the window trim with a razor or using the scraper/pull/scissors method.
4. At rounded window stool ends, make several adjacent scissor cuts until the wallpaper can lie flat in place against the wall. Trim away excess paper with a razor.

CHAPTER 7   **Painting and Wallpapering**   181

FIGURE 7.14
Wallpapering around outside corners is similar to working around inside corners, but here the wallpaper can extend onto the wall 1 1/2"–6".

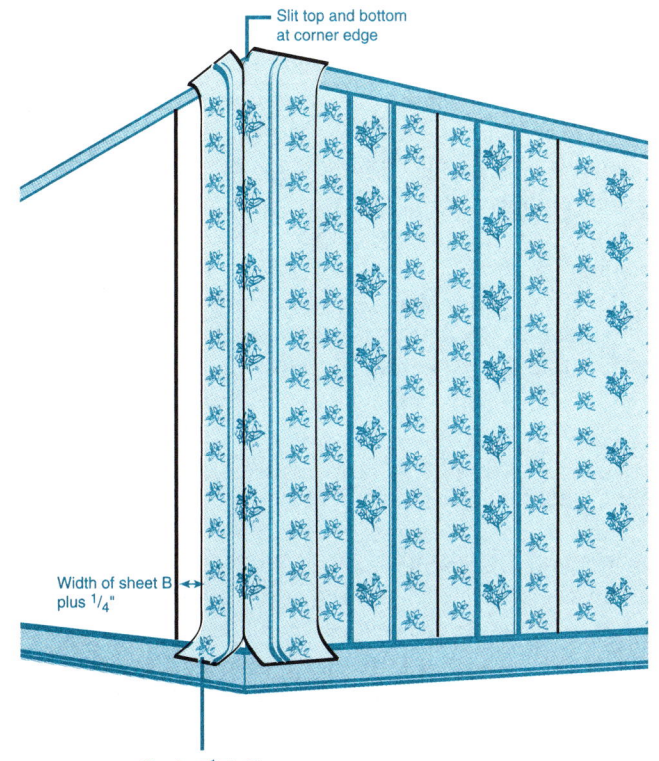

Slit top and bottom at corner edge

Width of sheet B plus 1/4"

Overlap 1 1/2"–6"

FIGURE 7.15
Trim the portion of the strip that covers the window, leaving 2" of overlap. Make a slit cut to the point where the window trim corner meets the wall.

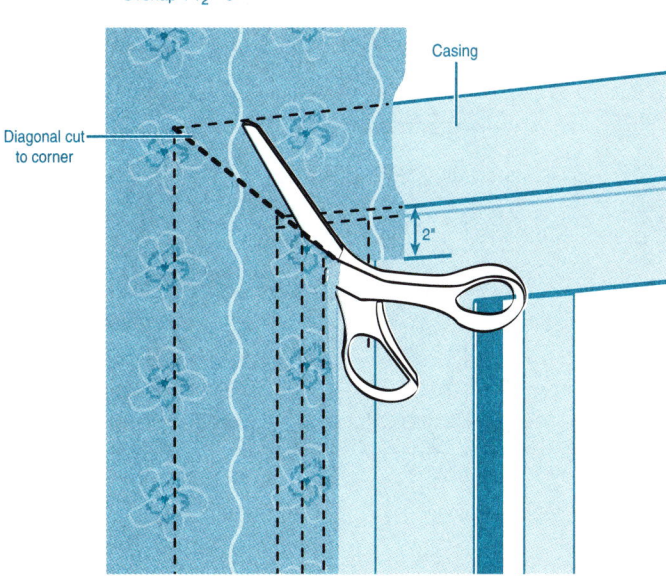

Casing

Diagonal cut to corner

2"

Dealing with Electrical Outlets and Switchplates

Electrical outlet plates and switchplates can be reinstalled as-is over wallpaper. But many people like the look of the plate covered with the pattern of wallpaper and matching the pattern around it. To paper around outlets and switchplates, and to cover the plates with wallpaper, follow these steps:

1. Turn off electrical power and remove the outlet cover or switchplate.
2. Paste the strip of wallpaper in place covering over the outlet or switch opening.
3. Feel for the opening beneath the wallpaper. Use a razor to cut through the wallpaper on both diagonals of the opening. Cut away all the wallpaper over the opening using the inside of the opening as a guide.
4. Reinstall the plate very loosely in its original position—you will have to make a slit for the toggle of a toggle switch. Hopefully the screw or screws are long enough for this; if they are not, use small nails through the screw holes to temporarily hold the plate in place.
5. Set a scrap of wallpaper larger than the cover plate over the cover plate and generally align it with the pattern on the wall. Perfectly align the scrap at the top of the plate with the pattern on the wall; then slip the scrap down 1/8" (doing so allows for the bevel of the plate and divides the very slight mismatch between the top edge and bottom edge). Fold the top of the scrap over the top of the plate and the bottom of the scrap over the bottom enough to make creases, as shown in Figure 7.16.

FIGURE 7.16

With the plate loosely in its place on the wall, match the pattern of the covering scrap to the wallpaper around it. Slip it down 1/8" and crease it over the top and bottom of the plate.

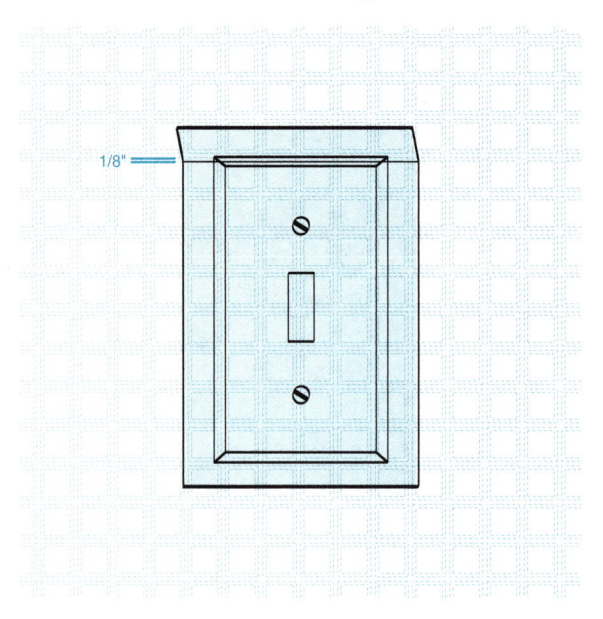

CHAPTER 7 **Painting and Wallpapering**   183

6. Do the same along the left side as you did along the top. Shift the scrap 1/8" to the right. Fold the scrap around the left and right edges enough to make creases.
7. Remove the plate from the wall and remove the scrap from the plate, taking care not to lose the position of the creases. Trim the scrap to fold around the plate by 3/4". Cut the scrap diagonally where the creases meet at the corners to allow for easy folding, as shown in Figure 7.17.
8. Apply paste to the plate and press the scrap to the plate. Fold the scrap around to the back at the creases.
9. Use a razor to cut out an opening for the switch's toggle or the electrical outlets. Press a wire through the screw holes. Reinstall the plate and turn the electrical power back on.

FIGURE 7.17
With the plate removed from the wall, lay it on the scrap with the creases aligned, as described in steps 5 and 6. Trim the scrap to slightly larger than the plate and cut away at a 45° angle at the corner. Paste the plate and crease the scrap around it a final time. Cut out holes for the switch's toggle or electrical outlets and poke the screw holes out.

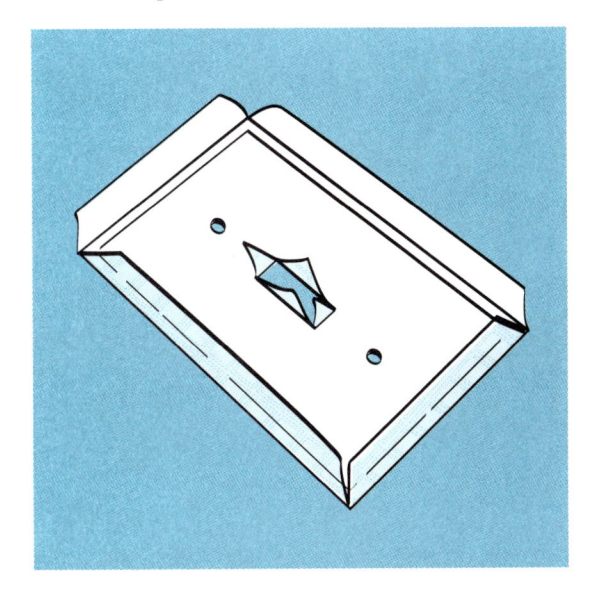

You'll have some cleanup to do when you've finished papering. Wipe the pasting table with water to clean it of all paste. Clean the brushes, scissors, and knives with water and a little household detergent. Wait until the table and tools are dry before putting them away. Wallpaper paste contains a fungicide, so do not pour unused portions down a drain. Instead, treat it as a hazardous waste and dispose of it according to your community's regulations.

Summary

This chapter discussed dramatic ways of altering the appearance of your rooms by painting and wallpapering. We reviewed the kinds of paint and finishes you can choose from and discussed where they are most often used to your best advantage. You learned how to paint whole walls and ceilings with rollers and how to paint doors, windows, and wood trim with brushes.

Wallpaper makes an even more dramatic statement than new paint, and several types lend themselves to do-it-yourselfers, including prepasted types. This chapter showed you how to determine where a pattern starts in a room and how to deal with inside corners, outside corners, windows, and electrical cover plates.

Now that you have made the inside of your home as stunning and vibrant as it can be, it is time to grab the portable radio and move outdoors. In the next chapter, you learn how to handle the chores that homes always demand for proper maintenance and how to undertake improvements—such as staining a deck and painting the exterior—that will make your home look great.

Outdoor Repairs and Maintenance

In this chapter:

* Repair and seal concrete and asphalt.
* Clean and stain a wooden deck.
* Repoint brick.
* Repair siding.
* Paint exterior walls.
* Repair and replace roof shingles.
* Clean gutters.

Home repairs means outside as well as inside. Some homeowners welcome that, and some do not. In any event, the best time to work outside is on beautiful autumn and spring days. Bring a radio or a CD player with you, and the weather almost makes the work a pleasure.

Weather and time are the two main instigators of outdoor repairs. Concrete and asphalt eventually crack and crumble along the top surface. Sun and wind wear at siding paint, so new coats have to be applied, or even some siding replaced. Higher up, leaves clog gutters, which can also be dented and dislodged. In addition, composition shingles eventually thin so that they curl up in a wind or crack. To postpone an entire reroofing job, you can replace these individual shingles that have gone bad.

Some of the outside of your home is horizontal (sidewalks, driveways, decks, and so on); some is vertical (your exterior walls); and some is very high (where the gutters and roofing material are). This is how I have sectioned this chapter: repairs to the horizontal, the vertical, and the high up.

Before we begin, however, let me pass along the first principle of home improvements outdoors: safety. Wear protective gear when using such chemicals as concrete and wood cleaners. Take extra precaution when working on ladders, and if your roof is two stories up or is steep, have professionals make repairs.

To do list

- ❑ Clean and patch concrete and asphalt.
- ❑ Seal concrete walks and drives.
- ❑ Clean wood decking and restain.

Problems Underfoot

Horizontal surfaces take a beating, not just from your feet and automobiles but also from rain, snow, ice, rock salt, and strong sunlight. These troublemakers make concrete, asphalt, and wood split and deteriorate at the surface if not properly protected. Proper preventatives—protective stains for wood and sealers for concrete—serve as coatings that keep the troublemakers from penetrating to where they can make damage. Where damage has already been done, modern science has produced compounds that fill cracks and hollows and that adhere strongly to surrounding undamaged material. Applied properly to clean areas, these are stronger than the sound material around them.

But surfaces to be treated have to be free of dirt, grit, grease, and oil. Some have to be dry (wood that has never before been stained) and some damp (concrete that will be receiving a patching compound). Always follow manufacturers' instructions.

The other unique element of working outdoors is the weather. Watch your weather report. Some compounds will not adhere properly if rained on shortly after application; some will be spoiled if subjected too soon to strong, hot sun or a hard freeze.

Things You'll Need

- ❑ Goggles
- ❑ Patching compounds in tubes or bags
- ❑ Cleaners and stains for decks
- ❑ Cold chisel and hammer
- ❑ Rubber gloves
- ❑ Work gloves
- ❑ Pan for mixing concrete or asphalt patching compounds
- ❑ Garden hose
- ❑ Roller and roller pan
- ❑ Square trowel
- ❑ For large areas, an 8 lb. sledgehammer

CHAPTER 8   Outdoor Repairs and Maintenance

Fixing Cracks and Bad Patches in a Driveway or Walk

Concrete walks and driveways often develop cracks owing to weight pressed from above or ground shifting from below. Narrow cracks—up to 1/2" wide and 1/2" deep—can be filled with a polyurethane material available in caulking gun cartridges, although these do not match the surrounding concrete in color and texture.

For larger cracks and damaged areas, buy premixed concrete patching materials. These include polymers that make bonds stronger than regular concrete and cure more quickly. You get a better grip with these products if you remove all damage back to sound concrete or asphalt and if you undercut the top surface so the patch cannot later lift out of the damaged area.

> **caution** Wear heavy gloves and goggles when working with any tool that can make concrete chips fly. Wear rubber gloves when working with concrete mixes because the contents can irritate the skin.

Work on days of moderate temperature with no rain in the forecast. Both freezing temperatures and hot or rainy days can interfere with the curing of the patching materials.

Patching asphalt is much the same as patching concrete. For small cracks, use a compound—they are black—available in caulking gun cartridges. For larger patching, buy premixed asphalt patching compound.

Follow these steps:

1. If the crack does not have crumbling sides and you do not think you can reasonably expand it, patch it using a caulking gun and patching compound in a caulking gun cartridge. Clean all dirt and loose material out of the crack as best you can. Use the caulking gun to squeeze the compound into the crack and smooth the compound with a putty knife.
2. For larger cracks, wear gloves and goggles. Use a cold chisel and hammer to cut into the crack, making it wider at the bottom than at the surface, as shown in Figure 8.1.
3. Clean out all the grit and dampen the area to be patched.
4. Wearing rubber gloves, add water to premixed concrete patching material. Avoid mixing more than you can work with in 30 minutes. Wait several minutes per manufacturer's instructions for the mixture to set up.
5. Trowel the mix into the damaged area. If the area of damage is more than 1/2" deep, make a primary layer of 1/2" and let it cure for one day, or according to the manufacturer's instructions. Add another layer on another day until the patching material is as high as the surrounding concrete. Then use a square trowel to smooth and level it.

> **note** When dealing with a large surface area of damaged concrete, break up the surface damage by lifting an 8 lb. sledge hammer and letting it drop of its own weight. Wear goggles. Sweep out the area with a stiff brush, and proceed as in steps 3 and 4.

FIGURE 8.1
Wearing gloves and goggles, chip out the damaged concrete. Try to undercut the solid concrete so that the new layer has a good anchor (see inset).

Sealing Concrete

Concrete is porous and absorbs water. In freeze-dry cycles, the water can freeze and crack off upper layers. Rock salt placed on sidewalks to melt ice in winter can also damage concrete. So can grease, oils, and acids. A preventative measure is to apply a sealer to the concrete and recoat about every six months. Popular sealers are water-based and contain either acrylics or silicone. One gallon covers 150–200 square feet and dries in about an hour.

If you would like to clean the concrete before you seal it, you can buy and apply concrete cleaners that brighten it. And although they might not completely remove oil and grease stains, they will make the stains lighter and less noticeable.

Things You'll Need

- ❑ Liquid concrete sealer
- ❑ Roller or squeegee with extension handle

To seal concrete, follow these steps:
1. Sweep the concrete clear of all dirt and debris.
2. Wear rubber gloves and rubber boots. Pour out a portion of sealer onto the concrete. Work it into the pores of the concrete with a roller or squeegee, and then move excess to the next area to be covered.

Staining a Deck

From the moment wood is placed horizontally to make a deck, it is under attack from natural forces. These include ultraviolet light, moisture, insects, and the fungi we call mold and mildew. Some people like to let their deck wood weather naturally, turning gray. But this is a risky tactic because even woods renowned for resistance to decay—redwood, cedar, and cypress, for example—are prone to degeneration over time. The family deck can therefore begin to look pretty dingy, if not in need of costly repair, when left for a long time without maintenance.

The remedy is to occasionally clean the deck and then coat it with a finish that protects its surfaces from natural enemies. Most people use a semitransparent stain made especially for decks. Such stains offer a good measure of protection as well as letting some of the natural surface of the wood show through. Paints and polyurethanes should be avoided because they trap moisture below the surface, moisture that then presses from below to cause pops and splits in the paint or coating. Stains more readily allow moisture to escape.

Some stains are heavy stains and do not readily let the wood grain show through. Lighter or semitransparent stains show more of the grain. These are more popular, although they generally need more frequent reapplication. Both come in a wide range of colors. Note that if mildew has been a problem on your deck in the past, you can buy a small package of fungicide at the stain dealer to pour into the stain before you apply it. The additive will resist further mold and mildew discolorations.

Take the advice of the manufacturer and, before you roll stain out onto the whole deck, test the new stain on an out-of-the-way place. Let it dry and see how you like it. Some stain companies will send you sample colors in small containers, and you can use these for testing the colors to see which you like best.

The surface of the wood should be clean and, for most stains, dry before a stain goes on it. Manufacturers make deck wood cleaners that remove stains and brighten the wood in anticipation of a stain being applied after the wood has dried. Use an acid-type cleaner (sodium hypochlorite, calcium hypochlorite, or sodium percarbonate) on decks discolored with mold and mildew; use a bleach (oxalic acid) to lighten wood that has grayed with age.

If your deck has already been stained, try to determine the manufacturer of the stain and whether the stain was water- or oil-based. It's always best to use a cleaner and new stain that is compatible with what has already been applied to the pores of the wood because the bond will last longer.

Things You'll Need

- ❏ Hose
- ❏ Bristle brush with a long handle extension
- ❏ Gloves and goggles
- ❏ Paint roller with a long handle extension
- ❏ Paint brush
- ❏ Possibly sandpaper and a power sander

Follow these steps:

1. Sweep the deck. Apply a wood cleaner following the manufacturer's instructions. Normally, this means diluting the cleaner, applying the solution to the wood, waiting an appropriate amount of time, and then scouring with a scrub brush before hosing the solution off.

2. Sand stubborn stains with 80-grit sandpaper. Where the stains are large or many, use a power sander.
3. Apply the stain according to the manufacturer's instructions. These might call for the deck to not have been exposed to rain or water for several days and in a period when rain is not expected for several days more.
4. Use a brush to stain around deck posts and other objects. Then move to using a pan and roller. Roll on stain to a manageable area and then go over the applied stain with a paintbrush to work it into the grain of the wood. Use a brush appropriate for either water or oil base.

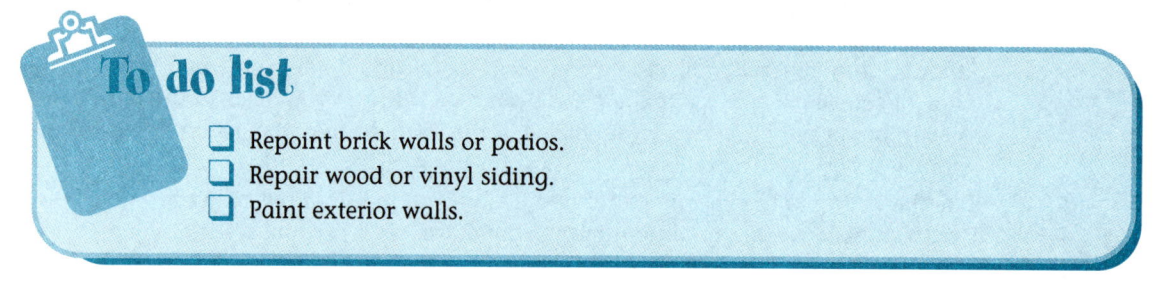

To do list

- ❏ Repoint brick walls or patios.
- ❏ Repair wood or vinyl siding.
- ❏ Paint exterior walls.

Working on Walls

Like sidewalks, driveways, and patios, walls can take a beating. But it's the wise homeowner who inspects the walls regularly and makes the small repairs, as well as applies a protective coating of paint when and where needed. As with most home improvement work, here a stitch in time saves nine.

A wall—whether of brick, wood siding, vinyl siding, or other—keeps rain, wind, and critters out of your home. If there are chinks in that armor, water can penetrate into the wall and cause rot—which is expensive to cut away and repair later. In addition, wind can bring in cold air that makes the heating system work harder than it should, or small animals or insects can reach living spaces or hiding places where they can do extensive damage.

Walk around your home twice a year and inspect the walls carefully. Keep an eye out for holes near the ground where animals could enter. Trim bushes and branches so they do not rub against walls, transferring rain water to them or scraping away their paint in a high wind. Check to be sure the paint isn't splitting on wooden siding, which typically should be painted every four to seven years.

Even brick, which seems set for the ages, has troubles when made into a wall. The mortar that holds the bricks together can deteriorate over time. Loose mortar needs to be scraped away and replaced with new before rain or wind can find a path from the outside in.

Working on brick walls and siding requires some tools that might not otherwise be in your toolkit. These are

- **Joint filler and jointer**—A joint filler, also called a *pointing tool*, has a wooden handle and a blade a little narrower than a mortar joint. It pushes

CHAPTER 8   Outdoor Repairs and Maintenance   191

mortar into the joint. A *jointer* is a tool with two blades, each of a different profile for smoothing mortar in the joint. The most common mortar joint profile is concave, so the blade for this one is convex. Other mortar joints might be V-shaped, flush, and the like.
- **Zip tool for vinyl siding**—This small hand tool helps separate one vinyl siding piece from another and conversely zips them together again. It is indispensable for vinyl siding work and is available where vinyl siding is sold.
- **Ladders, ladder braces, and scaffolding**—For work on walls, such as painting or repointing, sturdy ladders and ladder accessories are essential.

Things You'll Need

- ❏ Stiff brush
- ❏ Gloves and goggles
- ❏ Cold chisel and hammer
- ❏ Garden hose or water spray bottle
- ❏ Mortar mix and water
- ❏ Small trowel
- ❏ Flat board or hawk
- ❏ Joint filler and jointer

Repointing Brick

Brick, concrete block, cinder block, and more are held together with mortar, a combination of cement and sand. Mortar joints deteriorate, beginning with thin cracks and eventually crumbling. Mortar starting to go bad should be repaired. It will only get worse, and if it lets water into and behind the wall, greater damage and repair await.

The remedy is replacing the bad mortar—a task called *repointing* or *tuckpointing* in masonry parlance. The method calls for removing deteriorated mortar back to an area where secure bonding can take place and then pressing in new mortar. This work can be done on brick walls, as well as on flat surfaces such as patios.

> **tip** A flat board with a handle below comes in handy when jointing; you use the board to hold a quantity of wet mortar as you're applying it to the joints. Make one yourself or buy one (they are called *hawks*).
> If you have lots of repointing to do, you can also buy a chisel that more neatly fits the dimensions of the mortar joint than the one in your toolbox.

You can buy mortar to match the current mortar in your wall or on your patio. Take as large a piece of mortar as you can to a masonry store, where the salespeople can sell you the mortar and a colorant. Before you apply any of it to the wall or patio, mix up a small batch of mortar and colorant and let it dry. Compare its color to the existing mortar. Adjust colorant as necessary to get a good match.

Follow these steps to repoint bricks:

1. Wear gloves and goggles, and use the cold chisel and hammer to chip out the cracked or crumbly mortar. Clean it out to a depth of at least 3/4". If you reach the end of a brick, extend the cut 1" along it to the next brick; this will help anchor the new mortar.
2. Keep your goggles on. Use a stiff brush to scour out dust and debris. Alternatively, blow the grit out or hose it out.
3. Mix the mortar and colorant you have purchased. The consistency has to be a compromise between too runny (it would flow out of the joint and down the wall) and too stiff (it would be hard to work into position).
4. Spray the area with water. The brick and existing mortar should be wet to make a good bond. But wait until the water is absorbed; do not apply new mortar where there are puddles.
5. Place a batch of mortar on the hawk or board. Hold the hawk or board just under a horizontal joint. Using the joint filler (or alternatively, the jointer), push some mortar into the joint, as shown in Figure 8.2. Compact the mortar well and scrape away excess mortar with a small trowel.
6. Fifteen minutes later or when the mortar just holds a thumbprint, go over the joints with the jointer to shape the mortar so it conforms to the shape of the mortar around it. Shape the vertical joints first and then the horizontal ones. Wet the jointer from time to time. Again, scrape off excess mortar.
7. Keep the new mortar damp for three days by misting it with a hose or spray bottle. After five days, use a stiff brush to scour away mortar stains from the brick.

FIGURE 8.2
Use a joint filler to push mortar from a hawk or horizontal board into the gap of the joint. If you don't have a joint filler, use a small trowel. Press the mortar in well. When the mortar has stiffened slightly, go over it with a jointer to shape its profile.

Where a whole wall has poor mortar joints, the job overwhelms one person. It's best to call a pro in this instance and let him and his crew do the work.

CHAPTER 8   **Outdoor Repairs and Maintenance**   193

> **Pro's Tip:** Make concrete and mortar repairs in moderate weather. Freezing temperatures will interfere with the cement setting up. Similarly, very hot days can dry out the mortar too quickly, resulting in poor bonding.

Fixing Wooden Siding

Wooden siding can crack or be damaged if a heavy object strikes it. Although lapped siding looks tricky to remove, pieces of it can be pulled out and replaced with a bit of awkward sawing. It's some trouble, but not as bad as having to deal with rainwater getting behind siding and into the wall of the home.

The following procedure is for lapped siding, but its principles work for shingle and shake siding as well.

Things You'll Need

- [ ] Cedar shims
- [ ] Back saw
- [ ] Keyhole saw

1. Mark a vertical line up the piece of siding to one side of the damage.
2. Work a cedar shim under the vertical line on the piece of damaged siding. Work a second piece under the piece of siding just above the vertical line so that the end of the shim is almost completely under this upper piece (see Figure 8.3).

FIGURE 8.3
Drive cedar shims above and below where you intend to cut through the piece of siding that has the damage. The upper shim protects against butting into the upper piece of siding, and the lower shim protects against sawing into the lower piece of siding.

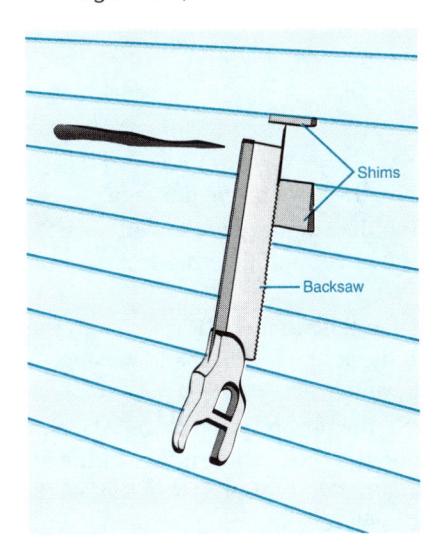

3. Use the back saw to saw along the vertical line. The two shims protect the good pieces of siding above and below the damaged piece.
4. When you have cut as far through the piece of siding as you can, shift the upper shim to one side and insert another close to it but on the other side of the line, as shown in Figure 8.4.
5. Finish cutting through the piece with a keyhole saw. Reverse the handle if you can because doing so makes it more comfortable to saw. If you cannot saw all the way through, saw as far as you can and finish the work with a sharp wood chisel and hammer.

FIGURE 8.4
Shift the upper shim to one side of the cutting line. Add a second shim to the other side of the cutting line. With a keyhole saw, work under the upper piece of siding to finish cutting through the board. Use the keyhole saw to finish any cutting below the level of the upper shim as well. Finish cutting through the siding with a sharp wood chisel and hammer if you have to.

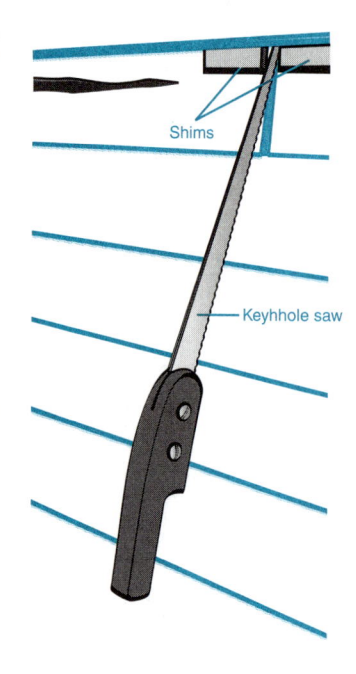

6. Repeat this for a line on the other side of the damage.
7. If a hidden nail(s) is holding the cut piece to the wall, pry it out some and look for the nail. You can often cut a nail with a hacksaw blade set into the handle of a keyhole saw.
8. Cut a piece of siding to match the old piece. Fit it up into the place of the old. If it resists going in, hold a block of wood to the lower edge and hammer upward with a hammer or mallet.
9. Use zinc-coated nails to hold the new piece in place. Alternatively, use regular nails, but countersink them to below the surface of the wood, fill them over with wood putty, and apply a paint primer to the patch. When the primer is dry, the new piece will be ready for painting.

CHAPTER 8   **Outdoor Repairs and Maintenance**   195

Repairing Vinyl Siding

Vinyl siding is immensely popular. It does not warp or split and does not require painting. But occasionally it is damaged and a piece has to be replaced. This is not difficult, but it does require a *zip tool*, or *zipper*, which is available where vinyl siding is sold.

You can remove an entire piece of vinyl siding, or you can cut out the damaged section. For cutting, use tin snips, a hack saw, or even repeated cuts of a sharp utility knife.

Things You'll Need

- ❏ Zip tool
- ❏ Replacement vinyl piece
- ❏ Vinyl siding nails
- ❏ Possibly a cutting tool such as a hacksaw, tin snips, or a utility knife

1. Work the end of the zip tool up under the bottom of the piece just above the piece that is damaged. Work it into the locking channel of the damaged piece. Pull down with one hand while moving the zip tool along the channel, releasing the grip that the upper panel has on the lower (see Figure 8.5).
2. Hold out—or have a helper hold out—the upper strip far enough for you to remove the nails along the upper part of the damaged strip. Remove the damaged strip.
3. Fit the replacement piece where the old one was, locking its lower portion to the upper portion of the piece or pieces below. Nail the replacement piece's nailing strip where the old one was. Leave the head of the nail a playing card's thickness out from the surface of the nailing strip to accommodate expansion in hot weather.
4. Use the zip tool in reverse of step 1 to lock the upper portion of the new piece to the lower portion of the upper piece.

FIGURE 8.5
Hook the zip tool into the locking channel connecting upper and lower pieces. Pull down and out with one hand while sliding the zip tool along the channel with the other. This unzips the connection between the two panels.

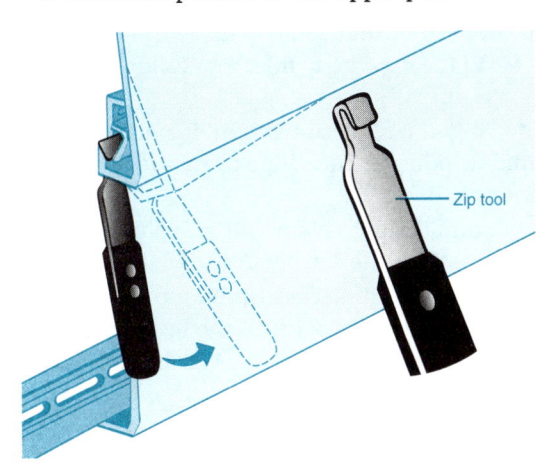

Repairing Aluminum Siding

Aluminum siding is harder to remove than vinyl siding. So, most repairs are done without replacing whole lengths of siding. Instead, dents are fixed with auto body filler. For larger areas, the damage is cut away with tin snips and a patch is glued in its place.

Things You'll Need

- ❑ Tin snips
- ❑ Drill, a sheet metal screw, and pliers
- ❑ Auto body filler, an applicator tool, and sandpaper
- ❑ Silicone caulk

1. For a dent, drill a hole into the dented area. Twist in a sheet metal screw and then pull out on its head with a pair of pliers. Repeat as many times and in as many places as it takes to restore the aluminum siding to almost its original position (see Figure 8.6).

FIGURE 8.6
Drill through the aluminum siding in the middle of the dent. Insert a sheet metal screw and then pull the head toward you with pliers.

2. Sand the damaged area with rough sandpaper. Mix the auto body filler according to the manufacturers' instructions. Spread it in the dented area with a plastic applicator that comes with it (or it can be bought with the auto body filler). Make the auto body filler mass slightly higher than the surrounding siding (see Figure 8.7).
3. After the auto body filler has cured, sand it smooth, beginning with rough sandpaper and working to fine. Wipe away the dust and paint the filler with a metal primer paint.
4. When it is dry, sand the primer smooth and paint it with an acrylic latex outdoor paint that matches the surrounding siding.
5. For more extensive work, draw vertical lines on the siding on either side of the damage. Stop the lines 1" beneath the lower edge of the piece above. Connect the ends of the two lines. Drill 1/2" holes where the lines meet.

CHAPTER 8 **Outdoor Repairs and Maintenance** 197

6. Wearing gloves to protect against sharp edges, insert the tips of tin snips into the holes and cut along the drawn lines. The bottom will come free (see Figure 8.8).
7. Cut a piece of new and matching aluminum siding 2" longer than the opening you have made. Cut the top portion off this new piece.
8. Apply silicone caulk to the back edges of the patching piece. Hook its lower edge where the old piece was and insert the top under the lower lip of the upper piece of siding. Press the patching piece along its edges, compacting the silicone caulk (see Figure 8.8).

FIGURE 8.7
Spread auto body filler across the damage. Apply it a little high and level it with sandpaper when it is dry.

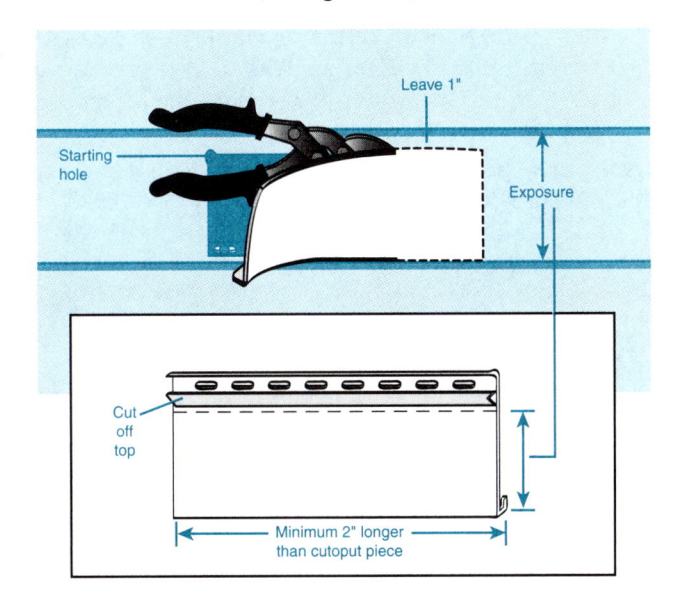

FIGURE 8.8
Cut out the damage using tin snips. Leave a 1" gap between the lower edge of the aluminum siding piece above and the horizontal cut you will make. Remove the piece. Cut off the top of the new piece. Make the length 2" longer than the opening. Apply silicone caulk to the back sides and top. Hook the lower edge in place and slip the top edge beneath the upper piece of siding.

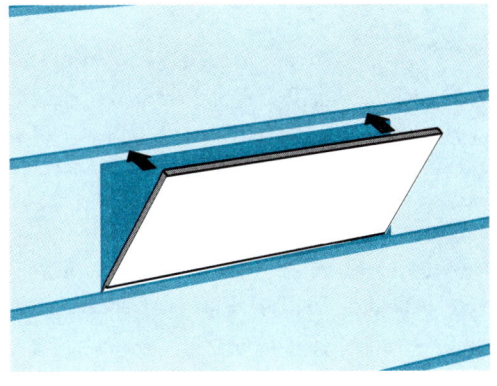

Power Washing a Wall

Exterior painted walls that look dingy can be freshened enough by a good cleaning to get by without a paint job for another couple of years. Washing is also a good idea for vinyl and aluminum siding every several years, and power washers can do the job quickly. Power washers can be rented from tool rental stores. With some experience, you can clean a home in half a day. Power washers require a connection to a garden hose and a connection to an electrical outlet.

Normally, power washing with water alone scours away enough grime to give a pleasing result. But most power washers have receptacles for detergents, which are fed into the water stream and add to the cleaning power. Many power washers have adjustable pressure settings; always begin with as little pressure as you can get away with to do the job to your satisfaction. Never make the pressure so high that it cuts into the wood or bends the aluminum.

Power washers can be helpful at more than cleaning. If you are going to paint the exterior walls of your home, a power washer can scour away grime as well as loose or brittle paint so the new paint adheres better and has a longer life.

While you have the power washer, you might think about using it on your driveway, patio, or deck. Ask rental store personnel which pressure settings on the power washer are best for various materials.

caution Avoid power washing on windy days. Even if you are not using a detergent, the blown water can be a nuisance.

POWER WASHERS ARE DANGEROUS TOOLS

When you rent a power washer, ask the rental store personnel to provide you with instructions and safety procedures, especially the latter. Power washers can deliver water 20–40 times the pressure coming out of a garden hose. It is therefore a dangerous tool. Never let children play with one; the water comes out with such force it can penetrate skin. Know where the electric power line overhead traverses your property. Never let the long wand of a power washer get within 10 feet of it; touching the wand to the power line can result in serious injury.

Wear safety goggles and rain gear. Never point the wand at yourself or any person. Avoid working from a ladder because the wand has a kick to it and can knock you off balance.

CHAPTER 8   **Outdoor Repairs and Maintenance**   199

Things You'll Need

- Power washer from a rental agency
- Detergent, if desired
- Goggles and rain gear
- Plastic to cover light fixtures and tape to cover electrical outlets

1. Cover plants and vents with plastic, and cover electrical outlets with tape. Read all the operating instructions and safety precautions.
2. Wear rain gear and goggles. Brace yourself when you turn on the wand. Keep the wand about 12" from the siding and at an angle of about 45°, as shown in Figure 8.9. Do not aim the wand at a window.
3. Move the wand steadily, keeping it pointed at an angle of about 45° to the siding. Do not point it at the underside of lapped siding; water can work its way between boards. If you are using a detergent, wash from the bottom up. When you rinse, rinse from the top down.

FIGURE 8.9
Make a pressure setting that will scour off grime but not damage siding. For high places, use an extender for the wand. Keep the wand off to the side so the spray strikes the siding at a 45° angle. Keep wand extenders well away from electrical power lines.

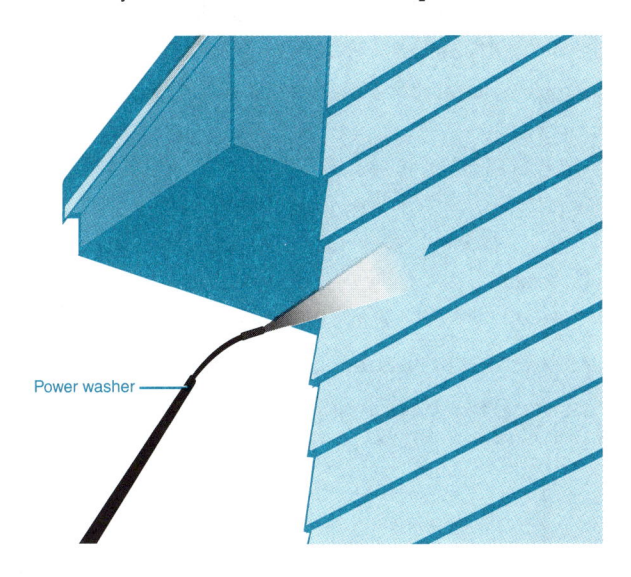

Power washer

Painting Exterior Siding

Exterior painting follows just about all the rules of interior painting that you learned in Chapter 7, "Painting and Wallpapering." The most important of these rules is to prepare the surface adequately. For such preparation work on your home's exterior, you might want to use a power washer, as described in the previous section. But in all cases, you need to caulk any small cracks or gaps in the siding, using exterior-grade caulk from a caulking gun. You'll also need to scrape and sand the surface using sandpaper, a scraper, and a wire brush.

USING LADDERS SAFELY

Pro's Tip

The two watch phrases for working safely with ladders are *Use proper clean equipment* and *Take your time*.

If you do not have good ladders at home, you can buy them or, if your need for them is limited, rent them. Types I and IA are the sturdiest and made for professional and industrial use. Type II is for commercial use, and Type III is for occasional home use. We recommend Type II and higher. Look for flat, not round, rungs; they are more comfortable to stand on.

Follow these safety guidelines when working with ladders:

* Know where the power lines on your property are—Keep ladders well away from them, even wood or fiberglass ladders.
* When ascending a ladder, use a tool belt for tools and supplies—This way, both hands can be free to hold onto the ladder. Wear sturdy shoes with a defined heel and a rubber sole.
* When on a ladder, do not lean out so far that your belt buckle crosses beyond the ladder side.
* Use a stepladder for work up to 10 feet on walls—Use extension ladders for work higher up. Use extension ladders that have rotatable feet so that a toothed edge can be placed into soil or grass and a skid-resistant surface on pavement.
* Prop an extension ladder against a house so that its feet are 1' out from the wall for every four feet of ladder height.
* Test the stability of a ladder—Do this by stepping on the first step. If the feet seem unstable, get off and stabilize them. If the soil is loose, place the feet on a board.
* If you think the feet might slip away from the house, secure the ladder by staking a board into the ground behind the feet—For pavement, screw a bolt into the house siding near the foundation and tie the lower sides of the ladder to the bolt.

You also can use ladder stabilizers and jacks to make your job safer and easier.

A *ladder stabilizer* clamps to the top of an extension ladder to prevent the ladder from twisting or sliding to one side. It also straddles a window, allowing you to work close to or on one, as shown in Figure 8.10.

FIGURE 8.10
Use a ladder stabilizer when you want to work near a window or when you want to get your upper body near a gutter but not lean the ladder against the outer gutter wall.

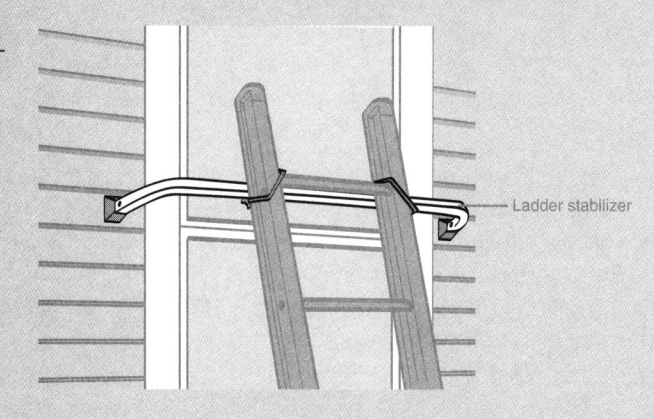

Ladder stabilizer

CHAPTER 8 Outdoor Repairs and Maintenance

Ladder jacks, shown in Figure 8.11, are devices that support scaffold boards, which in turn can support you and some equipment. They work in pairs with two extension ladders that are parallel and no more than 6' apart. The ladder jacks attach to the ladders and adjust to the ladder angle. You and a helper then carry two 2" × 10" scaffolding boards one at a time up the ladders and set them on the ladder jacks.

FIGURE 8.11
Use ladder jacks to support planks that can hold tools or serve as a working platform.

Ladder jacks

Like interior paints, exterior paint types have either an alkyd or latex base, but they are made somewhat tougher to stick to rougher surfaces and to endure temperature swings as well as exposure to sunlight, wind, and grit.

To estimate how much paint you will need, follow these steps:

1. Measure the length of each wall of the house. Add these lengths and multiply by 10' for each story of the home.
2. Subtract 21 square feet for each door and 15 square feet for each window. This gives a rough square footage of the siding you will paint.
3. Divide this by the square footage that one gallon of paint will cover (check the label of the paint you intend to buy for this information).
4. If you are painting trim such as shutters, windows, and doors, buy 1 gallon of trim paint for every 6 gallons you buy for the siding.
5. Double your estimates if you intend to apply two coats.

caution If your exterior paint contains lead (this includes the old layers beneath the current top layer), contact your local building department for ways of scraping and sanding while minimizing hazard.

Things You'll Need

- ❑ Paint
- ❑ Ladders
- ❑ S hook to hold a gallon paint can to a ladder rung, available in paint stores
- ❑ 4" paint brush suitable to the type of paint you are using

To paint wooden siding, follow these guidelines:

1. Make sure the surfaces are clean and sound. They can be slightly damp if you are going to use latex paint, but they need to be dry if you are using alkyd paint.
2. If you see rusty nails, sand the heads until they are shiny and coat them with a rust-inhibiting primer.
3. Paint in moderate weather and avoid painting in direct sunlight. Start in the morning and paint in shade; then move around the house, keeping in the shade as the sun moves across the sky. If the night is to be cold, stop painting two hours before temperatures drop below 40° F.
4. Work from large to small. Paint the siding first, then the window and door trim, and then things such as railings and posts.

note Bear in mind that using a brush is not the only way of painting exterior walls. You can also rent a sprayer. It applies the equivalent of two coats in one application, so the job is faster. But you also have to cover or move everything you do not want sprayed or touched with spray blown by a breeze, including windows, shrubs, and nearby cars.

note If you plan to apply two coats, note that alkyd paint takes a day or two to dry properly and latex takes from two to four hours.

caution Observe all the cautions for using ladders from the previous section.

To do list

- ❑ Find sources of leaks and problem shingles.
- ❑ Replace worn or cracked shingles.
- ❑ Clean gutters.

CHAPTER 8 Outdoor Repairs and Maintenance

Repairs on High: Working with the Roof and Gutters

Some outdoor work gets you up near, or even on, the roof. Gutters generally need to be inspected and cleaned out twice a year. And occasionally a shingle goes bad, requiring a replacement.

These jobs are not so bad so long as you are careful on ladders and keep your balance at all times.

You can work on a one-story roof that has a low slope; leave other jobs for professionals.

> **tip** — *Pro's Tip*
> Latex paint can be applied over oil or alkyd paint, but alkyd or oil over latex is not a good idea.
> To test the surface to be painted, rub the surface with clean fingers or—better still—a contrasting color cloth. If the surface shows chalkiness, the paint is probably oil- or alkyd-based. A second test involves wiping the surface with a rag wetted with rubbing alcohol; if paint comes away from the surface, it's latex. Oil- or alkyd-based paints cannot be softened or dissolved, but latex paints can.

Things You'll Need

- ❏ Binoculars
- ❏ Roofing cement
- ❏ Replacement shingles and roofing nails
- ❏ Small trowel and hose

Detecting Roofing Problems

Half the battle of repairing a leak is finding where it originates. This can be a baffling task. When water finds its way under a shingle, or under metal or built-up roofing on a horizontal roof, it can follow a twisted path to the point inside the house where you see it.

If you can find the point of origin on the roof, and if it is safely accessible, you can often make the repair yourself. If it is not accessible but you know where the problem is, you'll save the professional lots of time and thus save yourself money.

Many leaks in homes drip into a room at a light fixture. This does not mean the leak is above the light fixture, only that water has found its way to the upper surface of the ceiling and then has leaked through the fixture's ceiling opening. Look for water stains in the ceiling; these can lead you to the area where water is first reaching the ceiling.

Look at the roof through binoculars. You might detect damaged flashing (which is the metal around chimneys, vents, and the like) and in roof valleys. You can also detect damaged or curled roofing shingles.

If this sort of detective work fails, you can try simulating rain. With a garden hose, try squirting water up above a 6' × 6' section of roof. Let the water descend on the roof as rain would; if you squirt at the bottom of shingles, you can simply work pressured water up under them and create a new leak.

Have a helper inside wait at the point where the leak is visible inside the house. Wait an appropriate time to see whether any of your hose water is getting into the house. Test 6' × 6' sections nearest the eaves first; then work your way up toward the roof ridge.

Repairing a Composition Shingle

The most common form of shingle is the composition shingle, made of built-up layers of matting and asphalt, all topped with granules; these used to be called *asphalt shingles*. Composite shingles are meant to last 20 years or so, but cheaper ones might last only half that. Eventually, any composite shingle will lose its top granules and become thinner. Then it might curl up in a wind or pucker up, giving the roof a wavy appearance. It might also tear if struck by a falling branch. When a whole roof of shingles goes bad, they can be covered over with an entire new layer of good shingles (two or three layers, however, is the maximum). But individual shingles can often be repaired or replaced.

If you can reach a damaged shingle from a ladder set up by the eave, you can probably make this repair. If you cannot reach it, call a professional roofer. An exception might be a gently sloping roof only one story above ground—for example, a gently sloping roof on a garage or shed. There, if you are careful, you can maneuver on the roof to a damaged shingle, but observe the safety precaution of moving from a ladder to a roof (see the following Pro's Tip).

You will need roofing cement. This is a thick, black asphaltic substance that comes in a small tube you squeeze by hand, a cartridge for a caulking gun, or a gallon can. When you are working with composition shingles, it is best to work on a warm day. The shingles are more pliant then and not as apt to crack when lifted. In addition, the roofing cement, normally a thick and ornery substance, is more viscous and easier to work with.

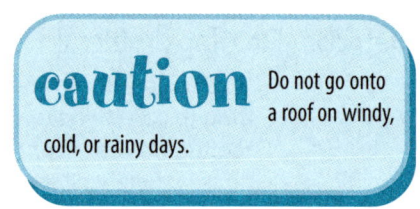

caution Do not go onto a roof on windy, cold, or rainy days.

Things You'll Need

- ❑ Putty knife
- ❑ Roofing cement from a can or tube

If a shingle has a tear or is curling up from the lower edge, you can repair it by following these steps:

CHAPTER 8 Outdoor Repairs and Maintenance 205

1. Shingles are meant to be held in place not only with nails, but also with thin asphalt patches just under the lower edge. Gently lift up the lower edge. If it does not come easily, slip a putty knife under the edge and lift it gently; lifting it too severely can crack the shingle.
2. Use roofing cement from a tube or can to spread a patch beneath the lower tab of the damaged shingle. Spread cement all the way to the shingle's lower corners. Make the patch of cement at least 1" wide top to bottom. Press the lower edge of the upper shingle down into the cement. If the shingle is torn, press roofing cement into the tear and smooth it out.
3. Generally, this should do; when the sun heats up the shingle, its underside will bond with the roofing cement. If the shingle has been badly warped, place a couple of bricks on the shingle for a day or so.

Pro's Tip

You can repair or replace shingles near the roofline by working from a ladder. If you want to get up onto a low sloping roof, extend the ladder three rungs above the eave. Climb to a rung approximately level with the eave. Holding onto the tops of the ladder sides, step off the ladder carefully onto the roof.

Pause for a moment to get used to the slope of the roof. Stay low and work on your knees or sitting down as much as possible.

Replacing a Composition Shingle

If a shingle is damaged beyond repair, you can replace it. Naturally, you will want its replacement to look exactly like its neighbors. Actually, you might have an exact replacement in your garage or storage area because when roofers finish a job, they generally have spare shingles left over and leave them with the homeowner. If you cannot find spare shingles around the home, take a piece of the damaged shingle to a roofing dealer. He will try to match it in color as best he can. He can also sell you appropriate roofing nails.

Composition shingles are about 3' long and normally separated into three tabs by cutouts that extend from the bottom edge about halfway up to the upper edge. When mounted with other shingles on a roof, the upper ends of the cutouts are concealed so that each tab looks like an individual shingle.

When replacing a shingle, take out the whole thing—that is, all three tabs—and replace it with a whole shingle. Work on a warm, but not a hot, day.

Things You'll Need

- ❑ Flat pry bar
- ❑ Hammer
- ❑ New shingle and roofing nails

1. Two rows of nails hold a shingle in place, one row halfway up the shingle and one near the upper edge. Lift the edge of the shingle two edges up from the damaged shingle and locate the nails; they are not difficult to spot

because they have broad heads. Let the edge down and lift up the lower edge of the next shingle down. Insert the pry bar flat end up to where one of the nails was and lift up on the shingle as shown in Figure 8.12. This raises the nail slightly. There are usually four nails to a shingle; do this for each nail.

2. Now you can let that flap go and return to the upper edge again. When you lift it this time, the heads of the nails should be raised slightly from where they were before. Slip the notched portion of the flat end of the pry bar under each nail head and pull up on each nail. Repeat this process for the four nails in the lower row of the damaged shingle.

FIGURE 8.12
Try to loosen nails by working the pry bar under the shingle on which the nail head rests. Then pull out the pry bar and lift the shingle edge covering the nail head. It should be loose. If it is not, work the front edges of the pry bar under the nail head, gouging the shingle if necessary, until the nail head is gripped by the claw of the pry bar.

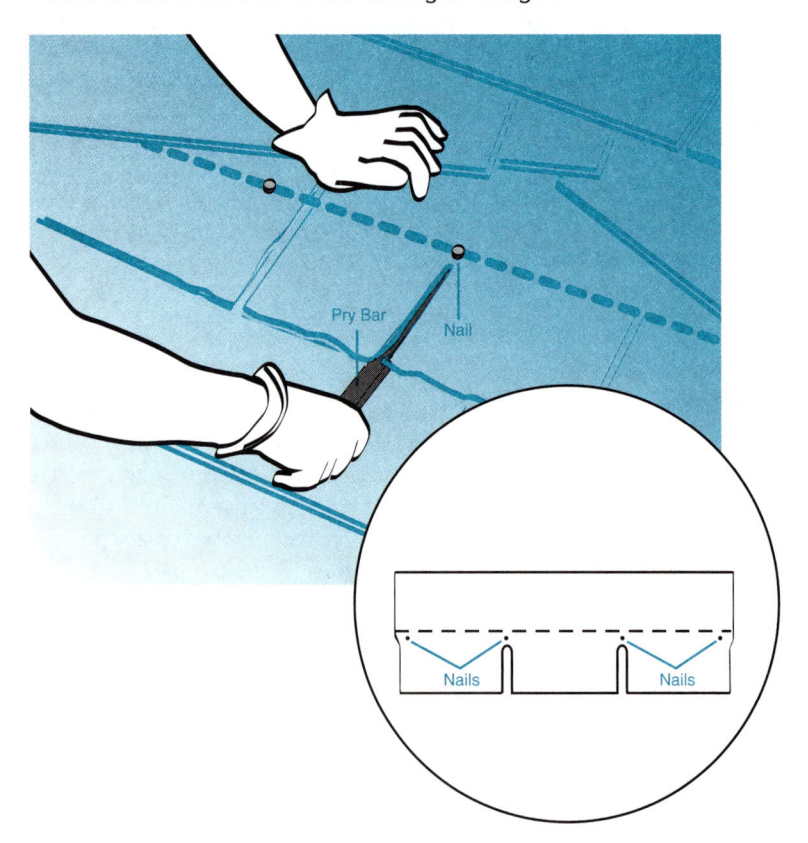

3. The damaged shingle should now be free. Gently pull it toward you; do not lose your balance.

4. Slip the new shingle into the place of the old. Try to use the old nail holes for the new nails. Nail the upper course of nails first. To hammer the nails without unduly lifting a shingle edge, use the flat end of the pry bar to press the nail into its place until it can stand by itself. Lift the shingle edge only enough to slip the flat end of the pry bar onto the top of the nail head. Hammer the shank of the pry bar, which transfers the blow to the nail head, as shown in Figure 8.13.

CHAPTER 8 Outdoor Repairs and Maintenance

5. Hammer the lower row of nails. With the putty knife, cover all the nail heads with a layer of roofing cement. Press the upper shingles down on the covered nail heads, which will now be out of sight.

FIGURE 8.13
Slip the flat end of the pry bar under the shingle edge and on top of a nail head. Hammer down on the pry bar shank, which transfers the blow to the nail. Cover the nail head with roof cement.

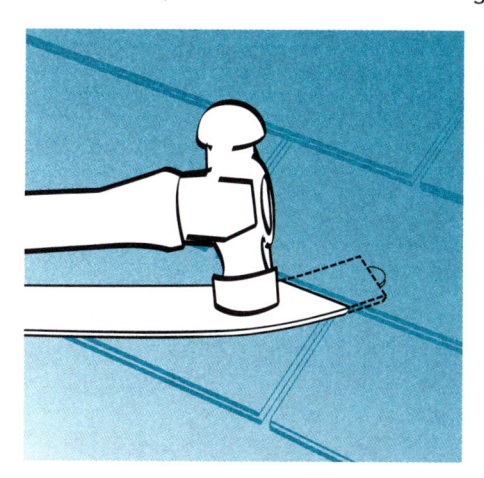

Cleaning Gutters

Gutters and downspouts are needed to carry rainwater and melting snow away from the walls and foundation of the home. If they clog, rain fills them and then spills over, wetting the walls and then saturating the ground near the foundation, where the water can find its way into your basement.

You should inspect your gutters at least twice a year, in spring and fall after most of the petals, seeds, and leaves have fallen from the trees. It's a good idea, too, if you have a thunderstorm season, to inspect the gutters at the onset of this period to make sure the gutters are going to be in top condition during a cloud burst.

Pro's Tip

If you are using an extension ladder to reach your gutters, you can use a ladder stabilizer, discussed in a sidebar earlier in this chapter, to prop the ladder away from the gutter wall. But with this arrangement, you cannot get much of your body above the gutter. For that, place a ladder-wide length of 2-by-4 in the gutter as you reach this level; the 2-by-4 will help to prevent the outer gutter wall from bending toward the house.

Things You'll Need

- [ ] Ladder and ladder stabilizer (or an 18" long section of a 2-by-4)
- [ ] Gloves and an old, small trowel
- [ ] Garden hose with spray nozzle
- [ ] Plumber's snake, if appropriate

1. Raise the ladder and ladder stabilizer; if you're not using a stabilizer, place the 2-by-4 in the gutter where the ladder will lean against it .

Use your gloved hand or the small trowel to scoop debris out of the gutter. If you use the trowel, be careful that its sharp point does not poke a hole in the gutter; this is why an old and dulled one is best for this work. A putty knife can do the job as well. Clear any debris from strainers placed over downspout outlets. These lift free of the outlets for cleaning.

2. As you move along, look for holes in the gutter, rusting parts, and loose gutter straps or gutter spikes. Mark trouble spots with tape on the outside of the gutter for repair later.

3. When the gutter is free of debris, have a helper pass up the hose. Flush the gutter with a blast of water; be careful about backsplashing in your face, though, because you are on a ladder. At a downspout outlet, point the spray down into the downspout to flush it out.

4. If there is a clog in the downspout that the water flow does not dislodge, work a plumber's snake down the downspout. If this fails, try removing a portion of the elbow assembly that angles the downspout from the gutter back to the house wall; this is where most clogs occur.

5. If slow flowing gutters and clogged downspouts keep recurring, consider buying and installing runs of gutter screen. These are strips or rolls of plastic mesh you can cut with heavy scissors to length. Lift the lower edge of the lowest shingles to slip under the upper edge of a length of gutter screen. Keeping the whole length convex, that is, crowned upward, set the other edge of the gutter screen against the inside of the outside wall of the gutter, as shown in Figure 8.14. Leaves will bounce off the gutter screen, but rainwater will find its way through and into the gutter. You might have to cut gutter screen lengths to fit around gutter straps or hangers.

FIGURE 8.14
To prevent leaf buildup in gutters, install strips of gutter screen, which can be cut to length with scissors. Install strips so the crown is up.

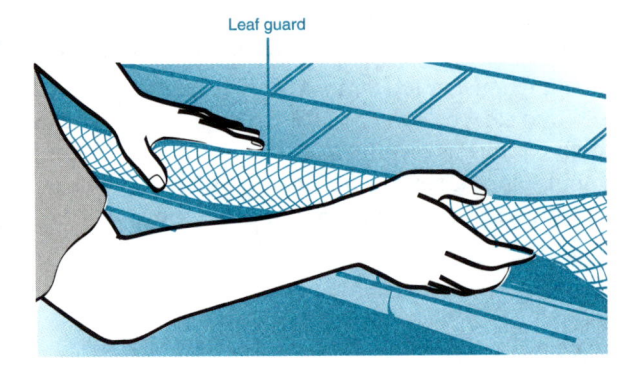

CHAPTER 8 Outdoor Repairs and Maintenance

Summary

The outside of a home is exposed to the elements and takes a beating. Boards weather; seams can develop gaps; shingles buckle. Any opening or other damage to your home's exterior must be repaired promptly to prevent it from worsening. This chapter examined repairs to the home's skin, including work with brick, wood siding, and roofing shingles. You also learned some simple repairs and maintenance techniques for keeping gutters clean and free of debris and a few techniques for maintaining driveways and decks.

References and Resources

Your local library is a valuable source of books on specialized topics. It likely has do-it-yourself books dedicated to flooring, wallpaper, painting, plumbing repairs, electrical improvements, patio construction, and the like. Ask librarians for help.

Home Improvement Magazines

Some good magazines for home improvements are

> *This Old House* (www.thisoldhouse.com)
>
> *Old House Journal* (www.oldhousejournal.com)

They can be bought on the newsstand, subscribed to, or accessed through their websites.

Useful Websites

If you use your favorite search engine to search under any common (or even not-so-common) home-improvement topics, you'll undoubtedly uncover thousands of sites offering information or suggestions. The following sections include some of my favorite sites for specific kinds of home repair topics and issues.

Do-It-Yourself Sites

> www.doityourself.com
>
> www.ehow.com

Energy Savings

www.eere.energy.gov (Office of Energy Efficiency and Renewable Energy, U.S. Dept. of Energy)

www.acee.org (American Council for an Energy Efficient Economy)

http://hes.lbl.gov (Home Energy Saver; you can get an energy audit if you input information about your home)

Stores

www.homedepot.com (Home Depot)

www.lowes.com (Lowe's Home Improvement Stores)

Safety

Asbestos (www.epa.gov; click Asbestos in Your Home)

Lead paint (www.hud.gov; for the brochure *Lead Paint Safety: A Field Guide for Painting, Home Maintenance, and Renovation Work*, click About HUD, then click HUD Offices—Lead Hazard Control, and click Helpful Tools—Lead Paint Safety Field Guide)

Tools

www.stanleytools.com

www.sears.com (click Tools)

Index

Numbers

2' levels, 12
6" joint compound blades, 14

A

aerators (faucet), cleaning, 97-99
air conditioners, 22
alkyd paint, 153, 168-169
Allen wrenches, 92
aluminum siding, 196-197
amp (ampere), 128
apartment maintenance, 23-24
armored cables, 133
asbestos flooring, 52
asphalt
  asphalt shingles, 204
  patching, 187
augers, 92, 107-108
autumn maintenance tasks, 21

B

backsaws, 13
ball faucets, 112-113
ballcock valves, 123
basements, 22
basin wrenches, 92
bathroom maintenance plans, 23
bathtubs, caulking, 99-101
bench vices, 13
beveled corner rollers, 150
bits (drill), 14, 31
blind stops, 63
blisters in flooring, deflating, 55
block planes, 13
blown fuses, 128
bolts, molly, 34-35
branches (plumbing), 90
brick wall repairs, 190-193
bristle combs, 152
broken window panes, 69-71
brush spinners, 152
brushes, 150
  choosing, 154-155
  painting tips, 161-162
  smoothing brushes, 171
bubble sticks, 171
buckets, 11, 15
building codes, 91
buying tips
  paint, 152-154
  paint brushes and rollers, 154-155
  plumber's supply stores, 94-95
  tools, 16-18
  wallpaper, 171-173
BX cables, 133

C

cable rippers, 126
cables (electrical). *See* electrical system
carpenter's wood glue, 48
casement windows, 64
caulking bathtubs, 99-101
caulking guns, 100
cedar shims, 14
ceilings, painting, 163-164

center punch, 34
ceramic tiles, 33, 43, 46-47
chandeliers, installing,
    140-141
channel-lock pliers, 11
chemical strippers, 158
chimneys, 21
chisels, 12, 31
chlorine bleach, 44
choosing. *See* buying tips
chop saws, 13
circuits
    grounded circuits, 128
    short circuits, 128
    testing, 129-130
    tripping circuit breaker, 128
clamps, 13
cleaning
    alkyd paint, 168-169
    faucet or spray hose nozzle
        aerators, 97-99
    grout, 43-44
    gutters, 207-208
    latex paint, 168
    pop-up sink stoppers, 103-104
    sink traps, 104-106
    tools, 15-16
clogs, removing
    drains, 107-108
    sink traps, 104-106
    toilets, 106-107
clothes washer hoses,
    replacing, 96
cold chisels, 31
cold water lines, 90
combination squares, 12
composition shingles
    repairing, 204-205
    replacing, 205-207
compression faucets, 108-110
compression fittings, 119
concrete, sealing, 188
continuity testers, 126
contracting professional
    repairmen, 24
coping saws, 13
cords (electrical), replacing,
    135-137
corner rollers, 163

corners, wallpapering,
    178-179
cracks
    in driveway/sidewalks, 187
    in plaster, 36-38
cylinder locks, installing,
    82-84

D

deadbolt locks, installing,
    84-87
decks
    autumn maintenance tasks, 21
    staining, 188-190
deflating blisters in flooring,
    55
dents
    in drywall, 41
    in resilient flooring, 53-54
dimmer switches, installing
    single-pole dimmer switches,
        142-143
    three-way dimmer switches,
        144-145
disk faucets, 115-116
door latches
    lock types, 82
    repairing by filing strike plate,
        80-81
    repairing by repositioning door
        stop, 81-82
door stops, repositioning,
    81-82
doors, 61, 76-77
    apartment maintenance plans,
        23
    autumn maintenance tasks, 21
    cylinder locks, 82-84
    deadbolt locks, 84-87
    latches, 80-82
    lock types, 82
    loose hinges, 78-79
    painting, 166
    shimming hinges, 79
    tools, 77
    wallpapering around, 180
    weatherstripping, 77-78

double-hung windows, 63,
    164-165
drain plungers, 92
drain-waste-vent (DWV)
    system, 90-91
drains, unclogging, 107-108
drills, 11
    drill bits, 14, 31
    drill guides, 87
    screw attachment drivers, 31
dripping faucets, 108
    ball faucets, 112-113
    compression valve faucets, 110
    disk faucets, 115-116
    single-handle cartridge faucets,
        114
    stem valve packing leaks, 111
driveways, fixing cracks in,
    187
dropcloths, 151
drywall repairs, 31-32, 40-43
    holes, 41-43
    lath, 31
    scrapes and dents, 41
    seams/joints, 32
DWV (drain-waste-vent)
    system, 90-91

E

edge guides, 151
edges of sheet flooring,
    resealing, 54-55
eggshell paint, 152
electrical outlets, wallpaper-
    ing around, 182-183
electrical system, 125
    chandeliers, installing, 140-141
    circuits, testing, 129-130
    cords, replacing, 135-137
    GFCI receptacles, installing,
        145-147
    jumper wires, 135
    lamps, 137-138
    light fixtures, installing,
        138-139
    permits, 133
    plugs, rewiring, 135-137
    principles of electrical wiring,
        127-128

installing 215

safety, 127-130
simple wiring connections, 132-134
single-pole dimmer switches, installing, 142-143
three-way dimmer switches, installing, 144-145
tools, 125-127
entrance locks, 82
entrance panels, 127
entryways, wallpapering around, 180
expansion shields, 35
exterior of home, maintenance of, 22
extra drill bits, 14

F

fall maintenance tasks, 21
faucets, 108
aerators, cleaning, 97-99
ball faucets, 112-113
compression valve faucets, 110
disk faucets, 115-116
handle pullers, 93
replacing faucets, 116-118
single-handle cartridge faucets, 114
stem valve packing leaks, 111
supply tubes, 118-119
winter maintenance tasks, 22
fiberglass mesh tape, 31
fiberglass window screens
repairing, 73
replacing on metal frames, 74-75
replacing on wooden frames, 73-74
files, 12
filing strike plates, 80-81
filters (water), installing, 99
finding
professional repairmen, 24
wall studs, 33-34
fireplaces, 21
flagged-bristle brushes, 154
flappers (toilet tank), 121-123

flat-head screwdrivers, 11
flat paint, 152
float cup valves, 123
floor repairs, 29
asbestos flooring, 52
hardwood floors, 48-52
resilient flooring, 52-58
tools, 48
winter maintenance tasks, 22
floorboards, replacing, 49-52
fluorocarbon tape, 94
foam weatherstripping, 66
foil wallpaper, 172
folding rules, 13
fuses, blown, 128

G

general-purpose saws, 12
GFCI receptacles, 145-147
glass cutters, 31
glazier's points, 62
glazing compound, 62
gloss paint, 152
glue, carpenter's wood glue, 48
ground fault circuit interrupter (GFCI) receptacles, 145-147
grounded circuits, 128
grout
cleaning, 43-44
replacing, 44-45
sealing, 45
staining, 46
grout floats, 31
grout saws, 31
gutters
autumn maintenance tasks, 21
cleaning, 207-208
spring maintenance tasks, 22

H

hacksaws, 13
hairline cracks in plaster, 36
hammers, 11
handsaws, 12

handymen. *See* **professional handymen**
hanging wallpaper
first piece, 176-177
second and subsequent strips, 177-178
hardwood floor repairs, 48-52
hawks, 191
heat guns, 158
heating systems, 21
hex wrenches, 92
hickeys (chandeliers), 141
high-gloss paint, 152
hinges, 78-79
hiring
painters, 170
repairmen, 24-25
holes
in drywall, 41-43
in plaster, 38-39
in resilient flooring, 53-54
hollow wall anchors, 34-35
home improvement stores, 16-18
home maintenance plans, 19-20
anytime maintenance tasks, 22-23
apartments, 23-24
autumn maintenance tasks, 21
spring maintenance tasks, 22
summer maintenance tasks, 22
winter maintenance tasks, 21-22
hook-blade scrapers, 150
hoses (washing machine), replacing, 96
hot water lines, 90
hot wires, 127

I

inlet valves (toilet tank), 123-124
inside corners, wallpapering, 178-179
installing
chandeliers, 140-141
cylinder locks, 82-84

How can we make this index more useful? Email us at indexes@quepublishing.com

deadbolt locks, 84-87
door weatherstripping, 77-78
GFCI receptacles, 145-147
light fixtures, 138-139
single-pole dimmer switches, 142-143
three-way dimmer switches, 144-145
toilet inlet values, 123-124
water filters, 99
window panes, 69-71
window weatherstripping, 66-68

J-K

jab saws, 31
joint compound, 31
joint filler, 190
jointers, 191
joints (drywall), 32
jumper wires, 135

keyhole saws, 31
kitchens, 24
knee pads, 12, 48
knives
    6" joint compound blades, 14
    putty knives, 12
    utility knives, 12

L

ladder jacks, 201
ladder stabilizers, 200
ladders
    ladder jacks, 201
    ladder stabilizers, 200
    painting with, 160-161
    safety tips, 200
    step ladders, 12, 151
lamps, 137-138
large pattern wallpaper, 172
latches. *See also* **locks**
    lock types, 82
    repairing by filing strike plate, 80-81
    repairing by repositioning door stop, 81-82

latex paint, 152-153, 168
lath, 31
lead paint, 67
light fixtures
    chandeliers, 140-141
    installing, 138-139
linoleum floor repairs, 52-53
    blisters, 55
    damaged sections, 56-58
    holes, dents, and scratches, 53-54
    loose edges, 54-55
lists (maintenance), 19-20
    anytime maintenance tasks, 22-23
    apartments, 23-24
    autumn maintenance tasks, 21
    spring maintenance tasks, 22
    summer maintenance tasks, 22
    winter maintenance tasks, 21-22
live wires, 128
locks. *See also* latches
    cylinder locks, 82-84
    deadbolt locks, 84-87
    types of, 82
loose hinges, 78-79
lubricants, 15

M

main shutoff valves, 90
maintenance plans. *See* **home maintenance plans**
masonry, 33-35
masonry nails, 35
mastic, 48
materials. *See* **tools and materials**
meeting rails, 63
metal window screens, 74-75
mildew, 157
miter boxes, 13
molly bolts, 34-35
multipurpose tools, 126
muntins, 63

N-O

nail sets, 52, 62
nails, 15, 35
needle-nose pliers, 11
nippers, 11
nipple bolts (chandeliers), 141
NM (nonmetallic) cable, 132
notched trowels, 48

oil, 15
opening stuck windows, 64-65
organic wallpaper, 172
outdoor repairs, 185-186
    aluminum siding, 196-197
    brick walls, 190-193
    composition shingles, 204-207
    concrete, sealing, 188
    decks, staining, 188-190
    driveway/walkway cracks, 187
    gutters, cleaning, 207-208
    painting siding, 199-202
    power washing walls, 198-201
    roof problems, 203-204
    vinyl siding, 195
    wood siding, 193-194
outlets, wallpapering around, 182-183
outside corners, wallpapering, 179

P

paint, 152
    alkyd paint, 153, 168-169
    estimating paint needs, 154
    flat paint, 152
    high-gloss paint, 152
    latex paint, 152-153, 168
    lead paint, 67
    satin paint, 152
    semi-gloss paint, 152
    stirring, 159
    varnishes, 153
paint brushes, 150
    choosing, 154-155
    painting tips, 161-162
paint mitts, 151

paint thinner, 153
painter's tape, 152
painting, 149-152
    alkyd paint, 153, 168-169
    brushes and rollers, 150, 154-155, 161-162
    ceilings, 163-164
    cleaning up, 168-169
    doors, 166
    estimating paint and work time, 154
    exterior siding, 199-202
    flat paint, 152
    high-gloss paint, 152
    ladder position, 160-161
    latex paint, 152-153, 168
    paint preparation, 159
    professional painters, hiring, 170
    room preparation, 156-157
    safety precautions, 155
    satin paint, 152
    semi-gloss paint, 152
    surface preparation, 157-158
    taking breaks, 166-167
    tools, 150-152
    varnishes, 153
    walls, 163-164
    windows, 164-165
parting strips, 63
passage locks, 82
paste, 171
pasting tables, 171
pasting wallpaper
    first piece, 176-177
    second and subsequent strips, 177-178
patching
    asphalt, 187
    drywall, 40-43
    plaster, 36-39
peeling paint, removing, 157
penetrating oil, 94
permits for electrical repairs, 133
pipe joint compound, 93
pipe wrenches, 92
pipe-thread tape, 94
pipes. *See* **plumbing**

plans, maintenance. *See* **home maintenance plans**
plaster repairs, 32, 35
    hairline cracks, 36
    holes, 38-39
    recurring cracks, 37-38
    wide cracks, 36
plastic shields, 34
plastic-sheathed NM (non-metallic) cables, 132
pliers, 11
plugs (electrical), rewiring, 135-137
plumb lines, 171
plumber's dope, 93
plumber's grease, 94
plumber's putty, 94
plumber's supply stores, 94-95
plumbing, 89
    ball faucets, 112-113
    bathtubs, caulking, 99-101
    building codes, 91
    clothes washer hoses, 96
    compression valve faucets, 110
    disk faucets, 115-116
    drain-waste-vent (DWV) system, 90-91
    drains, unclogging, 107-108
    faucet or spray hose nozzle aerators, cleaning, 97-99
    faucet, replacement, 116-118
    hot and cold water lines, 90
    main shutoff valve, 90
    materials and supplies, 93-94
    plumber's supply stores, 94-95
    shower heads, 96-97
    shutoff valves, 120-121
    single-handle cartridge faucets, 114
    sink pop-up stoppers, 101-104
    sink traps, cleaning, 104-106
    stem valve packing leaks, 111
    supply tubes, 118-119
    toilet inlet values, 123-124
    toilet tank flappers, 121-123
    toilets, unclogging, 106-107
    tools, 92-93
    traps, 91
    water filters, 99
    water supply, 90

plungers, 92
pointing tools, 190
polarized plugs, 135
pop-up sink stoppers
    adjusting, 101-102
    cleaning, 103-104
power drills, 11
power miter saws, 13
power sanders, 14
power washers, 198
power washing walls, 198-201
preparing to paint
    paint preparation, 159
    room preparation, 156-157
    surface preparation, 157-158
preparing to wallpaper
    room setup, 175-176
    wall preparation, 173-174
    wallpaper removal, 174-175
prevention. *See* **home maintenance plans**
privacy locks, 82
professional handymen
    finding and contracting, 24
    when to hire, 25
professional painters, hiring, 170
protective wear, 11
pry bars, 48, 62
putty knives, 12

Q-R

quick-connect plugs, 135

rabbets, 63
rags, 15
random texture wallpaper, 171
rasps, 12
razors, single-edge, 14
receptacles (GFCI), 145-147
recurring cracks in plaster, 37-38
regular pliers, 11
regular scrapers, 150
removing
    broken window panes, 69
    drain clogs, 104-106

How can we make this index more useful? Email us at indexes@quepublishing.com

removing

pop-up sink stoppers, 103-104
wallpaper, 174-175
window weatherstripping, 67
rental properties, 23-24
repairmen
finding and contracting, 24
when to hire, 25
replacement screening, 62
replacing
broken window panes, 69-71
ceramic tile, 46-47
clothes washer hoses, 96
door weatherstripping, 77-78
electrical cords, 135-137
faucets, 116-118
floor tiles, 55-56
floorboards, 49-52
grout, 44-45
sheet flooring sections, 56-58
shingles, 205-207
shower heads, 96-97
shutoff valves, 120-121
supply tubes, 118-119
toilet tank flappers, 121-123
window screens on metal frames, 74-75
window screens on wooden frames, 73-74
window weatherstripping, 66-68
repointing brick, 191-193
resealing sheet flooring edges, 54-55
resilient flooring repairs, 52-53
blisters, 55
holes, dents, and scratches, 53-54
loose edges, 54-55
sheet flooring, 56-58
tile replacement, 55-56
respirators, 14
rewiring
electrical plugs, 135-137
lamps, 137-138
rip saws, 12
risers (plumbing), 90
rollers, 150
choosing, 154-155
painting tips, 161-162
steam rollers, 171

roofing problems
composition shingles, 204-207
detecting, 203-204
rubber gloves, 48
rulers, 13

S

safety
autumn maintenance tasks, 21
electrical system, 127-130
ladders, 200
painting, 155
sanders, 14
sanding blocks, 13
sandpaper, 14
sash movement, improving, 65-66
satin paint, 152
sawhorse braces, 151
saws
backsaws, 13
coping saws, 13
grout saws, 31
hacksaws, 13
handsaws, 12
jab saws, 31
power miter saws, 13
scaffolding boards, 151
scissors, wallpaper scissors, 171
scrapers, 150
scrapes. *See* dents; scratches
scratches
in drywall, 41
in resilient flooring, 53-54
screen beads, 62
screens
fiberglass screen repairs, 73
replacing on metal frames, 74-75
replacing on wooden frames, 73-74
wire screen repairs, 71-72
screws, 15
sealing
concrete, 188
grout, 45

seams (drywall), 32
seasonal maintenance tasks, 20
autumn, 21
spring, 22
summer, 22
winter, 21-22
seat dressers, 109
seat wrenches, 109
self-adhesive fiberglass mesh tape, 31
self-adhesive foam stripping, 66
semi-gloss paint, 152
service entrance panels, 127
sharpening tools, 16
sheet flooring repairs, 52-53
blisters, 55
damaged sections, 56-58
holes, dents, and scratches, 53-54
loose edges, 54-55
shimming hinges, 79
shims, 62
shingles
repairing, 204-205
replacing, 205-207
shopping tips. *See* buying tips
short circuits, 128
shower heads, replacing, 96-97
shutoff valves
main shutoff valve, 90
replacing, 120-121
sidewalks, fixing cracks in, 187
siding repairs
aluminum siding, 196-197
painting siding, 199-202
vinyl siding, 195
wood siding, 193-194
simple wiring connections, 132-134
single-edge razors, 14
single-handle cartridge faucets, 114
single-pole dimmer switches, installing, 142-143

sink pop-up stoppers
   adjusting, 101-102
   cleaning, 103-104
sink traps, cleaning, 104-106
sliding windows, 63
small drywall saws, 31
small pattern wallpaper, 172
smoke detectors, 21
smoothing brushes, 171
snakes, 92, 107-108
sockets, replacing, 138
spline rollers, 62
splinters in hardwood floors, 49
sponges, 171
spring maintenance tasks, 22
spring metal weatherstripping, 66
spud wrenches, 92
stacks (plumbing), 90
staining
   decks, 188-190
   grout, 46
steam rollers, 171
stem faucets, 108
stem valve packing leaks, 111
stepladders, 12, 151
   painting with, 160-161
   safety tips, 200
stirring paint, 159
stop beads, 21
stoppers (sink)
   adjusting, 101-102
   cleaning, 103-104
stops (door), 63
stores
   plumber's supply stores, 94-95
   shopper tips, 16-18
   wholesalers, 18
straps (light fixtures), 139
strike plates, filing, 80-81
strippable wallpaper, 174
stripping wallpaper, 174-175
stub-outs (plumbing), 120
stuck windows, opening, 64-65
stud finders, 12
studs, finding, 33-34
summer maintenance tasks, 22

supplies. *See* **tools and materials**
surfaces
   preparing for wallpaper, 173-174
   preparing to paint, 157-158
sweeps (door), 77
switch loops, 143
switchplates, wallpapering around, 182-183

T

tail piece (sinks), 105
taking breaks while painting, 166-167
tape
   painter's tape, 152
   pipe-thread tape, 94
   self-adhesive fiberglass mesh tape, 31
tape measures, 11
testing circuits, 129-130
threaded-joint sealer, 93
three-way dimmer switches, installing, 144-145
tiles
   ceramic tile, 33, 43, 46-47
   replacing, 55-56
   resilient tile flooring, 52-58
tin snips, 62
toilet plungers, 92
toilets
   inlet values, 123-124
   plungers, 92
   tank flappers, 121-123
   unclogging, 106-107
   winter maintenance tasks, 21
tool aprons, 13
tool belts, 13
tool buckets, 11
tools and materials, 9-10
   2' level, 12
   6" joint compound blades, 14
   backsaws, 13
   basin wrenches, 92
   bench vices, 13

   block planes, 13
   bristle combs, 152
   brush spinners, 152
   bubble sticks, 171
   buckets, 15
   buying tips, 16-18
   cable rippers, 126
   care and maintenance, 15-16
   caulk, 100
   caulking guns, 100
   cedar shims, 14
   center punch, 34
   chisels, 12, 31
   clamps, 13
   cleaning, 15-16
   combination squares, 12
   continuity testers, 126
   coping saws, 13
   drill bits, 31
   drill guides, 87
   dropcloths, 151
   edge guides, 151
   expansion shields, 35
   extra drill bits, 14
   faucet handle pullers, 93
   files, 12
   folding rules, 13
   glass cutters, 31
   glazier's points, 62
   glazing compound, 62
   grout floats, 31
   grout saws, 31
   hacksaws, 13
   hammers, 11
   handsaws, 12
   heat guns, 158
   hex wrenches, 92
   jab saws, 31
   joint compound, 31
   jointers, 191
   knee pads, 12, 48
   ladder jacks, 201
   ladder stabilizers, 200
   ladders, 12, 151, 160-161, 200
   lubricants, 15
   masonry nails, 35
   mastic, 48
   miter boxes, 13

How can we make this index more useful? Email us at indexes@quepublishing.com

tools and materials

molly bolts (hollow wall anchors), 34-35
multipurpose tools, 126
nail sets, 52, 62
nails, 15
nippers, 11
oil, 15
paint mitts, 151
paintbrushes and rollers, 150
painter's tape, 152
paste, 171
pasting tables, 171
penetrating oil, 94
pipe joint compound, 93
pipe-thread tape, 94
pipe wrenches, 92
pliers, 11
plumb lines, 171
plumber's grease, 94
plumber's putty, 94
pointing tools, 190
power drills, 11
power sanders, 14
power washers, 198
protective wear, 11
pry bars, 48, 62
putty knives, 12
rags, 15
rasps, 12
replacement screening, 62
respirators, 14
rubber gloves, 48
sanding blocks, 13
sandpaper, 14
sawhorse braces, 151
scaffolding boards, 151
scrapers, 150
screen beads, 62
screws, 15
seat wrenches, 109
self-adhesive fiberglass mesh tape, 31
sharpening, 16
shims, 62
single-edge razors, 14
smoothing brushes, 171
snakes, 92, 107-108
spline rollers, 62
sponges, 171

spud wrenches, 92
stepladders, 12, 151, 160-161, 200
stud finders, 12
tape measures, 11
tin snips, 62
toilet/drain plungers, 92
tool aprons, 13
tool belts, 13
tool buckets, 11
toothed/notched trowels, 48
torpedo levels, 11
utility knives, 12
voltage testers, 126, 129-130
wallpaper scissors, 171
water trays, 171
wire nuts, 126
wood glue, 48
toothed trowels, 48
torpedo levels, 11
tradesmen
   finding and contracting, 24
   when to hire, 25
traps (plumbing), 91
traps, cleaning, 104-106
triangle scrapers, 150
tripping circuit breakers, 128
trowels, 48
tubs, caulking, 99-101
tubular flexible gasket weatherstripping, 66
tuckpointing brick, 191-193
two-conductor cables, 132

U-V

unclogging
   drains, 107-108
   toilets, 106-107
utility knives, 12

varnishes, 153
vents (plumbing), 91
vices, 13
vinyl siding, 195
vinyl wallpaper, 172
voltage, 128
voltage testers, 126, 129-130

W-X-Y-Z

walks, fixing cracks in, 187
wall fasteners
   masonry walls, 35
   molly bolts (hollow wall anchors), 34-35
   wall studs, finding, 33-34
wall repairs, 29-30
   ceramic tile, 33, 43, 46-47
   drywall, 31-32, 40-43
   grout, 43-46
   masonry, 33
   plaster, 32, 35-39
   tools and materials, 30-31, 190-193
   wall fasteners, 33-35
   wood paneling, 32
wall studs, finding, 33-34
wallpaper, 149-150, 170
   buying, 171-173
   choosing, 171-173
   electrical outlets and switchplates, 182-183
   hanging, 176-178
   inside corners, 178-179
   outside corners, 179
   removing, 174-175
   room setup, 175-176
   tools, 170-171
   wall preparation, 173-174
   windows, doors, and entryways, 180
wallpaper scissors, 171
walls. *See also* **siding repairs**
   painting, 163-164
   power washing, 198-201
   preparing for wallpaper, 173-174
   removing wallpaper from, 174-175
   winter maintenance tasks, 22
washerless faucets, 108-109
washing machine hoses, replacing, 96
water filters, installing, 99
water supply, 90
water trays, 171
watts, 128

weatherstripping
    installing on doors, 77-78
    installing on windows, 66-68
    removing from windows, 67
wholesalers, 18
window panes
    installing, 69-71
    removing, 69
windows, 61-62
    apartment maintenance plans, 23
    autumn maintenance tasks, 21
    broken window panes, 69-71
    casement windows, 64
    double-hung windows, 63
    fiberglass screen repairs, 73
    lead paint, 67
    painting, 164-165
    sash movement, 65-66
    screen replacement (metal frames), 74-75
    screen replacement (wooden frames), 73-74
    sliding windows, 63
    spring maintenance tasks, 22
    stuck windows, opening, 64-65
    tools, 62
    wallpapering around, 180
    weatherstripping, 66-68
    wire screen repairs, 71-72
window screens
    fiberglass screen repairs, 73
    replacing on metal frames, 74-75
    replacing on wooden frames, 73-74
    wire screen repairs, 71-72
winter maintenance tasks, 21-22
wire nuts, 126
wire window screens, 71-72
wiring (electrical). *See* **electrical system**
wood-frame window screens, replacing, 73-74
wood glue, 48
wood paneling, 32

wood siding
    painting, 202
    repairing, 193-194
wrenches
    basin wrenches, 92
    hex wrenches, 92
    pipe wrenches, 92
    seat wrenches, 109
    spud wrenches, 92

How can we make this index more useful? Email us at indexes@quepublishing.com

Do Even More ...In No Time

Get ready to cross off those items on your to-do list! *In No Time* helps you tackle the projects that you don't think you have time to finish. With shopping lists and step-by-step instructions, these books get you working toward accomplishing your goals.

Check out these other *In No Time* books, available now!

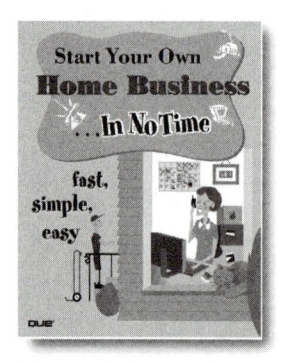

Start Your Own Home Business In No Time
ISBN: 0-7897-3224-6
$16.95

Plan a Fabulous Party In No Time
ISBN: 0-7897-3221-1
$16.95

Speak Basic Spanish In No Time
ISBN: 0-7897-3223-8
$16.95

Organize Your Garage In No Time
ISBN: 0-7897-3219-X
$16.95

Quick Family Meals In No Time
ISBN: 0-7897-3299-8
$16.95

Organize Your Family's Schedule In No Time
ISBN: 0-7897-3220-3
$16.95